LETTERS FROM
THE FEW

Best Wishes

For my many old correspondents and friends amongst The Few

LETTERS FROM THE FEW

UNIQUE MEMORIES FROM THE BATTLE OF BRITAIN

Dilip Sarkar MBE

AIR WORLD

AIR WORLD

LETTERS FROM THE FEW
Unique Memories from the Battle of Britain

First published in Great Britain in 2020 by
Air World
An imprint of
Pen & Sword Books Ltd
Yorkshire – Philadelphia

ISBN 978 1 52677 589 4

Typeset by Aura Technology and Software Services, India.

Printed and bound in England by TJ International, Padstow, Cornwall, PL28 8RW.

Pen & Sword Books Limited incorporates the imprints of Atlas, Archaeology, Aviation, Discovery, Family History, Fiction, History, Maritime, Military, Military Classics, Politics, Select, Transport, True Crime, Air World, Frontline Publishing, Leo Cooper, Remember When, Seaforth Publishing, The Praetorian Press, Wharncliffe Local History, Wharncliffe Transport, Wharncliffe True Crime and White Owl.

For a complete list of Pen & Sword titles please contact

PEN & SWORD BOOKS LIMITED
47 Church Street, Barnsley, South Yorkshire, S70 2AS, England
E-mail: enquiries@pen-and-sword.co.uk
Website: www.pen-and-sword.co.uk

Or
PEN AND SWORD BOOKS
1950 Lawrence Rd, Havertown, PA 19083, USA
E-mail: Uspen-and-sword@casematepublishers.com
Website: www.penandswordbooks.com

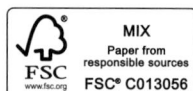

MIX
Paper from
responsible sources
FSC® C013056

Contents

Author's Note & Glossary

The aviation-minded reader will notice that I have referred to German Messerschmitt fighters by the abbreviation 'Me' (not 'Bf', which is more technically correct), or simply by their numeric designation, such as '109' or '110'. This not only reads better but is authentic: during the Battle of Britain, Keith Lawrence, a New Zealander, flew Spitfires and once said to me, 'To us they were just "Me's", "109s" or "110s", simple, never "Bf".'

In another attempt to preserve accuracy, I have also used the original German, wherever possible, regarding terms associated with the *Luftwaffe*, such as:-

Adlerangriff	Attack of the Eagles
Adlertag	Eagle Day
Eichenlaub	The Oak Leaves – a bar to the *Ritterkreuz*.
Erprobungsgruppe	Experimental group; for example *Erprobungsgruppe* 210, a skilled precision bombing unit.
Experte	A fighter ace. Ace status, on both sides, was achieved by destroying five enemy aircraft.
Freie hunt	A fighter sweep.
Gefechstand	Operations headquarters.
Geschwader	The whole group, usually of three *gruppen*.
Geschwaderkommodore	Group leader.
Gruppe	A wing, usually of three squadrons (*Staffeln*).
Gruppenkeil	A wedge formation of bombers, usually made up of vics of three.
Gruppenkommandeur	The wing commander.
Jagdbomber ('*Jabo*')	Fighter-bomber.
Jagdflieger	Fighter pilot.

Jagdgeschwader	Fighter group, abbreviated JG.
Jagdwaffe	The fighter force.
Jäger	Hunter, in this context a fighter pilot or aircraft.
Kampffleiger	Bomber aircrew.
Kampfgeschwader	Bomber group, abbreviated KG.
Kanal	The English Channel.
Katchmarek	Wingman.
Lehrgeschwader	Literally a training group, but actually a precision bombing unit, abbreviated LG.
Luftflotte	Air Fleet.
Oberkannone	Literally the 'Top Gun', or leading fighter ace.
Oberkommando der Wehrmacht (OKW)	The German armed forces high command.
Ritterkreuz	The Knight's Cross of the Iron Cross.
Rotte	A pair of fighters, comprising leader and wingman, into which the *Schwarm* broke once battle was joined.
Rottenführer	Leader of a fighting pair.
Schwarm	A section of four fighters.
Schwarmführer	Section leader.
Seelöwe	Sealion, the codename for Hitler's proposed seaborne invasion of England.
Stab	Staff
Stabschwarm	Staff flight.
Staffel	Squadron.
Staffelkapitän	Squadron leader.
Störflug	Harrassing attacks, usually by lone Ju 88s.
Stuka	The Ju 87 dive-bomber.
Sturkampfgeschwader	Dive-bomber group, abbreviated StG.
Vermisst	Missing.
Zerstörer	Literally 'destroyer', the term used for the Me 110.
Zerstörergeschwader	Destroyer group, abbreviated ZG.

Each *geschwader* generally comprised three *gruppen*, each of three *staffeln*. Each *gruppe* is designated by Roman numerals, i.e. III/JG 26 refers to the third *gruppe* of Fighter Group (abbreviated 'JG') 26. *Staffeln* are identified by numbers, so 7/JG 26 is the 7th *Staffel* and belongs to III/JG 26.

AUTHOR'S NOTE & GLOSSARY

Rank comparisons may also be useful:-

Gefreiter	Private 1st Class
Unteroffizier	Corporal, no aircrew equivalent in Fighter Command.
Feldwebel	Sergeant
Oberfeldwebel	Flight Sergeant
Leutnant	Pilot Officer
Oberleutnant	Flight Lieutenant
Hauptmann	Squadron Leader
Major	Wing Commander
Oberst	Group Captain

In photograph captions, ranks are as they were when the image was taken.

RAF abbreviations-

AAF	Auxiliary Air Force
AASF	Advance Air Striking Force
A&AEE	Aeroplane & Armament Experimental Establishment
AFC	Air Force Cross
AFDU	Air Fighting Development Unit
AI	Airborne Interception radar
AOC	Air Officer Commanding
AOC-in-C	Air Officer Commanding-in-Chief
ATA	Air Transport Auxiliary
ATS	Armament Training School
BEF	British Expeditionary Force
CAS	Chief of the Air Staff
CFS	Central Flying School
CGS	Central Gunnery School
CO	Commanding Officer
DES	Direct Entry Scheme
DFC	Distinguished Flying Cross
DFM	Distinguished Flying Medal
DSO	Distinguished Service Order
E/A	Enemy Aircraft
FAA	Fleet Air Arm

EFTS	Elementary Flying Training School
FIU	Fighter Interception Unit
FTS	Flying Training School
ITW	Initial Training Wing
LAC	Leading Aircraftman
MRAF	Marshal of the Royal Air Force
MSFU	Merchant Ship Fighter Unit
NCO	Non-Commissioned Officer
ORB	Operations Record Book
OTC	Officer Training Corps
OTU	Operational Training Unit
PDC	Personnel Distribution Centre
RAFVR	Royal Air Force Volunteer Reserve
RFS	Reserve Flying School
RN	Royal Navy
RNAS	Royal Navy Air Service
SASO	Senior Air Staff Officer
SOO	Senior Operations Officer
SSC	Short Service Commission
UAS	University Air Squadron
U/S	Unserviceable

Acknowledgements

Naturally, I must thank all of my sadly deceased correspondents, and the late Wing Commander Pat Hancock OBE DFC, one-time Honorary Secretary of the Battle of Britain Fighter Association.

I must also thank my friends Air Marshal Cliff Spink; Christina Avramakis, Operations Manager, together with staff and essential volunteers at Bentley Priory Museum; Martin Mace and all at Pen & Sword; Andy Long; Nicolette Perry; Alan Wright; David McIntyre; Roman Poplawski; Peter Drobinski; Edward McManus, Battle of Britain London Monument; Jan Kansik; Rob Oliver and Derek Boyling.

Unless otherwise indicated, all photographs are from the Dilip Sarkar Archive and collated over forty-years researching the Battle of Britain period; most originate from the collections of The Few themselves.

Foreword

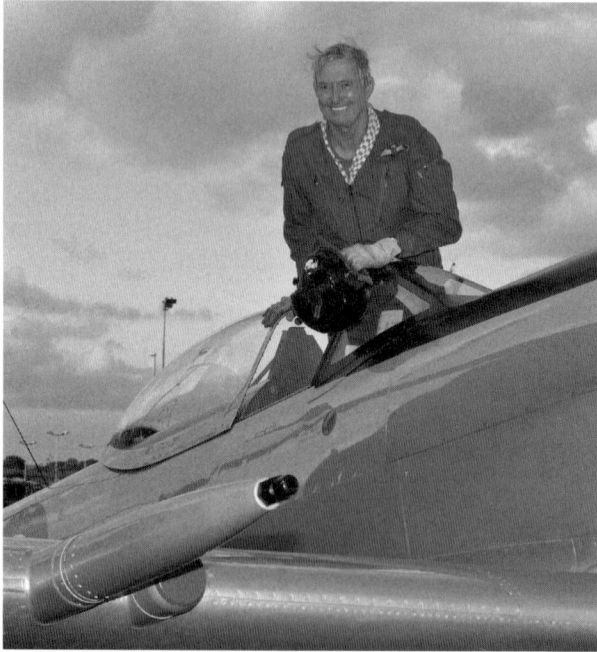

It is now over twenty years ago that, like Dilip Sarkar, I was the guest at two of the Battle of Britain Aircrew Association Annual Dinners at Bentley Priory. How did I get so lucky? Well, I was privileged to be the AOC of the combined 11/18 Group with my Headquarters at Bentley Priory at that time, and this august assembly had kindly afforded me an invitation. Just to sit in the presence of these wonderful people was quite breath-taking and to hear their stories – normally only obtained with much persistence on my part and always told with supreme modesty and understatement – was awe inspiring. Dilip went on to establish a unique relationship with these gallant gentlemen over many years, and the correspondence that he had with so many of them has provided a remarkable and very personal insight into their stories – and much more. History really does come alive when you read these letters and Dilip has done wonders weaving together a book that brings out just about every aspect of flying fighters in those dark days in WW II. More than that you also get a real sense of the overall pressures and tensions that existed when not strapped into a Spitfire or Hurricane.

I have been enormously privileged to have flown the Spitfire and Hurricane over the past 29 years, the Spitfire in particular. However, my flights were done in the best of weather (mostly) and I certainly did not have an enemy trying to shoot me down. As I engaged in a bit of free-wheeling mock combat in a Spitfire with another fighter, high above the green fields of England, I could only imagine what it was like to do this in the cauldron of war. Dilip's book brings this arena into sharp focus with these penetrating first-hand accounts, and it is impossible not to live the moment with these heroes.

Sitting next to Sir Christopher Foxley-Norris at one of those splendid dinners all those years ago he reflected quietly "What a splendid bunch they are!". Indeed they were, and I commend this Dilip Sarkar book which so wonderfully illustrates the humanity and courage of these extraordinary men.

Air Marshal Cliff R Spink CB CBE RAF (Rtd)
Keyston
January 2020

Prologue

The Battle of Britain, at the time an air battle of unprecedented scale, was fought between 10 July and 31 October 1940 – the stakes infinite.

During those epic sixteen weeks of high drama, closely following the catastrophic Fall of France, RAF Fighter Command – a multi-national force – and the German *Luftwaffe* jousted daily for control of the air over southern England, aerial supremacy being a prerequisite for Hitler's proposed seaborne invasion of south-east England. Ultimately the *Luftwaffe* failed to achieve this essential control of the skies, Fighter Command thereby delivering the first reversal of Germany's pre-eminence in the war. Although neither side was decisively defeated, Fighter Command had ensured that

Some of Few pictured during the 60th anniversary year. Dilip Sarkar enjoyed personal friendship with numerous members of the exulted Battle of Britain Fighter Association, facilitating a unique perspective and access to their memories.

Britain remained free, still in the war, and had a base from which, in due course with American help, the liberation of Nazi-occupied Europe could one day be launched. Largely responsible for this victory were those at the sharp end: the pilots, navigators, air gunners and observers of Fighter Command – immortalised by Churchill when he famously said, 'Never in the field of human conflict has so much been owed by so many to so few.' And so, this 'band of brothers' became forevermore known as The Few.

Growing up in the 1960s, I was very conscious that the Second World War remained omni-present. Family members, neighbours, teachers, had all been in it, and boys were subjected to a relentless barrage of war films, jingoistic comics, action toys and scale plastic models. Escaping from the war was impossible. Personally, I never wanted to. I became obsessed by everything connected with it, especially aeroplanes, and as a child loved listening to older people talking of their wartime experiences. Then it happened: in 1969, after several years of promotion, the film *Battle of Britain* was released. As an 8-year-old boy, for me, watching dogfights on the big colour screen was life-changing. Most other films at that time were black-and-white with crude 'special effects'. *Battle of Britain* was different. Here we had *real* Spitfires and Hurricanes, and although the 'Me 109s' and 'He 111s' were actually Spanish-built post-war and powered by Rolls-Royce Merlin engines, they looked authentic and impressive to any schoolboy. Over the years, the Battle of Britain story has, by necessity, been much propagandised, and is now so heavily myth-laden that achieving an accurate assessment and interpretation of events is challenging. But in 1969, that mattered not. Britain was losing its place in the world, its Empire evaporating, and it needed to remind everyone of its critical part in Total Victory – the pivotal moment in modern world history. A whole new generation bought into this, unreservedly. *Battle of Britain* popularised the Battle of Britain story – the heroes of which were, of course, the Few. From the day I watched *Battle of Britain*, my interest in those who fought this tumultuous battle in the clouds became part of my DNA.

Battle of Britain also triggered my interest in restoring vintage 'warbirds' to flying condition, increasing my opportunities to see and hear first-hand these incredible machines from yesteryear. I also became interested in 'aviation archaeology' – the discovery of aircraft crash sites and recovery therefrom of remaining wreckage. Indeed, a veritable plethora of amateur groups and museums sprang up in pursuit of this activity, especially in south-east England, over which the Battle had mainly been fought. Then, in 1980, *FlyPast* appeared, a monthly magazine focussed, at that time,

Dilip Sarkar's privileged relationship enabled him to assemble line-ups of the Few and other wartime personalities, providing the public a unique opportunity to meet men and women from the pages of history. Pictured here at the launch of *The Invisible Thread: A Spitfire's Tale* in Great Malvern, 1992, are, from left (* = one of the Few): Dr Gordon Mitchell; Wg Cdr Bernard Jennings AFC DFM*; Fred Roberts (armourer, 1940); Flt Lt Hugh Chalmers (65 Squadron, 1941); Flt Lt Peter Hairs MBE*; Flt Lt Tadek Turek (Polish); Flt Lt Michael Graham DFC (504 Squadron post 1940); Bob Morris (engine fitter, 1940); WO Bob 'Butch' Morton (616 Squadron 1941, PoW); Sqn Ldr Lionel 'Buck' Casson AFC DFC*; Flt Lt William Walker*; Flt Lt Kazek Budzik (Polish, 308 Squadron, 1941); Flt Lt Richard Jones*; Fg Off Ken Wilkinson*. All are now deceased.

on aircraft restorations, recoveries and aviation history. That same year, the Battle of Britain's fortieth anniversary, Winston Ramsay edited and published the encyclopaedic *Battle of Britain: Then & Now*, placing in the public domain details of both sides' aircraft and aircrew losses, recoveries and memorials. Many of us at that point, I think, really began to grasp that the Battle of Britain was not a romantic game, but, like any other battle, a violent confrontation in which young lives were lost. Inspirational though the sacrifices of the 'Finest Hour' were, sobering they were too. And I began to think about my obsession in a very different way.

In 1985, as a young policeman, I was posted to work at Malvern, in Worcestershire in the West Midlands, far from south-east England. Having already been on the periphery of aviation archaeology locally, in 1986 I had my 'lightbulb moment' when a friend, Andy Long, then aged only 17 to my 25 years, mentioned that a Polish Battle of Britain pilot, Flying Officer Franciszek Surma, had baled out of a Spitfire just outside the town owing to an engine fire. That was it: the start of a journey which is still on-going. I began researching the life of 'Franek' Surma, discovering that he had been reported Missing in Action over Dunkirk on 8 November 1941. The history of the Spitfire involved, R6644, was also investigated, and slowly I began tracing pilots who had either flown with Surma or who had soared aloft in R6644. In this endeavour I received invaluable assistance from Wing Commander Pat Hancock, Honorary Secretary of the Battle of Britain Fighter Association, who would pass my letters on to members of the Association I needed to contact. The choice was theirs whether or not to respond. All did.

Over the years my research into various individual casualties, aircraft and combats substantially increased in scale and scope, always firmly rooted

At the same event, another line-up, from left: Grp Capt Gerry Edge DSO DFC*; Wg Cdr Bernard Jennings AFC DFM*; Fred Roberts; former *Luftwaffe Leutnant* Hans Wulff (KG53, ZG26, JG6); Flt Lt Hary Welford*; Flt Lt William Walker*; Fg Off Ken Wilkinson*; Fg Off John Lumsden (Mosquitos and Brigands, post-war); Sqn Ldr Buck Casson AFC DFC*; Flt Lt Richard Jones*; Flt Lt Peter Taylor (65 Squadron 1942); WO Butch Morton; Flt Lt Peter Hairs MBE*; Flt Lt Hugh Chalmers; Polish Flt Lts Tadek Turek, Kazek Budzik and Tadek Dziedzic.

in the human experience. A constant stream of research projects generated prolific correspondence with the surviving Few. This was never random: initial contact always concerned a specific question; and nor did I contact survivors simply for the sake of it. At this time, the Few were in their late sixties or early seventies, many only recently retired, and so for the first time had both the opportunity and desire to reflect on the past and rekindle auld acquaintance. Most had disappeared into happy obscurity, their wartime reputations and 'names' forgotten. In many ways I became both a catalyst and conduit for this process, helping provide information to reconnect with the past.

From 1990 onwards, it was a privilege to assemble several times a year, and for some years ahead, large numbers of the Few at my book launches, exhibitions and lectures. Indeed we became a kind of extended family, an unofficial reunion association, if you will. So, I came to know many of the Few as friends. These relationships, and our correspondence arising, enabled me to collate a substantial and unique archive of first-hand material and photographs, the priceless historic value of which I am only now beginning to realise.

In the years after the Second World War, the famous aces – men like Douglas Bader, Johnnie Johnson, Al Deere and Bob Stanford Tuck – either published their memoirs or were the subject of biographies. Most of the survivors, however, had neither considered producing such a record, or sought a platform from which to share those experiences. Indeed, most could not imagine anyone else being interested in their war. I was, though. Very much so. All of these experiences, from the most celebrated ace to the most junior member of the support team, are vital to enabling a true appreciation and understanding of 'what it was like'. None should be ignored. Academia may have a cautious approach to oral history, but what follows in this book surely shows the value of the information which is only obtainable from eye-witnesses – those elderly men were a primary source in themselves.

It was also obvious from the start that the Few were getting fewer as time marched on. Some 2,900 Fighter Command aircrew are known to have fought in the Battle of Britain; 544 lost their lives during the summer of 1940, over 700 more by the war's end. In 1998, I dined at Bentley Priory, Fighter Command's one-time HQ, with only just over 100 of the Few at that year's annual reunion; at the time of writing, there are but three members of the Association living, and one non-member. There may be others still alive who never joined the Association, but there may be none.

With the foregoing in mind, and sitting here over thirty years after beginning my work with very modest resources, I hold the fulfilment of a vision.

PROLOGUE

For decades, I eagerly awaited the postman's arrival every day, never quite knowing what would drop through my letterbox, or from whom, or where.

For some, the Battle of Britain remained, as one correspondent described it, 'a kaleidoscope of memories'. For others, their part or time in it had been short and relatively inconsequential. There was little science attached to selecting those for inclusion in this book, and it was a difficult choice: so many to choose from and all deserving. Some of the following chapters concern aces, at least two of which were household names; both also remained so long after the war – but for very different reasons. Most are proud to represent the many amongst the Few who simply did their 'bit' – without considering themselves in any way heroic or worthy of a verse. All but one of the RAF pilots in this book flew either Spitfires or Hurricanes, only because those types are my primary interest and were therefore the focus of my research.

Another Great Malvern gathering, launch of *Through Peril to the Stars: RAF Fighter Pilots Who Failed to Return,* 1993; from left: Wg Cdr Bernard Jennings AFC DFM*; Sqn Ldr TA 'Steve' Stevens DFC (19 Squadron 1941); Sqn Ldr Bob Pugh AFC (Wellington pilot); Flt Lt Tony Minchin, 122 Squadron; Sqn Ldr Buck Casson AFC DFC*; Wg Cdr George Unwin DSO DFM*; Fg Of Ken Wilkinson*; Flt Lt Tadek Dzeidzic; Flt Lt Denis Nichols*; Flt Lt Ron Rayner DFC (41 Squadron, 1941); Flt Lt Duncan Spruce (118 Squadron 1943); Flt Lt Iain Hutchinson*; Flt Lt William Walker*; Flt Lt Richard Jones*; Grp Capt Gerry Edge DSO DFC*.

LETTERS FROM THE FEW

The Few are all holders of the coveted Battle of Britain Bar to the 1939-45 Star – but no such acknowledgement was ever given those who served on the ground. Moreover, those in less glamorous supporting roles were never admitted to the Battle of Britain Fighter Association. Again, the experience of those on the ground, without whom the Few could not have fought, is important. For that reason, the reader will find the story of an armourer included in this book, representing those who also served. Finally, the human experience of the Battle of Britain cannot be exclusive; to properly contextualise and fix the whole narrative in time and space, we must hear from our former enemy – which in the Epilogue we do.

After the Second World War, survivors were just expected to get on with their lives, which, with new priorities to concentrate on, including earning a crust and raising families, they largely did. This, perhaps, helped them forget traumatic experiences, or at least temporarily put them aside. A number of survivors told me that they were unable to discuss the past with family members who had not shared the wartime experience. Indeed war experiences were hardly party conversation, and God forbid that anyone should consciously 'shoot a line', which is to say exaggerate or seek recognition for their deeds. The letters I received, therefore, were a first attempt by some to articulate and record their experiences, inevitably written in such a way, usually, as to downplay their own achievement. At face-value, the letters and extracts reproduced in this book appear innocent enough, but in some of them there are undoubtedly echoes of what today would be identified as Post Traumatic Stress Disorder and 'Survivor Guilt'. To a degree, then, perhaps for some of my correspondents this exercise was sub-consciously therapeutic – but I only surmise. All of the men in this book, regardless of role or side, are sadly now deceased. It was an honour and a privilege to know them all, to differing degrees, and call them friends.

And now, you too can share in my excitement at opening and reading … letters from the Few.

Dilip Sarkar MBE FRHistS

Chapter One

Flight Lieutenant Richard Jones AE
Spitfire Pilot

It was in 1991, that Richard Leoline Jones and I became great friends: one of the Few who had flown Spitfires with 64 and 19 Squadrons during the Battle of Britain. On 30 September 1991, Richard wrote to me, having read my first book, *Spitfire Squadron*, published in May 1990, concerning 19 Squadron 1939-41. I was soon on my way to meet Richard and his wife, Elizabeth, at their Witney home, there finding a delightful couple, so warm and welcoming. It was the start of a long and valued friendship.

Richard's original letter included a yellow sticky notelet with scribbled details of his RAF service. Having joined the RAFVR in November 1938, he had, according to the note, undertaken elementary flying training at Woodley, near Reading, on 'Magisters/Hawker Harts and Hinds'. Mobilised on 1 September 1939, after induction at Cambridge, Pilot Officer Jones learned to fly Harvards at Tern Hill in Shropshire. Then, on 6 July 1940, he arrived at 5 Operational Training Unit (OTU) at Aston Down, near Stroud, for conversion to Spitfires. According to his logbook, a copy of which the 'sticky' was attached to, on 8 July Flight Lieutenant Gough checked Richard out in a Harvard, following which he made two 'Experience' flights in a Miles Master. On 11 July, Pilot Officer Jones soared aloft for the first time in a Spitfire (P9824), making twenty-four further training flights and accumulating a respectable 19.40 hours on Spitfires before the course concluded on 26 July. The record showed that Wing Commander 'Bull' Hallahan, a veteran of the fighting in France with 1 Squadron, gave Pilot Officer Jones's abilities as a fighter pilot a rare rating: 'Above Average'. Richard was then on his way to join 64 Squadron at Kenley for 'London Defence' – by which time the Battle of Britain had started.

Over the years, Richard sent me many notes on those far off days:-

'From a very early age I lived quite near a very large RAF station and used to go up and watch the aircraft. At that time there were Hawker Harts and all those other Hawker variants, and as soon as the Volunteer Reserve started up I immediately applied, and luckily was accepted. I started flying almost immediately, about two years before the war.

'Upon arrival at Kenley, I remember being met by the CO, an absolutely charming man and a real gentleman in every sense of the word, Squadron Leader Don MacDonell. He immediately made us new pilots feel at home, he called us his "Chicks". We would find our CO a quiet but determined leader and an excellent fighter pilot. He looked after the best interests of all who served under him and he had the respect of all.

'To give us battle experience as quickly as possible whenever the time allowed, we were paired off with a senior battle-experienced pilot to practise dog-fighting and yet more dog-fighting to give us both experience and confidence in the Spitfire and combat conditions. We were lucky to have that extra-curricular training, which would have been impossible had we been posted to 64 later on that summer, and for obvious reasons.

Pilot Officer Richard Jones pictured at Fowlmere, September 1940.

'The operational focal point of every squadron was dispersal, which was a hut containing 12 beds, and an Orderly Clerk with a telephone. I well recall the three states of Readiness. The first was "Readiness", which meant all pilots kitted up and ready to go. The next was at "15 minutes", which meant that you had to be in the Mess and available to be ready for flight in 15 minutes. Finally, "30 minutes", which meant that you could relax a bit, play billiards or go to the local cinema. From that state you could be called to "15 minutes" and so on.

'If you were on Readiness, then that day you would rise very early, at around 0400 hrs, so that you were at the aerodrome and ready before dawn in the event of an emergency. Immediately, you would be served a remarkable breakfast and the attention that we received from staff was amazing. After breakfast we used to get into what we called the "Cattle Truck" to be driven over to Dispersal. We would then get kitted up, excepting our helmets and parachutes, which were placed on or in the aircraft, also at the ready, and waited in the Crew Room for something to happen. If you were not down on the board to fly, then it was a long day, waiting around. Most pilots spent their waiting time playing cards, chess, reading or sleeping.

3

Suddenly the tranquillity would be shattered by the telephone's bell, Immediately, everyone was tense, in anticipation of orders to scramble. Certainly, the telephone stirred our senses quicker than anything else that I have ever experienced.

'If it was a scramble, we ran to and got into our Spitfires, engines started and away. We would be given immediate instructions, such as "Scramble Angels 10 over Dungeness". We knew that because our radar-based system of early warning, wherever we were sent there was always a good chance of meeting the enemy. If we did meet the Germans then of course we would engage them to the best of our ability.

'When we came back, anybody who had been successful, perhaps in shooting down an enemy aircraft, might do such a thing as a "victory roll", but those were not encouraged because it was not always known whether one's own aircraft was in fact damaged. Immediately upon landing the IO would take full details from each pilot of what had happened, whilst the groundcrew prepared the aircraft for immediate take-off. We then started the waiting process all over again, until such time as we were either scrambled again or relieved of Readiness by another squadron. We would then drop back to 15 minutes, then 30 minutes, and so the cycle went on. In fairness,

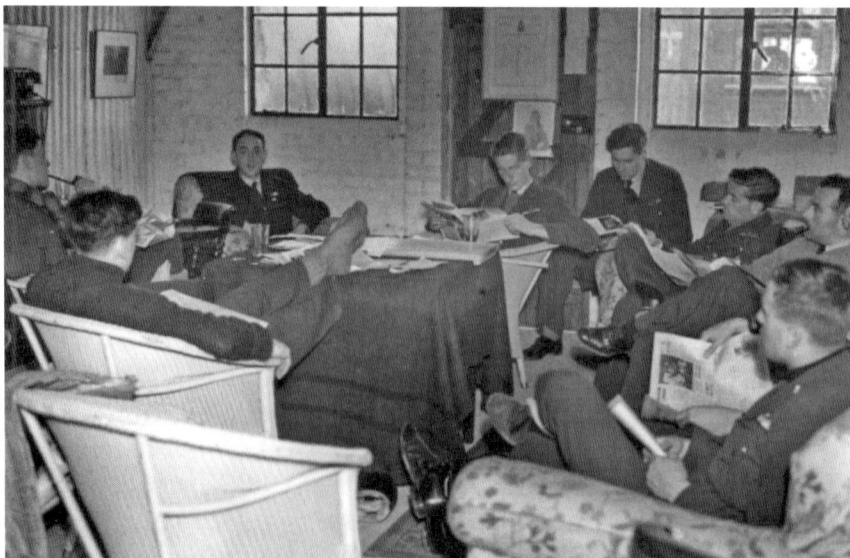

A mixture of 19 and 616 Squadron pilots pictured at Fowlmere during the Battle of Britain; extreme left, with pipe, Fg Off Colin MacFie (616); clockwise: Sqn Ldr Brian Lane DFC (19); Plt Off Hugh Dundas (616); Plt Off Richard Jones (19).

despite the actual state of Readiness, we were always pretty much ready for most eventualities.

'One incident of many that I can still recall was when we of 64 Squadron were visited by the Air Minister, Sir Archibald Sinclair. We were all lined up to meet him, standing in front of our Spitfires. He congratulated us on the work that we were doing and in his opening words thanked us as *Hurricane pilots of 12 Group*! Clearly the Minister knew not the difference between a Spitfire or Hurricane, much less the disposition of Fighter Command's Groups. We were not impressed.

'I well remember my first operational engagement with the enemy. We were about nine Spitfires against thirty or forty enemy fighters and before meeting them I had real butterflies in my stomach, wondering what to expect. When they were spotted we waded into them and once engaged all fear disappeared. We immediately realised it was them or us. All hell appeared to be let loose with aircraft everywhere. The next moment we were all on our own, everyone had disappeared.

Richard and Elizabeth Jones married during the Battle of Britain – only parting with Elizabeth's death in 2009.

'In fact, in the panic of my first engagement I don't think I even fired a shot, as it appeared to me to take all my time avoiding a collision with other aircraft. I felt it was the most valuable experience I had received in my life – I returned to base a more mature individual and felt extremely lucky to have survived to tell the tale.

'There were so many incidents that it is almost impossible to single the odd one out, but there is one particular incident that immediately comes to mind. On that particular day we were on duty down at Hawkinge, near Dover, and had the 'phone call and immediate scramble. I rushed to the aircraft, got in but it would not start under any circumstances, so I was left behind. No sooner had the Squadron taken off, Hawkinge was bombed. On the Dispersal Point that I was on there was only one very small shelter,

Flight Lieutenant Richard Jones pictured while serving as a test pilot.

about three or four people would fill it, so everybody rushed for it. When I entered, the aerodrome was being bombed. I was being pushed to the back, then we were all pushed forward. I came out of the shelter, we all went around again, entering the back of the shelter, and so we all kept going around, in and out, whilst being bombed! It wasn't very funny at the time, but when you look back, having survived the experience unscathed, it was most amusing!

'The Spitfire was the most wonderful aircraft *ever*. Perfect. Predictable in most ways, very fast. Wonderful. Everybody loved it. Our Spitfires could get up to nearly 40,000 feet, so we used to tackle the German fighter escorts. If a pilot was posted to a Hurricane squadron, that was the finest aircraft he had ever flown; if posted to a *Spitfire* squadron, however, you were flying the finest aircraft *ever*.'

On 12 September 1940, Pilot Officer Jones was posted from 64 in 11 Group to 19 Squadron in 12 Group, based at Fowlmere, the Duxford satellite. At that time (and more of which later), 19 Squadron was operating as a top cover Spitfire squadron in Douglas Bader's 'Big Wing'. Another yellow 'sticky' on Richard's logbook reads, 'My first week with 19 – apart from the last entry, not very interesting'. The flights comprised ferrying aircraft about, a scramble to 29,000 feet on 23 September; another scramble that day prompted the observation 'Chased a recco 109 into 10/10 cloud – very amusing!!!' The last entry concerned the events of 28 September – on which day a single *gruppe* of Ju 88s headed for London, protected by three *jagdgeschwadern* of Me 109s. Soon 19 Squadron was up, Pilot Officer Jones flying Spitfire P7432:-

'When patrolling over the Tenterden area at 29,000 feet, the Controller informed us that as there were apparently no enemy aircraft in the vicinity we could "pancake". I was "Arse-end Charlie" and relaxed slightly as we descended to 20,000 feet. Suddenly about four feet of my starboard wing just peeled off. My initial thought that it was a poor show on a new aircraft.

Then a loud bang followed and a hole appeared above the undercarriage. I was obviously the target of an enemy fighter positioned up sun. Immediately I took evasive action but simultaneously my engine cut out, so suddenly I was in a high-speed stall and spin. As my radio was U/S I was unable to inform the Squadron, the other pilots of which returned to base blissfully unaware that I had been shot down.

'As the aircraft's controls were not responding I did not recover from the spin until at 10,000 feet, and at that time I realised that the hood was jammed shut. Subsequently I crash-landed with a dead engine in one of only two suitable fields in a heavily wooded area just outside Hawkhurst. Unfortunately, I did so amongst a flock of sheep and unfortunately several were killed. I was rescued by the Army and taken first to the Hawkhurst doctor who treated a flesh wound to my leg, then to their Mess prior to returning safely to Fowlmere.

'My Spitfire had a broken propeller and radiator, a few holes and some missing parts but was otherwise relatively undamaged. For some reason the incident was not recorded in the 19 Squadron ORB, but in my log book I wrote, "Shot down and crash-landed at Hawkhurst, Kent. Killed three sheep. What a bloody mess!!!" – which it was!'

Richard Jones was always a popular guest at events, pictured here at Worcester Guildhall in 1998 with the author and Lady Bader.

On 15 November 1940, Richard was returned to 64 Squadron, with which he remained until April 1941, when seconded to the Ministry of Aircraft Production and 'lent' to the De Havilland company as a test pilot. Consequently, Richard test flew Spitfires and Hurricanes that had been repaired at the factory, a job which he retained until leaving the RAF (as a Flight Lieutenant) in 1946.

Interestingly, having served in both 11 and 12 Groups, Richard was well-placed to comment on the experience of having flown small tactical formations and with the 'Big Wing', about which he wrote to me on 1 February 1997:-

'My immediate impression [when posted to 19 Squadron in 12 Group] was the experience of flying with a Wing comprising four or five squadrons of both Spitfires and Hurricanes, instead of at Kenley taking off on a "flap" with anything between five to ten aircraft – to intercept hundreds of enemy aircraft.

'To me, this experience gave me enormous confidence, when you looked around and saw anything from fifty upwards of friendly fighters keeping me company. Also, I presumed that there was perhaps time being wasted in forming up etc after take-off and the using of valuable fuel en route to the south coast. At the same time, I felt it must have had a very great effect in lowering the morale of the enemy, who for the first time encountered such a formidable opponent.'

As we will see, the views of pilots regarding the 'Big Wing' remain divided, even amongst those of the same squadron. These, therefore, are invaluable recollections.

Post war, Richard Jones enjoyed a long career in the motor industry, then in 'retirement' worked as a part-time court usher at Witney Magistrates' Court. Always a popular guest at our many events, Richard had time for everyone, a truly charming, gentle, man. Richard and Elizabeth married during the Battle of Britain, and were only parted by Elizabeth's passing, following a long illness, on 28 May 2009. Richard soldiered on but left us on 7 March 2012. To me, Richard never seemed to look any older, the 'Peter Pan' of the Few – but sadly, nobody lives forever.

Chapter Two

Group Captain Peter Townsend CVO DSO DFC*

Hurricane Pilot

On my desk, as I write, is a yellowing copy of the *Daily Express* newspaper, priced at 1½d and dated Tuesday, 1 November 1955. The front page and much of the content within is devoted to a story concerning one of the Few – but the story is far from what could normally be expected. Indeed, the front pages that day concerning that particular fighter 'ace' – who through protracted correspondence I later came to know well – were probably the most widely read on a global basis that year. For this story – a controversial royal romance – had the world's attention.

A handsome man in a civilian suit appears on the front page, alongside a photograph of a pensive looking Princess Margaret, the younger sister and only sibling of Queen Elizabeth II. The headline reads 'Romance is off'. The Princess's 'personal message' beneath begins, 'I would like it to be known that I have decided not to marry Group Captain Peter Townsend' – the man in the suit – emphasising that 'I have reached this decision entirely alone, and in doing so I have been strengthened by the unfailing support and devotion of Group Captain Peter Townsend.' It was the sad end to two years of speculation and a scandal rocking the Royal family – not because Townsend was a commoner sixteen years older than the headstrong Princess, but due to him being divorced – an insurmountable hurdle given that Princess Margaret's elder sister, the Queen, was Head of the Church of England, which insisted that marriage was 'indissoluble'.

Flight Lieutenant Peter Townsend while serving with 43 Squadron at Wick during early 1940, pictured with his Flight Rigger, Duxbury (left) and Engine Fitter, Hacking.

GROUP CAPTAIN PETER TOWNSEND CVO DSO DFC*

It was in February 1944 that the dashing and decorated Group Captain Townsend had been assigned to the Royal Household as Equerry to King George VI. At that time, Peter had been married to Rosemary Pawle for three years. In 1950, Peter was made Deputy Master of the Household, becoming a key courtier, but in 1952, Rosemary and he divorced. That year, the King died, Elizabeth became Queen, and Group Captain Townsend was elevated to Comptroller to the Queen Mother. Queen Elizabeth II's coronation took place in 1953, a lavish state occasion and after all those years of war and austerity a golden pageant uplifting the nation and Commonwealth. There, the sharp-eyed coronation press were delighted to note and photograph the Comptroller and Queen's 23-year-old sister, Margaret, beaming at each other, their secret romance blown in a momentary lapse when the Princess brushed some fluff from the war hero's smart uniform.

With the media's spotlight firmly focussed on the fact that Margaret's would-be suitor was divorced, a crisis developed. Peter had proposed, and the Princess was inclined to accept. Under the Royal Marriages Act 1772, however, because Margaret was under 25, the Queen had to approve the marriage. Less than twenty years previously, King Edward VIII had abdicated over his determination to marry the American commoner and divorcee Wallis Simpson – rocking the monarchy in the process. So seismic a scandal was the abdication that it remained an open sore. With that in mind, and very much influencing events, the British Cabinet refused to countenance the proposed marriage of Princess Margaret and Group Captain Peter Townsend. Churchill informed the Queen that the dominion leaders were unanimously opposed to the match, and Parliament would not countenance a marriage unrecognised by the Church of England – unless Margaret, like her uncle before her, renounced her rights to the throne. It was decided that the troublesome Townsend would effectively be banished from the realm for two years, as Air Attaché in Brussels, until Princess Margaret was 25 and legally able to make her own decision. Public opinion, however, firmly supported the lovers, a further indication that the establishment was increasingly out of touch with the people, failing to keep up with the social changes in Britain.

After two years' separation and exile, Group Captain Townsend returned for an answer. Having been guests of Lord Rupert Nevill at Uckfield House, on Monday, 30 October 1955, Margaret returned to Clarence House in London while Peter went back to his friend the Marquis of Abergavenny's flat in Knightsbridge. The world's press awaited news with eager anticipation. Soon a decision would be announced. That evening the couple met in a drawing room at Clarence House, Peter recording the

Princess's press statement in pencil. At 1817 hrs, his green Renault was espied by clamouring reporters leaving – for the last time. An hour later, the statement was issued, ending eighteen days of intense media scrutiny and public interest, and two years of controversy: Princess Margaret would not be marrying Group Captain Townsend.

Afterwards, public opinion remained divided, the Princess having been seen by many to put duty before love and personal happiness. Eventually the tumult subsided. In 1956, Peter retired from the RAF and, unsurprisingly perhaps, moved permanently to the continent, enjoying a varied career as a wine buyer, United Nations advisor, and author. In 1959, Peter married a Belgian, Marie Luce Jamagne, the couple settling happily in France. Ten years later, Group Captain Townsend joined an impressive array of technical advisors on the epic movie *Battle of Britain* – by which time he was writing his excellently researched and lively *Duel of Eagles*, chronicling the Battle of Britain, published in 1970. Eight years later, his autobiography followed, *Time & Chance*, providing a rare personal comment on the Princess Margaret affair: 'She could have married me only if she'd been prepared to give up everything – her position, her prestige, her privy purse.' Documents released in 2004, however, confirm that in 1955 the Queen and new Prime Minister, the divorced and sympathetic Sir Anthony Eden, formulated a plan making that unnecessary: the only change to Princess Margaret's royal life and status would be removal from the line of succession. In other words, the Princess would have retained her royal title, allowance, remained in the country and continued public duties. Like Peter, Margaret largely kept silent, even in private, regarding the affair, but did disclose to her biographer, Christopher Warwick, that the real reason she ultimately rejected Townsend was because after two years apart there was uncertainty as to whether the love between them remained 'strong enough'. Nonetheless, the available evidence suggests that Margaret was unaware of the plan devised by her sister, the Queen, and the Prime Minister until *after* her decision had been reached and announced. Whether that would have made any difference will always remain speculative.

Why, the reader may justifiably wonder, rake over these old coals again here? That is because today, sixty-five years after Margaret's decision was made public, there are subsequent generations who very likely know nothing of the scandal involving the Princess and dashing Battle of Britain fighter pilot – and to understand the Peter Townsend I knew, thirty years after those headlining personal events, it is necessary to be aware of this trauma in his life, lived out in the media's full-glare. Afterwards, it was dealt with as expected by an English gentleman: with utmost propriety, integrity and dignity. There was, though, a great deal more to Peter Townsend, a highly intelligent, sensitive, creative and kind man who was one of the greatest humanitarians it has been my privilege to know, through protracted correspondence and long-distance telephone calls. The problem for Peter, of course, was that the Princess Margaret affair was to a degree omnipresent, firmly placing him outside the establishment he had served so well. He never joined, for example, the Battle of Britain Fighter Association, although as the then Hon. Sec. Wing Commander Pat Hancock told me, 'The Group Captain would be made extremely welcome.' A very private person, Peter was also a busy man, travelling around the world, always working on some literary or humanitarian project or other. Indeed, he often wrote to me between connecting flights, as he dashed around, suitcase in hand. He was, I think, an exceptional man by any standards.

Peter Wooldridge Townsend was born in Rangoon, India, on 22 November 1914, the son of Lieutenant Colonel Edward Copleston Townsend and his wife, Gladys. The family home, though, was in less exotic Devon. The young Peter was educated at Wychwood Preparatory School, Bournemouth, before going up to Haileybury and Imperial Service College, near Hertford. In 1933, with all the necessary credentials for an officer and gentleman, the 19-year-old school-leaver opted not for the church – a popular choice

The first German aircraft to fall on English soil since 1918, destroyed by Flight Lieutenant Townsend's Blue Section. The He 111 of KG26 crashed near Whitby.

Characteristically, Peter Townsend – ever the humanitarian – visited the wounded radio-operator and air gunner Karl Missy in hospital. They met again years later while Peter was researching *Duel of Eagles*.

for his family – but for a career in the RAF. That year, Flight Cadet Townsend entered the RAF College Cranwell – and became a Prize Cadet. With this early indication of potential behind him, upon graduation, on 27 July 1935, Peter accepted a Permanent Commission. Pilot Officer Townsend first joined 1 Squadron at Tangmere, flying Hawker Fury biplane fighters, but was then, strangely, posted to fly twin-engined Vickers Vildebeest torpedo-bombers with 36 Squadron in Singapore. The climate, however, adversely affected his health, and so Flying Officer Townsend, as he now was, returned to Tangmere, on 27 June 1937, again flying the Fury, this time with 43 Squadron. After a specialist navigation course at Manston, he was posted to 217 Squadron, a reconnaissance unit also at Tangmere. A bout of protracted illness followed, after which Peter – 'Much to my delight' – re-joined 43 Squadron, 'The Fighting Cocks', in September 1938. It was not the best start to a flying career perhaps, but a period of stability followed, during which Peter sufficiently impressed to be promoted flight lieutenant in January 1939, and was appointed commander of 'B' Flight in August. A day later, Germany invaded Poland. Two days after that, Britain and France declared war on Germany, Hitler having ignored their ultimatum to withdraw back behind the German border. Peter Townsend, the Prize Cadet, was going to war.

On 18 November 1939, 43 Squadron moved north, to Acklington in 13 Group, near Newcastle-upon-Tyne, tasked with providing aerial protection to convoys within five miles of the British coastline. Of those days, Peter wrote:-

'Dilip, it was bleak. Very. The weather was often filthy, and our job was to patrol over convoys off the east coast. Remember that we had no dinghies, Air Sea Rescue was virtually non-existent, so if our sole engine let us down,

14

we were entirely dependent upon merchantmen for rescue. We faced the weather and the sea, but rarely the enemy. One day, my great friend Caesar Hull intercepted and shot at a *Heinkel*, but these raiders usually avoided our attention by flying into cloud immediately our Hurricanes were sighted. For this reason, we decided to keep low, very close to the sea, so less visible and able to use maximum boost to climb and catch them, before we were sighted and the usual disappearing act occurred. On 30 January 1940, Caesar used this tactic to good effect and destroyed a *Heinkel*.'

At dawn on 3 February 1940, He 111 *Werke Nummer* 3232, 1H+FM of II/ KG26 took off from Schleswig to intercept a convoy travelling south off Britain's north-east coast, a return trip of five hours duration. At 0903 hrs, Danby Beacon Radar Station gave warning of unidentified aircraft sixty miles out to sea, approaching the British coast at 1,000 feet. Minutes later, Flight Lieutenant Townsend, leading 43 Squadron's Blue Section of 'B' Flight, with Flying Officer 'Tiger' Folkes and Sergeant Jim Hallowes, was scrambled:-

'We received information that a Bandit was attacking a ship off Whitby. We spread out in search formation, line abreast, very loose, just above the waves and made all haste. Suddenly, I saw a He 111 just below cloud. It all happened very quickly, because had the German seen us, he could have easily escaped into the cloud. We stepped on it, and when the bomber filled my sights, opened fire. That burst killed the observer, *Unteroffizier* Peter Leushake, and mortally wounded the flight engineer, *Unteroffizier* Johann Meyer. The rear gunner, *Unteroffizier* Karl Missy, returned fire but was badly wounded.'

Peter's official combat report succinctly describes the engagement, which took place at 300 feet, five miles south of Whitby:-

'Speed of E/A 180. Seen climbing for clouds, flying NNW. Fighters' speed 240. Carried out No 1 Fighter Command Attacks five times. E/A lowered undercarriage after third attack. Under and top rear gunner firing from E/A. All attacks except the first one made with full deflection. E/A turned east, landed, undercarriage collapsing, crashed through hedge and stopped fifty yards from farmhouse.'

Only Missy and his pilot, *Unteroffizier* Hermann Wilms, survived and were captured, although Missy lost a leg and was so badly wounded that he was returned to Germany in a 1943 prisoner of war exchange. Peter visited the wounded Missy in Whitby Hospital the following day:-

'Yes, that's right, I did. I felt I should. I took him some cigarettes. I felt sorry for him but did not regret my actions. The Squadron buried Missy's friends with full military honours at Catterick. Twenty-eight years later we met again, at Missy's home in Germany, when I was researching the German side of the story for my book *Duel of Eagles*. He bore me no ill-will and welcomed me as a friend.'

The bomber was one of three destroyed that day, and, having force-landed at Bannial Flat Farm, Whitby, Yorkshire, became famous as the first German aircraft to be brought down on English soil during the Second World War.

On 22 February 1940, Peter destroyed another He 111, engaged on a reconnaissance of Carlisle. Thirty miles off the Farne Islands, the raider crashed into the sea with great force – there were no survivors. Peter 'felt utterly nauseated'. The next day, 43 Squadron moved further north, to Wick in Scotland, from where it was to provide aerial cover for the great naval anchorage at Scapa Flow in the offshore Orkneys. On 8 April, Flight Lieutenant Townsend and Sergeant Hallowes were scrambled after dark to intercept some twenty raiders bound for Scapa Flow. Peter found a He 111, the return fire from which was ferocious, until the Hurricane's eight machine guns silenced the opposition. With navigation lights on, the bomber 'landed in the sea', Peter reported. All aboard were lost. Back at Wick there was a surprise: Sergeant Hallowes had attacked another Heinkel, which force-landed on 43 Squadron's airfield, causing great excitement. The crew, however, insisted that they had been shot down by a Spitfire, even though there were no Spitfires in this sector, inspiring Peter to coin the phrase 'Spitfire snobbery'. Peter told me that:-

'During the Battle of France, the Germans saw "Spitfires" everywhere – even though there were only Hurricanes. There was more kudos, it seemed, being bested by the Spitfire, the performance of which was superior to the Hurricane.'

An analysis of *Luftwaffe* combat claims indicates an impossibly high proportion of Spitfires, considering the overall size of the Spitfire force in action over southern England. For example, between 10 July and 31 October 1940 the Germans claimed 711 Hurricanes and 1,940 Spitfires destroyed! If we take the figure of twelve operational aircraft per squadron, there were actually only 396 Hurricanes and 228 Spitfires. This means that the overall ratio of Hurricanes to Spitfires was 1.7, in the former's favour. Interestingly, the Germans were 1.7 times more likely to claim a Spitfire destroyed than a Hurricane. While factually impossible, owing to numbers available and the Spitfire's demonstrable technical superiority, this does confirm Peter's allegation of 'Spitfire Snobbery'. Indeed, *Leutnant* Heinz Knocke, an Me 109 pilot with I/JG52, wrote that 'The Supermarine Spitfire, because of its manoeuvrability and technical performance has given the German

Squadron Leader Peter Townsend drawn by Cuthbert Orde while commanding 85 Squadron.

formations plenty of trouble. "*Achtung*! *Spitfeur*!" is a warning German pilots have learned to pay particular attention to when hearing it in their earphones. We consider shooting down a Spitfire to be an outstanding achievement, which it most certainly is.'

On 21 February 1989, Peter wrote to me again on the subject:-

'I must honestly say that while my admiration for the Spitfire and its pilots are unbounded, I always have a pang of regret concerning the Hurricane, a squadron of which, 85, I commanded during the Battle of Britain and Night *Blitz*. There were, as you know, thirty-three Hurricane squadrons and nineteen Spitfire squadrons in the Battle of Britain, and the Hurricanes, while doing considerably greater execution, suffered heavier aggregate losses. However, I do not wish to dwell on this fact.'

What Peter says regarding the Hurricane 'doing considerably greater execution' than the Spitfire has long been accepted. But is that actually true, there being a big difference between a combat claim and a confirmed aerial victory, cross-referenced with an actual loss? According to my own studies of combat losses and claims, the *Luftwaffe* lost 1,273 aircraft during the Battle of Britain; Spitfire and Hurricane pilots alone, however, claimed to have destroyed 2,051 – 1,109 by Hurricanes, 942 by Spitfires.

17

Even if those figures for claims accurately reflected losses, the Hurricane's 'execution' was only 167 more aircraft than the Spitfire. Considering that there were fourteen more Hurricane squadrons, I would argue that this figure is not 'considerable'. In fact, being less numerous, the Spitfire was actually 0.32 per aircraft more successful than the Hurricane.

In 1996, an American, John Alcorn, published his 'Statistical Study of the Battle of Britain' in *Aeroplane Monthly*. Following years of work, endorsed by the late Dr Alfred Price, John completed an exhaustive survey of losses and claims. In conclusion, John argued that the nineteen Spitfire squadrons destroyed 521 enemy aircraft, while the thirty-three squadrons of Hurricanes destroyed 655 – an average of twenty-seven kills per Spitfire squadron and twenty-two per Hurricane squadron. According to this data, therefore, the Spitfire was 1.25 times more successful in combat than the Hurricane. In 2000, the same magazine carried John's 'Update', in which he challenged 'anyone to significantly improve on my findings', which were arrived at after 2,000 hours 'using just about all of the references available'. The Update, however, changed nothing substantially, John's conclusion remaining that 'the Spitfires were somewhat more successful on average': 2.32 enemy aircraft destroyed per Spitfire, 1.81 by each Hurricane. Of these, 282 Spitfire kills and 222 Hurricanes kills were Me 109 single-engined fighters. Thus, on average, the Spitfire squadrons accounted for fifteen 109s each, whereas the Hurricanes managed 7.5 – and therein lies the rub, as the New Zealander Battle of Britain ace Air Commodore Alan Deere explained:-

'There can be no doubt that victory in the Battle of Britain was made possible by the Spitfire. Although there were more Hurricanes than Spitfires in the Battle, the Spitfire was the RAF's primary weapon because of its better all-round capability. The Hurricane could not have won this great air battle, but the Spitfire could have done so.'

The reason for this was that the Spitfire was able to perform at all altitudes, even as high as 30,000 feet, whereas the Hurricane could not. Had Fighter Command only been Hurricane-equipped, it would have been decimated by the high-flying Me 109s. It has, however, been argued that the Hurricane was better able to attack the bombers, while the Spitfire fended off the 109s higher up. That is true, but the point is that the Spitfire could do both. That is not to say that nineteen squadrons of Spitfires could have prevailed alone, without the Hurricane. Air Chief Marshal Dowding, for example, had made clear that he required fifty-two squadrons to guarantee Britain's aerial defence – the sum of both Spitfire and Hurricane squadrons. So, while we now know that the long-accepted claim that Hurricanes executed greater damage on the enemy is a myth, the fact always remains that owing to there being insufficient Spitfires, the Hurricane was essential to the defence of this country. Peter Townsend, however, was sadly no longer with us when John Alcorn's ground-breaking argument and evidence-based conclusions were published; what Peter would have made of it, we will never know.

Returning to Peter's war, on 30 April 1940, his DFC was gazetted: 'In April 1940, whilst on patrol over the North Sea, Flight Lieutenant Townsend intercepted and attacked an enemy aircraft at dusk and after a running fight shot it down. This is the third success obtained by this pilot and in each instance, he has displayed qualities of leadership, skill and determination of the highest order, with little regard for his own safety.' This was, of course, a very early award, even before the Battle of France, and appropriate recognition for the dangerous flying 43 Squadron was undertaking, in which, as Peter said, the pilots faced not only the enemy but equally, if not more so, the dangers of the weather and sea. Flight Lieutenant Townsend was, by now, an experienced fighter pilot and flight commander, one of the small number of British pilots who had actually engaged the enemy during this 'Phoney War' period. On 10 May 1940, Hitler's long-awaited assault on the west erupted. The effect of *Blitzkrieg* – Lightning War – was shocking: armour and motorised infantry with close air support punched through Allied defences, covering ground quickly. The German fighters enjoyed total aerial superiority, enabling the ground forces to operate largely unimpeded by air attack. Sensibly, Air Chief Marshal Dowding had preserved his precious and superior Spitfires for home defence, deploying only Hurricane squadrons in France with the Advance Air Striking Force supporting the British Expeditionary Force. Among those Hurricane-equipped units embroiled in the continental turmoil was 85 Squadron – which by 16 May 1940 had lost two commanding officers already. On that day, Peter was signalled to the effect that he was promoted squadron leader and given command of 85. It was a just reward for hard-won experience and obvious leadership ability.

Squadron Leader Townsend would not join his new Squadron in France however. On 19 May 1940, as Peter spent the day 'quietly at my mother's home in Sussex', most of the Hurricane squadrons were withdrawn from

France – and such were 85 Squadron's losses that the unit was rendered 'non-operational' and sent to Debden, on the east coast of Essex:-

'85 Squadron was re-forming after the shambles in France. My job was to take a dozen boys not long out of school, together with our new Hurricanes, and create an efficient fighting unit. Both of my flight commanders had fought in France, Dicky Lee and Jerrard Jefferies, although Dicky, godson of the "Father of the RAF", "Boom" Trenchard, would sadly soon be killed, and Jerrard went on to 310 (Czech) Squadron, being replaced on 85 by a most charming man and able fighter pilot, Harry Hamilton, a Canadian. The new pilots were boys of 20 or less, with just ten hours on Hurricanes. This was the problem. In a single-seater fighter you have to do everything yourself, fly, navigate, fight, with nobody there to help you. It had taken years for me to gain what experience I had, but I didn't give much for my chances of survival even so. The new boys' chances were even less. Some of my pilots, however, had fought in France, and so could pass on that experience. First, we had to teach the new boys to fly the Hurricane properly,

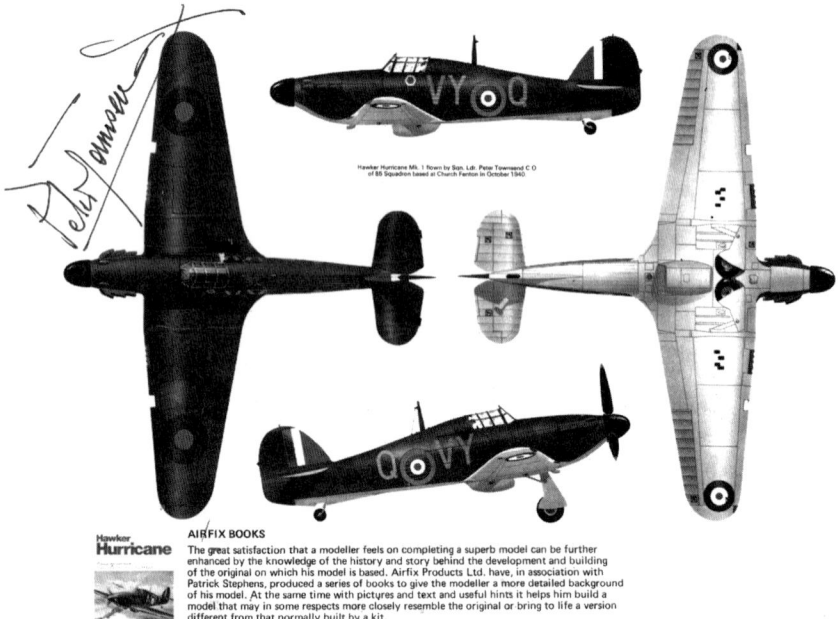

Hawker Hurricane Mk. 1 flown by Sqn. Ldr. Peter Townsend C O
of 85 Squadron based at Church Fenton in October 1940.

AIRFIX BOOKS

Hawker Hurricane

The great satisfaction that a modeller feels on completing a superb model can be further enhanced by the knowledge of the history and story behind the development and building of the original on which his model is based. Airfix Products Ltd. have, in association with Patrick Stephens, produced a series of books to give the modeller a more detailed background of his model. At the same time with pictures and text and useful hints it helps him build a model that may in some respects more closely resemble the original or bring to life a version different from that normally built by a kit.

Having kept the instructions to his Airfix 1/24 Hurricane, purchased and built in 1979, Group Captain Townsend would later sign Dilip's keepsake – a unique addition to the archive.

to search the sky, always look out, practising dogfighting and absolutely emphasising that in combat you never climb or dive in front of a 109. The Hurricane's greatest advantage and best defence was that it could turn tighter than the *Messerschmitt*, and so in combat you turned, tight, and turned again and again if necessary. As this programme progressed, the new boys went off patrolling convoys off the east coast – excellent training under operational conditions.'

The day after the Battle of Britain began, throughout the morning of 11 July 1940 enemy reconnaissance bombers were very active over the east coastal area. A Do 17 on a weather flight was shot down off Cromer, and Squadron Leader Peter Townsend, on a solo dawn patrol, engaged another Do 17 near Harwich:-

'The weather was filthy, heavy rain and cloud. I encountered the Dornier in cloud, managed to get up close and fire, causing a lot of damage, but the rear gunner, Werner Borner, shot it out with me. His MG15 was actually knocked out of his hands in the exchange, but beforehand Werner hit my Hurricane. There was an explosion in the cockpit and I broke away, trailing smoke. My engine packed up. So, I was 200 miles from land in one direction, and twenty from the British east coast. No option but to bale out, which I did, and fortunately got picked up quickly by a passing trawler. I was taken back into Harwich, well plied with rum. The Do 17, of II/KG2, got home, crash-landing at St-Léger, Arras, with three wounded men aboard.'

Being north-east of London, 85 Squadron continued to be engaged on convoy protection. On 10 August 1940, control of the Debden Sector passed from 12 to 11 Group. Three days later, the squadron ceased dispersal to Debden's satellite airfields, concentrating on and operating from the Sector Station. By 18 August, the *Luftwaffe* was firmly focussed on attacking Fighter Command's bases in the south-east. At 1740 hrs on this critical day, 85 Squadron fought its first squadron-strength combat, at 10,000 feet, east of the river Crouch. Peter's combat report provides an exciting account of the action, written minutes after landing:-

'85 Squadron ordered to patrol at 1730. Ordered to steer 160°. At 1740 sighted approximately 200 E/A steering west. Main formation consisted of 160 approx. in 6-8 formations, stepped up. Smaller separate formations of approx. 20 Me 110s. Steered to intercept largest formation but met 20 Me 110s on the way. Attacked 1 Me 110 after evading Yellow 1, went straight across me. Fired in a left-hand turn, full deflection. After 2-3 second burst, E/A heeled over and went into vertical spiral. Saw it thus for some 3,000 feet. My height 10,000 feet. P/O English and Sgt Howes also intercepted E/A descending in vertical spiral, out of control. Sgt Howes followed it to 3,000 feet but could not catch up with it. Sgt Howes certain it could not recover control. 1 Me 110 claimed destroyed but unconfirmed.

'A general engagement was now taking place, E/A consisting chiefly of Me 110. Main formation of bombers had now turned east. After a bit of general milling around with Me 110s, encountered 4 or 5 Me 109s. Attacked one in left-hand climbing turn. After 3 second burst, E/A flicked over to right, with flames and white smoke from underneath. Spun down burning well and lost sight of. 1 Me 109 claimed destroyed, unconfirmed. Shortly after attacked by another Me 109. No difficulty in getting on its tail, and again in left-hand climbing turn gave it short burst. Appeared to break up, roof came off and pilot baled. Parachute opened OK as far as I could see. 1 Me 109 claimed destroyed, unconfirmed. Chased 2 or 3 more Me 109s out east. After long chase, plug pulled, was hardly gaining on him. Gave him a burst at 400-500 yards, no effect but dive increased. Waited until a little closer and gave it another very short burst, then ammunition ran out. My position now approx. 30 miles south of Margate. Fell in with Green 1. Sighted 1 dinghy about 10 miles due east of Margate with 3 survivors. Sighted 1 Hurricane US-? [author's note: 56 Squadron aircraft] on mud flats between Isle of Sheppey and mainland. Landed Debden 1850.'

To me, Peter wrote: 'Our job was to get the bombers. Fighters were of no interest, because they were not dropping bombs (at that stage). We tried to avoid the fighters as best we could, but obviously their job was to protect the bombers and prevent us from attacking them, so it was often impossible to avoid getting tangled up with the German fighter escort.'

Peter knew how interested I was in the tactics used by the fighters of both sides during the Battle of Britain. Before the Second World War, it was believed that any air attack against Britain would be made from bases in Germany, making landfall over Britain's east coast. Moreover, owing to the distance involved these attacks were not expected to be escorted by single-engined fighters. Indeed, there were those in high places between the wars who believed that owing to the new monoplanes' high performance offset against the human body's limitations, fighter-against-fighter combat may not even be possible. Consequently, Fighter Command's tacticians' thinking revolved around set-piece attacks based upon the squadron of twelve aircraft. Each squadron was divided into two flights, 'A' and 'B', each of two sections of three aircraft. These, it was perceived, should fly closely together in 'vics' of three, in a 'V' formation, thus able to collectively bring twenty-four guns to fire simultaneously, as opposed to a lone fighter's eight. In Spain, though, the Germans worked out that in fighter combat, height and flexibility was essential, developing the *Schwarm*, the section of four aircraft, 200 metres apart, spread out, stepped-up in line abreast, providing mutual cover and each pilot able to search the sky for enemies without fear of collision with his neighbour. In action, the four broke into two pairs, the *Rotte*, each comprising leader and wingman, the latter's job being to guard the leader's tail while he concentrated on making the kill. The Fall of France, however, changed everything, Hitler's unprecedented advance to the Channel ports putting even London within range of the Me 109 – meaning that bombers would be escorted and proving the *Fighter Command Book of Tactics* to be a useless document. Time and time again, however, RAF fighter squadrons arrived in the battle area none the wiser – and paid the price in pilots' lives. As Peter wrote to me on 10 May 1989, 'Squadrons began experimenting with tactics themselves, there being no clear overall briefing, everything had changed. As your friend George Unwin rightly said, the Fighter Command Area Attacks were "all very well for the Hendon Air Pageant, but not for anything else". We were all learning on the job, as individual squadrons, really, during the actual battle.'

Peter's subsequent letter of 26 June 1989, was, I thought, illuminating:-

'In my Squadron, 85, we never flew in tight vics of three when in action, only during "air drill" or displays, as well as occasionally to save time on take-off. In going into action or on patrol, I put each section of the Squadron into line astern; this reduced the Squadron's front, increased its mobility and allowed each pilot more freedom to look about and behind him. You must remember that the conditions facing us were much different to those facing the German fighters. We were on the defence, they were attacking, either as escort or on a sweep.'

'We were under orders from the ground controller. For this reason, we had to maintain a reasonably compact (not tight) formation. Another reason was that (apart from the Duxford Wing) we were deployed in squadrons of twelve aircraft (in 11 Group there was not enough time to form up as wings). With twelve aircraft against perhaps fifty or more of theirs, we had to stick together to launch an effective attack.'

On 17 July 1989, Peter wrote again:-

'Between two aeroplanes: many, many thanks for your interesting letter… In (open or search) line astern, you had three weavers or tail-end Charlies, who, if they did their job properly, had no business to be the first to be shot down. On the contrary, you were covered by three look-outs – except in one tragic case with 85 Squadron when a Spit joined us (almost certainly piloted by Richard Hillary, who might have known better). With the Spit's front silhouette very similar to the Me 109's, our tail-end Charlie who saw it was a fraction of a second too late in warning that the aircraft following were Me 109s. That lost us a super flight commander, Hamilton from Canada.'

This is fascinating stuff, straight from a highly successful squadron commander during the Battle of Britain – dispelling myths about inflexible, tight formations as standard, emphasising that different tactics were dictated by defence or offence, and, most importantly, putting flight to the mistaken belief that 'weavers' were the most vulnerable to surprise attack. Those three paragraphs in those two letters, hand-written on translucent blue aerograph paper, are, to me, worth their weight in gold leaf.

On 19 August 1940, 85 Squadron moved from Debden to Croydon – in the thick of it. Heavily engaged for the rest of that month, Peter recorded more personal combat successes amongst 85's 'bag'. The last day of the month would be traumatic for the 25-year-old squadron leader:-

Squadron Leader Townsend prepares for a sortie.

'We were scrambled from Croydon and could see smoke rising from the Sector Station at Biggin Hill. Over Tunbridge Wells area we caught up with a circle of Me 110s, but then the 109s came down on us. I hit one in a climbing left-hand turn before singling out a 110. A 109 got in the way, so I attacked it. It disappeared. So focussed was I then on a 109 intimately close beneath me that I failed to realise that the 110 ahead with winking nose-guns was firing at me! My Hurricane was hit by 20mm. My left foot was violently kicked off the rudder pedal and petrol splashed into the cockpit. I was so shocked that for a few seconds I lost control and dived steeply. Miraculously the aircraft did not catch fire but straightened out. I baled out, landing on my backside amongst some fir trees. My left foot was a mess, so I sat smoking a cigarette whilst awaiting assistance. The funny thing was that the drive through the Kentish lanes with the local policeman to Hawkhurst Cottage Hospital was the most frightening thing since I took off from Croydon! By 2200 hrs that night, I was on the operating table at Croydon Hospital, where my big toe was amputated. From an operational perspective, that was me out of the Battle of Britain.'

In just over a fortnight of intense aerial combat, 85 Squadron had claimed the destruction of fifty enemy aircraft, in addition to others probably destroyed and damaged. The price, however, was high: four pilots had been killed in action, including two flight commanders, and six more, including the squadron commander, had been wounded (one of these would later succumb to his injuries). By 2 September 1940, 85 Squadron's strength was such that it could only patrol as a flight. The following day, the squadron was relieved by 111, and withdrew north to Castle Camps, there to re-form once more. That month, Peter was awarded a Bar to his DFC, the citation acknowledging that 85 Squadron's success was 'due to Squadron Leader Townsend's unflagging zeal and leadership'. Three weeks after being wounded, Peter returned to the squadron, able to at least lead from the ground if not, temporarily, in the air.

Having again received new pilots and led a comparatively nomadic existence, based variously at Church Fenton, Kirton-in-Lindsey and Gravesend, on New Year's Day 1941, 85 Squadron returned to Debden. By that time, the aerial battle had changed. The daylight battle won, Fighter Command was now dealing with the *Nachtangriff* – the Blitz on British cities by night. Lacking dedicated night-fighting aircraft, at first Spitfires and Hurricanes, although designed and intended as day fighters, were pressed into service at night, along with Blenheims and the Defiant turret-fighter.

Squadron Leader Townsend now had to convert 85 Squadron to a night-fighting unit, at first continuing to operate the Hurricane. On 22 April 1989, Peter wrote:-

'As you know, in its day version the Hurricane had kidney-shaped exhausts like the Spit. When we switched to night-fighting, these were replaced by six-stub exhausts on each side, to dampen the flames. The aircraft was, of course, pitch black, with the Squadron crest, a white hexagon. There may have been other changes also in the colour of national markings, eliminating white, I can't remember the exact form.'

By February 1941, the Blitz was in full swing. At 2015 hrs on 25 February, Squadron Leader Townsend was sent off from Debden into the dark winter sky. The enemy's effort that night was on a comparatively small scale, with some sixty aircraft of *Luftlotte* 2 operating over Britain. Peter reported that:-

'Vectored at 12,000 feet to East and then over to Channel B (GCI frequency). Orbited over balloon barrage (master lights visible) at 13,000 – 14,000 feet. Reported considerable activity to Controller NW of me (flares, searchlights etc). Proceeded in that direction but told "bad area" (this probably from R/T point of view and should be looked into as it was a very GOOD area from activity point of view). Continued orbit, then given vector 210 (this was last available information from Controller until end of combat, owing to confusion in chase and identification, hood being open and helmet becoming insecure – I wish they would think of a decent way of securing chin-strap of helmet so that friction buckle does not slip. Why not ordinary buckle, holes and strap?). Proceeded on vector 210, protesting, as to south of me on that vector there was only one vague searchlight which soon doused. After few minutes, 3 x3 searchlights suddenly shot up and immediately illuminated an aircraft proceeding east. Gave Tally Ho, height 12,000 feet, and asked Controller not to speak to me. Altered course to SE to intercept. At range 800 – 1,000 feet aircraft lost by lights, as it was now out to sea and I was in and out of lights. Lights doused and a moment later sighted aircraft with navigation lights coming towards me from SE, at 12,000 feet. Turned in to intercept, suspecting trickery. On crossing coast, searchlights immediately exposed an aircraft. Closed in to identify to about 200 feet. Imagine it was a Ju 88 owing to long cowling of engines and wing plan. Identification difficult owing to intensity of searchlights and was anxious not to reveal my identity by coming close to target, which was almost too good to be

Pressed into the night-fighter role as an emergency measure, Squadron Leader Townsend taking off for a patrol over London during the Blitz.

true, flying straight and level, with navigation lights ON! Now passed out to port beam of target for further identification and to avoid searchlights. As I passed port quarter imagined I saw twin rudders, suggesting Dornier, and from port beam decided aircraft was Dornier. Asked Controller if E/A was in vicinity, reply inaudible. Asked for searchlights to be doused, so as to come in really close, unseen, for final identification. No dousing. From port beam decided to shoot aircraft down as it appeared to be a Dornier and was observing no recognition procedure – navigation lights on, no colours of the day or recognition letter. As there was ample illumination and too much for me below E/A, decided to execute attack from above, slightly unorthodox, admittedly. Accordingly closed from port beam to line astern. E/A diving slightly, otherwise no evasive action. At point blank, line astern, slightly above, gave 1-2 second burst. Effect of De Wilde [illuminating tracer] ammo terrific and was unable to say if there was any return fire – probably not. Pulled out, up and right to avoid collision. Banked left and saw E/A diving down, belching white vapour, top rear gunner firing wildly, but not very near me. Shower of large sparks appeared to come from starboard side, followed by explosion and red pyrotechnic cartridge. E/A then zoomed up into stalled turn and dived, spiralling, to crash (with navigation lights still ON!) and exploded. Three parachutes were seen to open in searchlight beams. Landed Debden 2215 hrs.'

The 'E/A' – 85 Squadron's first nocturnal victory – was a Do 17Z-2 of 4/KG2 raiding London. Three crew-members baled out safely, as Peter described, but a fourth was killed when his parachute failed to open. The bomber crashed at Little Waldingfield, near Lavenham, Suffolk. Quite why the German pilot was flying around a hostile sky with his navigation lights 'ON', we will never know.

Peter's experiences as a pioneering night-fighter pilot and leader were published in his excellent memoir *Duel in the Dark* (see Bibliography). After probably destroying a Ju 88 in the early hours of 10 April, and damaging another the following night, his personal score of aircraft destroyed rose to at least eleven, with three shared, two 'probables' and four damaged. On 13 May 1941, Peter's appointment to the DSO was gazetted, in recognition of his leadership of 85 Squadron, particularly in the nocturnal role; the citation paid tribute to his 'outstanding powers of leadership and organisation, combined with great determination and skill in air combat. By his untiring efforts he has contributed materially to the success of his Squadron.'

Peter was promoted and posted to HQ 12 Group as Wing Commander Night Operations. Subsequently, Wing Commander Townsend DSO DFC & Bar commanded both RAF Drew and West Malling, in addition to another

Under Squadron Leader Townsend's leadership, 85 Squadron became a successful night-fighter unit.

night-fighting unit, 605 Squadron, and attended staff college. His was a distinguished service record by any standards, leading to his appointment as Equerry to King George VI in 1944. And therein, as we know, lies another tale.

Fast forward to that night in 1955 when the Princess Margaret's personal message was issued – and Group Captain Peter Townsend returned to his exile as Air Attaché in Brussels. A year later, Peter left the RAF, and became a writer. Travelling around the world alone, he wrote of his experiences in *Earth My Friend*. Then he began work on *Duel of Eagles*, masterfully weaving his personal memories into the wider context of the Battle of Britain story. Concurrently, he was sought out to be an advisor on the 1969 movie *Battle of Britain*. Journalist Leonard Moseley was on hand to record the story of the film's production; of Peter Townsend, who joined the film set in San Sebastian, he wrote that:-

'He was quite the politest man I have ever met, even when the Spanish reporters started to ask him questions about his relationship with Princess Margaret.

'"You really must not ask me anything about that, *mon vieux*," he would say, smiling gently. "You wouldn't want me to embarrass other people, would you, any more than you would want to embarrass me."

'But about anything else he would talk endlessly, about his childhood, his air battles, his travels, in a soft monotone which did not change even when he was describing the shooting down of the first Heinkel. He posed for pictures with Galland, with Hein Reiss in his Goering uniform, and with the *Messerschmitts*, and showed no sign of impatience when the cameras were clicking. He was always first to a door to hold it open for anyone, male or female, who was passing through. He handed money out to street urchins and smiled and listened with every sign of attentiveness when middle-aged women, complete strangers, came across the room and gushed over him. One began to understand why he had won so many hearts during his service with the Royal Family.'

That was the man I knew, incredibly charming and kind. A people person.

Perhaps less widely known than Peter's distinguished war record and, of course, the Princess Margaret affair, was his humanitarian and philanthropic work. After leaving the RAF, Peter covered the Arab-Israeli war for a newspaper, visiting the Golan Heights, scene of a great battle – where he saw a dead body for the first time. He told me that

Group Captain Peter Townsend (right) pictured with another ace, the great Squadron Leader James 'Ginger' Lacey, during the making of *Battle of Britain* in 1969.

'Although I was personally responsible for the deaths of many men, I never saw any of them. We were shooting at the aircraft, detached from the men inside whom our bullets were hitting. To see that carnage on the Golan Heights was profound, really underlining the violence, suffering and futility of it all.' Although he wrote several other well-received books, including *The Last Emperor*, a biography of King George VI, and his autobiography, *Time and Chance*, a significant title, emphasising Peter's humanitarian interests, has to be *The Girl in the White Ship*, the story of a young female Vietnamese, the sole survivor of her ship brimming with refugees. Indeed, Peter was deeply moved by the plight of child victims of war – and typically resolved to do something about it. In 1979, the United Nations 'Year of the Child', he travelled the world meeting child war victims, inspiring his book about the 'Boat People', and *The Postman of Nagasaki*, telling the story of a boy maimed during the atomic attack on that Japanese city. In 1988 he found 'lying around in a bag at the bottom of a drawer' his flying logbooks, medals and awards. Thinking it 'sensible to put them to some use', in November that year the collection was auctioned, raising $35,200 – which Peter wrote to me about on 24 March 1989:-

'Your guess is bang-on: it is with Leonard Cheshire that I have been talking with a view to helping one of his homes, and although it is less likely now that my "medal money" will go in that direction… While there is no organisation that I can imagine more deserving than the LC Homes, they do not fit exactly into my plan and special wish that the money should help child-victims of war. Only recently I discovered from an old friend, who has worked for years in this area (UN High Commissioner for Refugees & UNESCO), that the International Red Cross have specific plans for aid to child and women victims of war. I am therefore following this line, but it will not be until May that I hear more about creating a trust fund within the framework of the International Red Cross or possibly the UN Commission for Refugees, who have helped me the world over for texts on child-victims.'

And so, the money from Peter's personal wartime memorabilia was used to benefit not himself but child victims of war.

As previously related, Peter happily married Marie Luce, the couple having three children and enjoying a wonderful life together at St-Léger-en-Yvelines. Princess Margaret married Anthony Armstrong-Jones, later Lord Snowdon, the match ironically ending in divorce. Although Peter wrote to me that 'I must confess that I dislike, more and more, publicity of any kind – inseparable, I know, from writing books!', his life-story will always include the Royal love affair. This will never go away, and therefore cannot be ignored. Indeed, even as recently as 2016, the story broke again, with broadcast of the Netflix television series *The Crown*, in which Peter was played by Ben Miles. Arguably that is separate to his wartime past – but to understand the man, the whole must be considered. In the final reckoning, taking all into account, Group Captain Peter Townsend emerges as an exceptional individual in all respects, a perfect English gentleman.

Peter died of stomach cancer, aged 80, on 19 June 1995.

To Peter Townsend himself goes the last word, extracted from the foreword he kindly contributed to my book *Through Peril to the Stars* (1993):-

'Once, when describing an air combat with my eight-year-old son, he asked "But why did you have to kill them?" Truthfully, I never wanted to kill anybody, and least of all a young man of my age who shared with me a passion for flying, young men in their late teens or early twenties. That is the tragedy of war.'

Chapter Three

Wing Commander Roger Boulding
Spitfire Pilot

In July 1940, a unique phenomenon gripped wartime Britain's Home Front: the 'Spitfire Fund'. Voluntary collections sprang up all over the country and in the dominions to present Lord Beaverbrook, the Minister of Aircraft Production, with a cheque for £5,000 – the price tag set on a Supermarine Spitfire fighter. At the time, Britain was under aerial bombardment and threatened by invasion during the Battle of Britain. The Spitfire Fund therefore provided the opportunity for civilians to indirectly hit back at the *Luftwaffe*. As towns and cities all vied to make their contribution, there was intense rivalry. Housewives happily parted with their aluminium cooking utensils from which the 'Beaver' promised to make even more Spitfires.

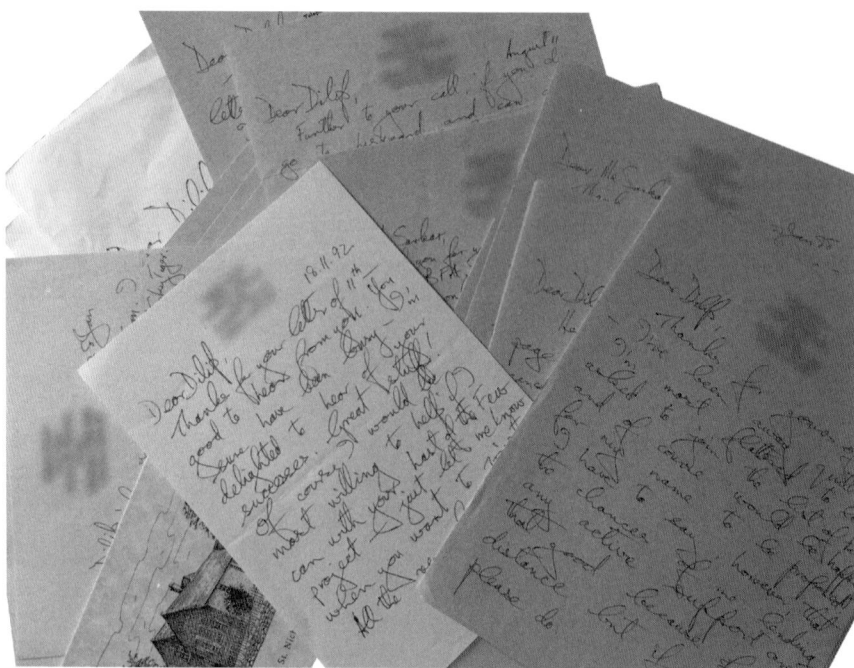

The provincial city of Worcester became an early and enthusiastic donor, raising over £10,000 – the equivalent of about £2 million today – and presented two Spitfires to the government: Castle Bromwich Aircraft Factory-built Mk IIAs, P8045 and P8046, *City of Worcester I* and *II*. As Worcester is my hometown, from an early age I had a keen interest in these two 'presentation' Spitfires – leading to my friendship with several pilots who once flew them, including Wing Commander Roger John Eric Boulding.

On 11 March 1941, P8046 was taken on charge by 74 'Tiger' Squadron at Manston. This was an interesting time for Fighter Command. The architects of victory during the Battle of Britain, Air Chief Marshal Sir Hugh Dowding and Air Vice-Marshal Keith Park, had been replaced as Commander-in-Chief and Air Officer Commanding 11 Group by Air Marshal Sholto Douglas and Air Vice-Marshal Leigh-Mallory respectively. The new men were enthusiastic supporters of the use of mass fighter formations in both defence and offence – a controversy over tactics having erupted during the Battle of Britain which ultimately involved Churchill himself. Now, with Douglas and Leigh-Mallory at the helm, 'Big Wings' were pushed through and adopted as standard – wrongly, as things turned out. Nonetheless, Fighter Command was reorganised in the spring of 1941, the Spitfire replacing the Hurricane completely as the RAF's frontline fighter, and each sector station becoming home to three Spitfire squadrons, collectively forming a 'wing'. A new post was created of 'Wing Commander Flying', the fighter pilot's dream job, as Air Vice-Marshal Johnnie Johnson, wing leader *par excellence*, explained: 'Being a wing leader was the best job in the air force. A commander has a lot of administrative tasks and duties as a rule, taking up a lot of time, but not so for the wing leader, who was able to concentrate on leading in the air and fighting.' Amongst the first wing leaders appointed was Wing Commander A.G. 'Sailor' Malan, the legendary South African who had commanded 74 Squadron throughout 1940. The 'Sailor' became Wing Leader at Biggin Hill, that famous fighter station south of London, and left 74 Squadron at Manston the day before *City of Worcester II* arrived. His place at 74's helm was taken by one of his two flight commanders, Squadron Leader John Mungo-Park DFC. It was an exciting time. The weather was improving, the Germans had been held off during the Battle of Britain, and Fighter Command's new bosses looked forward to 'reaching out', 'leaning into Europe', and taking the war to the *Luftwaffe* across the Channel in north-west France – in a complete reversal, in fact, of the Battle of Britain scenario.

Above left: Roger Boulding learning to fly with the RAFVR at Sywell in 1938.

Above right: Pilot Officer Roger Boulding proudly sporting newly awarded 'wings'.

At Manston, 74 Squadron's code letters, ZP, were applied to the fuselage of Spitfire P8046, which was given the individual aircraft letter L, and as a new machine became the personal mount of a flight commander, Flight Lieutenant Tony Bartley DFC, newly arrived on promotion himself from 92 Squadron. An ace, Tony survived the war with a distinguished service record, after which he married the movie star Deborah Kerr and went into the film and television industry (the couple divorced in 1959). From his home in County Cork, Tony wrote to me on 9 January 1988 providing copies of his logbook entries for flights in Spitfire 'L'. The record showed that Flight Lieutenant Bartley flew this Spitfire on twelve occasions between 18 March and 10 April 1941. These flights included 'Fighter Patrol' and, on 6 April 1941, 'Rhubarb – St Omer Area'. A 'rhubarb' was the codename for usually a pair of Spitfires nipping across the Channel at zero feet ('down amongst the rhubarb'), popping up over the French cliffs, striking inland and attacking targets of opportunity. Owing to the ever-present dangers from flak and fighters, these were dangerous sorties and cost Fighter Command many experienced and irreplaceable pilots. On this occasion, Tony, flying with Pilot Officer Bob Spurdle, strafed the German fighter airfield at St Omer,

Spitfire P8046, *City of Worcester II*, outside the flight sheds at Castle Bromwich Aircraft Factory.

Pilot Officer Roger Boulding and 'Sam'.

shooting up an Me 109 on the ground. On the way out, the Spitfires were 'Attacked by Me 110 near Calais – Me shot down by P/O Spurdle'. Four days later, Tony was over France in 'L' again when 'Ear drums packed up while diving to intercept Me 109s'. Back at Manston, the Flight Commander was grounded by the Medical Officer, and remained so until 26 May 1941.

The day after Flight Lieutenant Bartley's 'Ear drums packed up', P8046 was flown three times by Flying Officer Roger Boulding, who largely took over the aircraft as his personal mount for the next few days. On 6 January 1988, Roger replied to my letter of inquiry, sending a copy of his logbook detailing the flights concerned, adding that 'The first trip in P8046 on 15 April 1941 was as escort to a Lysander, also based at Manston, on ASR duties. The second trip was abortive because the other squadrons were unable to make the rendezvous on time. The third trip was some offensive sweep which was completed with only Ack Ack opposition. I was apparently leading the Squadron on this one.' Roger went on to say:-

'I well remember many of the pilots you list as having flown P8046, and am delighted to hear that Johnnie Freeborn is OK – I last met him at the Battle of Britain 40th anniversary at the Guildhall in London – please give him my regards when next you are in touch. Pilot Officer Parkes was a New Zealander,

74 Squadron pilots at readiness, Biggin Hill, early 1941; from left: Flying Officer Roger Boulding (and Sam!); Pilot Officer Henryk Szczsney; Flight Lieutenant John Freeborn DFC and Pilot Officer Harbourne Stephen DSO DFC.

Flying Officer Boulding (right) and Pilot Officer Szczsney on readiness with an unknown 'Tiger' Squadron pilot at Biggin Hill, spring 1941.

Flying Officer Roger Boulding (and Sam!) at Gravesend in 1941, with another presentation Spitfire, P8394, *Gibraltar*.

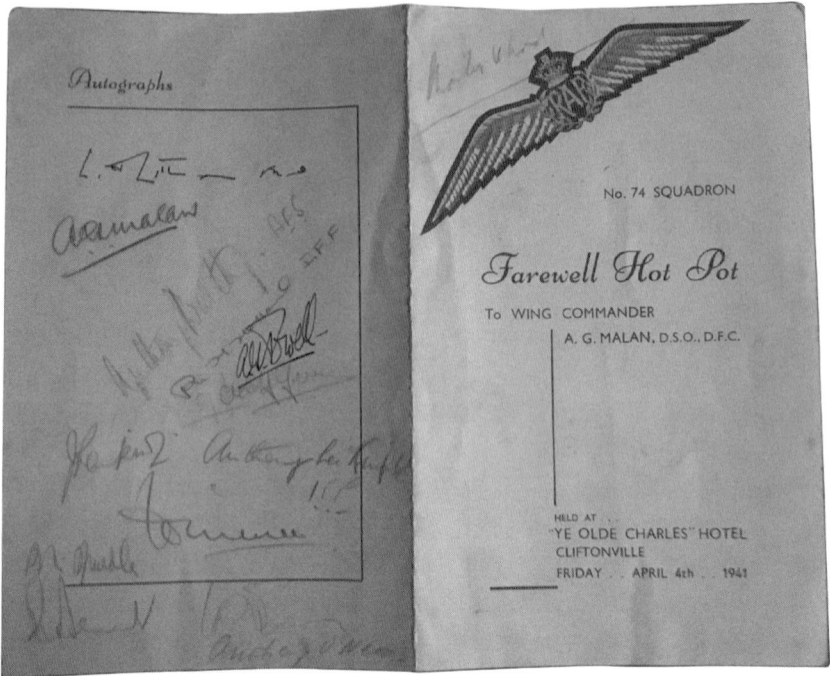

The signed menu celebrating Wing Commander 'Sailor' Malan's promotion to lead the Biggin Hill Wing, signed by the man himself and other Biggin Hill luminaries including 92 Squadron's Jamie Rankin.

The He 111 of 5/KG53 shot down by Flying Officer Boulding during the early hours of 11 May 1941. The enemy aircraft force-landed at Kennington, near Ashford.

The same view today (Alan Wright).

my No 4 and also taken PoW on the same trip as myself. Peter Chesters killed himself doing a "victory roll" over Manston. Squadron Leader Wood was, I think, attached to us to gain experience before posting to his own unit. Mungo-Park was the Squadron Commander.

'As an after-thought, I think the reason I flew P8046 so often for a brief period would be because after Tony Bartley became non-operational I was Acting Flight Commander. He had been posted in to run the Flight after Mungo-Park's promotion to CO, when "Sailor" Malan (our CO) became Wing Leader.

'I wish you every success in your work. If you can think of anything else I might be able to help with, please do let me know. Memory is not what one would wish, but you never know!'

At the time, the Malvern Spitfire Team, a research society founded in 1986 by Andy Long and I, was most active, Roger soon joining our list of Patrons which, as Dr Gordon Mitchell, son of Spitfire designer 'RJ' and our President, observed, 'Reads like a *Who's Who* of the Battle of Britain'. Roger became an enthusiastic supporter, attending several of our early events and engaging in protracted correspondence. I came to know him as a warm and amusing man with a great sense of humour – the latter clear from his address: 'Gribbit House' in Frog Lane! In the spring of 1988, I visited both Roger and another former 74 Squadron pilot who had also become a friend, namely Bob Poulton DFC, who had flown Spitfire P8047 *The Malverns*. During that meeting, I was able to tease a little more out of Roger Boulding:-

'I was born Roger John Eric Boulding at Grays, Essex, on 19 November 1919, the son of a dentist. I took a Short Service Commission in the RAF and learnt to fly at 6 EFTS, Sywell, with Paddy Finucane, later to find great fame and success as a fighter pilot before going missing over the Channel. My "Pilot's Licence for flying land machines" was issued on 30 September 1938.

Above, below and opposite: More views of the Kennington He 111.

I then continued flying training at Montrose, Shawbury and Penrhos. Operationally, I first flew Fairey Battles with 52 Squadron at Upwood, Kidlington and Benson, then with 98 Squadron at Hucknall before going to France with 142 Squadron as part of the AASF. When things turned a bit sour over there I managed to escape, flying back to England from Dieppe in a Tiger Moth, landing at Hawkinge on 22 May 1940. I remember that on that day, 22 May 1940, Boulogne Harbour was being heavily dive-bombed.'

142 Squadron, based at Berry-au-Bac, was actually the first RAF squadron to attack the advancing Germans on 10 May 1940 – losing a staggering thirteen Battles that fateful day. There is no record of Pilot Officer Boulding having flown operationally during the Battle of France, and nor is it recorded why he was sent home, alone, before the squadron was withdrawn from the chaos on the continent in June. Unfortunately, the question was one I never thought to ask, as at the time I was so firmly focussed on the Battle of Britain itself.

Upon return to England, Pilot Officer Boulding then continued flying Battles, at Waddington, before spending a month with 98 Squadron, flying from Kidlington. Then, in July 1940, Roger re-joined 142 Squadron at Binbrook, operating from Eastchurch. On 3 August 1940, Roger's logbook records a sortie that evening (with Sergeants Hemmings and Ducas flying as his navigator and air-gunner) to dive-bomb Boulogne Harbour – where enemy vessels were assembling in preparation for the invasion of England. Diving from 8,000 to 5,500 feet,

Left: After repatriation, Roger Boulding took at Permanent Commission, enjoying a varied career and retiring as a Wing Commander.

Below: Squadron Leader Roger Boulding over Egypt in a Vampire during the 1950s – an exciting time for aviation.

Pilot Officer Boulding and crew bombed the south jetty and harbour entrance, noting fires burning all around the basin. Roger:-

'Of course, during the summer of 1940, the RAF needed fighter pilots, to make good losses suffered in France and already during the Battle of Britain, which started in July. I therefore answered the call and, much to my delight, converted to Spitfires. On 22 August 1940, I was posted to 74 Squadron, the famous "Tigers", at Kirton-in-Linsey, where the Squadron was re-forming after involvement in the Dunkirk air fighting and early stage of the Battle of Britain. Our CO was the highly successful fighter pilot and leader "Sailor" Malan.

I first flew a Spitfire the day after my arrival on the Squadron. On 5 October, flying from Coltishall, I shared a Do 215, east of Harwich, and on 5 December, by which time we were operating from Manston, I got my first Me 109 over Dover. We got into a scrap over Margate with some more 109s on 7 May 1941, I got one and damaged another but was shot up myself in the process. My Spitfire's petrol tank and coolant system were damaged, so I crash-landed back at base with petrol pouring into my cockpit and leaking glycol. I was flying Spitfire P7316, ZP-S. Later that day I patrolled over Canterbury, but another Section Leader collided with me, damaging the rudder and airscrew of my Spitfire, P8018, ZP-T, so I had to crash-land at Detling.

'By that time the Germans were bombing our cities, particularly London, very heavily by night. Nocturnal defences were poor, radar etc embryonic, and so desperate was the hour that even Spitfires were pressed into a night-fighting role. The Spitfire, however, is not a good aircraft to fly at night, and indeed it was never intended to be by the designer. Visibility was poor because the bank of exhausts on either side of the nose and in front of the pilot glowed red-hot and ruined night vision. The narrow track undercarriage, coupled with the fact that when landing the pilot's view of the airfield below was virtually non-existent, also made night flying pretty dodgy.

'At that time, we were operating from West Malling, the general idea being that, over the full moon period, the AA guns were restricted to their shells exploding no higher than 12,000 feet over Central London. Over Outer London they could fire up to the maximum, and outside the barrage night-fighters operated under close control. We day fighters were sent up to the Central Area at intervals of 500 feet, to patrol individually.'

The early hours of 11 May 1941 would prove eventful for Roger, and I quote his letter of 13 December 1988:-

'The theory was that you got through the barrage into the patrol area via a "gate", marked by two green searchlights fixed in a vertical position, but I don't think in practice this bit ever worked very well!

'Anyway, I had been on patrol for quite a while, in Spitfire Mk IIA, P8380, coded ZP-Q, throughout which time Central London appeared to be at the base of a huge pyramid of flame. I hadn't seen a thing, except the flames, shell bursts and the odd aircraft in flames over the outskirts. Didn't really expect to see anything with two great rows of glowing exhaust ports ruining my night vision! So, when I began to have a bit of a problem controlling the revs, I headed for base and called control.

Almost immediately, I saw this large twin-engined thing in front of me, going the same way! I had only to line up on him and press the button – it obviously wasn't one of ours! I hit him underneath and the effect was of an enormous burst of sparks, which I perforce flew through. The *Heinkel* stuck its nose down and headed for the deck, meaning that it was difficult to see against the dark background of the earth – but, of course, his rear gunner could easily see me silhouetted against the light moonlit sky, so he opened up on me every time I got into position to give him another burst – very adjacent he was too!

'We carried on like this until the German pilot was indulging in some rather fancy low flying across Kent. I don't think that I hit him again and eventually lost sight of him so circled the area and obtained a radio fix from base, which established my position, and returned to West Malling. There we found signs of damage to my Spitfire (very minor), to the debris guard over my oil cooler inlet, indicating that I had hit a small piece of debris. When my radio fix coincided with the discovery of a He 111 on the ground, it was credited to me; the rest of the Squadron had stooged around all night and saw absolutely nothing!

Group Captain Brian Kingcome DSO DFC, unknown, Wing Commander Bob Stanford Tuck DSO DFC, Wing Commander Roger Boulding and Squadron Leader 'Gandi' Drobinski DFC with the famous White Hart blackboard signed by innumerable wartime fighter pilots.

WING COMMANDER ROGER BOULDING

I seem to remember a total of thirty-three were shot down that night, mostly by night-fighters – and this was the best night score to date. The rest you know.'

To locate and destroy an aircraft at night, especially in a machine unsuited to nocturnal operations, was no mean feat. The night in question – a full moon – had, in fact, seen the most devastating attack on London during the night Blitz. The enemy bombers first identified targets by moonlight, then by the glare of 2,000 fires. The firefighters were hard-pressed to deal with this conflagration: water mains flowed only early on, before demand exceeded supply and pipes were fractured. The night also coincided with a low spring tide, the Thames resembling a much smaller river with dangerous mud flats for fifty yards either side. Fireboats managed to run their hoses over the flats, but were unable to supply sufficient water to the volume of pumps demanding it. So desperate was the situation that any water supply, including ponds, canals and swimming pools, was used, and even sewers. And the bombs continued raining down, as the hundreds of night raiders flew a shuttle service to and from their continental bases. When the 'All Clear' sounded the following morning, numerous fires were out of control, and many Londoners were without basic services. A thousand Londoners were killed and 2,000 injured, although fortunately this terrible night was the last major raid on Target *Loge* – appropriately named after the Norse fire god.

Wing Commander Boulding with the Polish Flight Lieutenant Kazek Budzik at the opening of the 'Spitfire!' exhibition, courtesy of the author and team, at Tudor House Museum, Worcester, on 4 June 1988.

The He 111 Roger shot down was *Werke Nummer* 3976, A1+JN, of 5/KG53 *Legion Condor*, based at Wevelgem, in Flanders. The aircraft force-landed at Kennington, near Ashford in Kent, at 005 hrs on 11 May 1941. The crew were all captured. The bomber crash-landed in a field behind the home of a Mr Charles Field, in Church Road: 'When this bomber with its five-man crew crashed, it was midnight. I had just gone to bed when I heard a noise. It didn't sound like an aircraft. Then there was a scraping noise as the plane apparently brushed against trees. When it had reached Ashford it was down to roof-top height. It was moonlit, otherwise the pilot could never have seen to land. He came down in the field and ended up against my garden fence. Part of the wing ploughed through my freshly sown carrot-row. I went outside to the back of the house and saw the plane on the ground. One, who I presumed was the pilot, who was injured, was talking to a British soldier. The commander was thrown out and broke a leg. The other three crew were standing nearby. They were all taken to Canterbury Hospital. Soldiers were on the spot immediately, because a house opposite was a guard post. It took the military authorities several days to examine and remove the plane.'

What now remains: Wing Commander Boulding's log books, medals and membership cards for the Battle of Britain Fighter Association and Caterpillar Club.

Wing Commander Boulding's brochure and tickets for the 1969 premier of *Battle of Britain*.

Thirty-seven years later, Mr Field had a surprise when the bomber's commander, the former *Hauptmann*, Albert Huffenreuter, knocked on his door: 'He said, "I have taken thirty-seven years to find you!" Now a teacher in Hamburg, he had been to see the local vicar, Reverend Dudley Harvet, who sent him along to see me. I took him along to see Peter Huckstepp, whose late father, Fred, was the first-aider who pulled the pilot from the plane. We spent an hour together.'

For Albert Huffenreuter and *kamaraden*, years followed as prisoners. That night was KG53's last attack on England. A month later the unit was withdrawn to Poland, thereafter operating on the *Ostfront*. Surviving Roger's bullets and being captured was, perhaps, the better option.

For Flying Officer Boulding, the war continued as, with the improved daylight weather, Fighter Command's operations intensified. On 21 January 1988, Roger wrote to me regarding his exit from the air war:-

'On 17 June 1941, I was on a sweep over France, flying a Spitfire VB, W3251, leading a section of four 74 Squadron Spitfires. "Sailor" Malan was leading 74 Squadron as Wing Leader, flying Top Cover.

Above left: Proud daughter: Nicolette Perry displays her late father's memorabilia in 2019.

Above right: 'There but for the grace of God': the grave of Flying Officer Ricalton at Sittingbourne – who joined 74 Squadron at the same time as Roger Boulding.

Having dived down onto some Me 109s, and in accordance with the standard drill of that time, we didn't follow all the way down but attempted to re-form, climbing towards the sun and weaving. I was following "Sailor", and another Spitfire was following me. After a while "Sailor" came on the radio telling someone to "Look out behind!" I quickly did so and saw the chap still behind me, and screwed my head around some more, still looking for the trouble. Then I saw "Sailor" below me, violently rocking his wings. Suddenly there was an almighty bang on the armour plating behind my seat and it became rather obvious that the chap behind me had been replaced by someone rather less friendly! With controls gone I had to jump out and floated down from 12-15,000 feet in broad daylight. Naturally I found a substantial reception committee waiting. And that was that, as the Germans kept on saying "For you ze var is over!"'

By then, Roger had flown 164 operational sorties. According to Roger's 'Wartime Log For British Prisoners', a diary supplied by the YMCA to those in captivity, his time behind the wire began at *Dulag Luft*, a reception centre, then going to *Oflags* IX, VIB and XXIB, before ending up at the notorious *Stalag Luft* III at Sagan, from where the 'Great Escape' was launched – and as a result of which fifty prisoners were murdered by the *Gestapo*. In February 1945, Roger and his fellow prisoners joined the long trek west, as the Germans retreated from the Soviet advance, trudging through dreadful winter conditions with inadequate clothing and supplies. At 1150 hrs on 2 May 1945, it was, thankfully, all over, and Flying Officer Boulding was liberated at Lubeck. Roger:-

'For myself, there is not much else to tell. After the war I remained in the service with a Permanent Commission and was CO of 35 Squadron (Lancasters) and 249 Squadron (Vampires in Egypt), followed by various administrative command and staff jobs until retiring in November 1966.'

In truth, Roger enjoyed an exciting post-war career, during which he variously flew Wellingtons and Lancaster bombers before Meteor and Vampire jet fighters. Somehow he even managed to get in the pilot's seat of an American B-29 Super Fortress! By 1951, his logbook records a total of 1,161 flying hours and an 'above average' rating as a pilot. Roger's 'administrative' jobs also included commanding no less a Station than RAF Coningsby, now home to the much-loved Battle of Britain Memorial Flight's Spitfires, Hurricanes, Dakota and Lancaster.

Having married Doreen Barnet in 1947, after leaving the RAF the Bouldings ran various pubs, restaurants and hotels until closing the doors of Minehead's Merton Hotel for the last time and retiring in 1985. Doreen, a former WAAF, died in 1987; Roger on 2 March 1993, leaving behind a daughter, Nicolette, and grandchildren, Luke and Hannah.

In August 1940, another 142 Squadron Battle pilot, Flying Officer Alan Ricalton, joined 74 Squadron with Pilot Officer Boulding. An experienced pilot who had flown operationally during the Fall of France, on 17 October 1940 the 26-year-old Ricalton was hacked down by 109s over Maidstone; his grave can be found in Sittingbourne Cemetery. As Roger said, 'There but for the grace of God…'

Chapter Four

Squadron Leader Dennis Adams
Spitfire Pilot

In 1989, I was researching the history of yet another Spitfire, this time Mk IIA P7323, in which Sergeant Kenneth Pattison was killed on 11 October 1940 – the only operational crash in my home county of Worcestershire in the Midlands. Amongst the pilots identified who had flown this aircraft with 611 Squadron was Pilot Officer Dennis Arthur Adams, who was born in Banbury on 6 May 1913, joined the RAF Reserve in 1936, left as a squadron leader in 1943, and emigrated to South Africa. It was there, in Natal, that I located him, and from where he wrote me many letters. The first, dated 19 November 1989, rather set the scene regarding his open and non-conformist character:-

'When writing to me in future, please, none of the comic wartime ranks. My name is Dennis!'

It is, of course, customary to address a retired commissioned officer by their rank, and some get tetchy should you not, but clearly not Dennis. Regular correspondence followed, much of which, leafing through the aerographs in front of me, concerned our mutual interest in fishing. But I digress – so let us return to Spitfire P7323 and the reason for my inquiry to Dennis Adams in faraway Natal.

Originally the Spitfire was designed and produced at Supermarine, a comparatively small factory on the banks of the river Itchen at Woolston, Southampton. Wartime demand for Mitchell's superb fighter, however, exceeded Supermarine's ability to supply. Moreover, after the Fall of France, this high priority target, just sixty miles away from the German airfields around Cherbourg, was extremely vulnerable – as events during the Battle of Britain confirmed. It therefore became a matter of urgency to disperse production and translate manufacture into mass production. The new site chosen for a 'Shadow Factory' was at Castle Bromwich, Birmingham, the intention being to adopt the automotive industry's line-type production methods to construct Spitfires in number. Lord Nuffield, pioneer of the mass produced and comparatively inexpensive automobile, was chosen to oversee the all-important project. The Castle Bromwich Aircraft Factory (CBAF) began mass production of the first Spitfire Mk IIs in June 1940. The aerial testing of these new machines was the responsibility of Alex Henshaw, a famous pre-war aviator and holder of various records, who was determined that his experience should be put to good use in wartime. Appointed Chief Test Pilot at CBAF, under Henshaw's leadership an intensive flying programme began, ongoing from dawn to dusk, regardless of the weather. Ultimately, CBAF would produce and test most of the 22,000 Spitfires built.

At the time of Dunkirk and the early stage of the Battle of Britain, the Me 109E was found to enjoy certain advantages over the Spitfire and Hurricane Mk Is, including fuel injection, 20 mm cannons, and a Constant Speed propeller. Altering the angle of a propeller's 'bite' is similar to changing gear in a car. At first, propellers were two-bladed, made of laminated wood and fixed. German developments led to the RAF fitting the two-pitch propeller, offering 'coarse' or 'fine' pitch, but nothing in between. The German airscrew, however, provided the pilot with a wide-range of settings, enabling the optimum pitch to be selected for any given situation. This was why the CS propeller was important, giving RAF pilots parity with their enemy. The new propeller was also driven by an improved Rolls-Royce Merlin engine, the XII, this combination increasing the Spitfire's ceiling by 2,000 feet. The new engine ran on the more efficient 100, as opposed to 85, octane, and was fitted with an automatic Coffman starter, so no longer required the

Pilot Officer Dennis Adams in an early Spitfire Mk I, lacking both armoured glass windscreen and rear-view mirror, at Ternhill in 1940.

cumbersome external trolley accumulator battery. The first Spitfire Mk II produced by CBAF, P7280, initially flew in May 1940; the first delivered to a squadron (152) was P7286, and in August 1940, 611 Squadron became the first fully-equipped Mk II unit.

In 1989, Alex Henshaw checked his logbooks and confirmed that on 10 August 1940 he successfully gave P7323, the forty-third Spitfire built at CBAF, its production test flight. On 28 August, Spitfires P7320, '21, '22 and '23 were delivered by 9 Maintenance Unit (MU) to 611 Squadron, based at Digby in Lincolnshire. Other CBAF-built Mk IIs soon began arriving, the squadron's Mk IAs being relegated to training with 7 Operational Training Unit (OTU) at Hawarden. 611 'West Lancashire' was an Auxiliary Air Force (AAF) unit based on the territorial principal and had become a fighter squadron in early 1940. Commanded by Squadron Leader James McComb, 611 had participated in the Dunkirk air-fighting, flying from Hornchurch, and during this period based at Digby was another squadron providing protection to convoys steaming within five miles of the east coast. Spitfire P7323's first flight with 611 Squadron was made by Flight Lieutenant Kenneth Stoddart on 27 August 1940, on which date the unit flew south to Duxford. 611 Squadron found itself dispersed to Duxford's nearby satellite at the old First World War aerodrome at Manor Farm, Fowlmere, there joining 19 Squadron's Spitfires. Over the next few days, P7323 was flown by Flying Officer Barrie Heath, and Pilot Officers David Scott-Malden, James Walker and Dennis Adams, 611 Squadron flying daily from Digby to the Duxford Sector and back, used for local defensive patrols or as extra reinforcements.

The job of Duxford's squadrons was to protect the industrial Midlands and north, patrolling convoys and covering 11 Group's airfields in the south-east, while Air Vice-Marshal Park's squadrons were engaged further forward.

In order to preserve limited resources, and to provide the greatest tactical flexibility, Air Chief Marshal Dowding and Air Vice-Marshal Park carefully shepherded their fighters, intercepting the enemy with 'penny-packet' formations of flight- or squadron-strength. The Germans, however, were determined to lure Fighter Command to battle for destruction *en masse* – which is exactly what Dowding and Park's tactics were intended to avoid. Consequently, the brunt of the battle was borne by 11 Group, while 12 Group's squadrons stood comparatively idly by – much to their frustration. This was intolerable to the headstrong and determined Squadron Leader Douglas Bader, commanding 242 Squadron at Coltishall. On 30 August 1940, 11 Group called for reinforcements and 242 Squadron sallied forth, engaging German bombers over Hatfield. It was the first time Bader and his pilots had engaged a big German formation, and in their excitement many claims were made – and confirmed with little or no analysis by 12 Group. The impression was that 242 Squadron had executed great damage to the enemy. Bader saw his chance: he submitted a report arguing that with more fighters under his command, the execution would be greater still. This, however, was a misconception right from the start – because primary evidence confirms that fighters from 11 Group squadrons were also engaged simultaneously with 242, meaning that there were, in fact, already more fighters present than just those of 242. Bader's AOC, Air Vice-Marshal Leigh-Mallory, agreed with his charismatic and forceful subordinate's assessment, though, ordering that in future 242 Squadron would operate from Duxford with the Hurricanes of 310 (Czech) Squadron, while the Fowlmere-based Spitfires of 19 Squadron provided top cover. This Bader-led 'wing' first saw action on 7 September 1940, but was caught on the climb by German fighters over London. Nonetheless, the Wing claimed twenty enemy aircraft destroyed, with more probably destroyed or damaged. More recent research, however, suggests that the Wing overclaimed on that occasion by 3:1.

At 1530 hrs on 11 September 1940, Squadron Leader Brian Lane DFC led off his own 19 Squadron from Fowlmere at the head of an all-Spitfire 12 Group Wing, the other squadrons being 266, 74 and 611. Pilot Officer Dennis Adams was flying Spitfire P7323, 'FY-P'. The ensuing combat was 611's first against a mass German formation. 611 Squadron would have more action on 15 September 1940 – recognized as the turning point for the hard-pressed defenders and still annually commemorated as 'Battle of Britain Day'. Again, Dennis flew P7323: 'It was very confusing. Aircraft everywhere. So many that I was unable to get in position to fire at anything, and the AA fire was very distracting. If the German aircrews thought we were down to our last few Spitfires and Hurricanes, they must have got quite a shock when Bader turned up over London with fifty of us!' And that, for all the evidence confirming the Big Wing's actual inefficiency, contrary to beliefs at the time, had to be a decisive blow to enemy morale.

Further patrols followed, until 19 September 1940, when 'A' Flight of 611 Squadron, including Pilot Officer Adams, was sent to operate from Ternhill in Shropshire. 'B' Flight continued supporting Wing operations, Spitfires from 616 Squadron making up the numbers. It was this period of the squadron's history, in fact, that had prompted my correspondence with Dennis.

In that first letter, Dennis also wrote that:-

'From the time we got squadron letters, I had "P", and stuck with it wherever possible. My first "P" was destroyed when Sgt Levinson went night-flying and got caught by the local searchlight chaps. He baled out. This was when I was on leave in February 1940. Funny thing about that leave, I wasn't very patriotic as I got <u>German</u> Measles and spent most of the time u/s. Nice leave!!

'I do not know the serial numbers of any of the aircraft I flew from the time I joined in April 1936, as my beautiful leather-bound "Pilot's Lying Logbook" disappeared along with my Caterpillar Club badge, both items prized by me.'

611 Squadron had, in fact, deployed a flight to Ternhill from Digby, prior to operations with the Duxford Wing. On 22 July 1940, Pilot Officer Adams was patrolling in Spitfire N3062, about which he wrote to me on 9 January 1990:-

'Regarding the forced landing at Colwyn Bay, it was a stupid thing that caused the engine to overheat and seize. A fitter had tightened the hose clamp too tightly on the header tank and when the motor got warm and the metal expanded, it stripped. I suppose the clamp cost sixpence. Just shows, doesn't it? I was trying to make Sealand aerodrome, but the motor started to seize and the glycol was coming back and stinging my eyes. So, I looked for a place to park, and only just in time, as the motor gave a heck of a jerk and seized. So my mind was made up for me.'

Fortunately, the Spitfire was pulled up onto the promenade, away from the incoming tide, by some 'Brown Jobs' and saved.

On 21 September 1940, Pilot Officer Adams was scrambled from Ternhill in Spitfire P7323, to investigate a 'bogey' at 20,000 feet over Liverpool.

611 Squadron dispersal at Digby, summer 1940. From left, back row: Sgt Levenson; Plt Off MacFie; Sgt Burt; Plt Offs Scott-Malden, Jones and Adams; Sgt Darling; Fg Off Heath; unknown. Middle row, seated: Fg Off Watkins and Flt Lt Leather. Front row: Plt Off Brown; Flt Lt Stoddart and Plt Off Pollard.

Having climbed through cloud, Dennis found a Do 215 of 2(F)/121 engaged on a photographic reconnaissance sortie. The enemy aircraft flew west, trying to escape. Dennis's letter of 19 November 1989, recalled this combat:-

'The Do 215 was at about 30,000 feet when I caught up with it, and I climbed to a couple of hundred feet above on the starboard side before attacking. Two guns on the starboard side (third and fourth) fired about two rounds each, then stopped. The armourers believe that the lubricant they used froze. Another point that was omitted [from Dennis's original combat report], I tried to get the 215 to turn to land at Speke. From that height he could have made either easily. But no success. I must say, he was a single-minded pilot, he just went straight ahead and I think he was lucky that the small field, just over a road, was there. It's pretty rugged country.'

The Dornier crashed at Trawsfyndd, Merioneth, North Wales. One of the four-man crew were killed, the others captured.

By this time, Dennis had some experience, having also destroyed a *Stuka* and an Me 109 over Dunkirk on 2 June 1940. A week after shooting down the Dornier, Dennis and several other 611 Squadron pilots were posted as replacements to 41 Squadron. Dennis set off from Ternhill to Hornchurch with a colleague, Pilot Officer Peter 'Sneezy' Brown, in his Rover sports car.

On 2 October, flying with 41 Squadron, Dennis shared in the destruction of an Me 109. According to other published accounts, on 7 October he was shot down by return fire from a Do 17, baling out of Spitfire N3267 and alighting at Douglas Farm, Postling. The cause of his parachute landing, however, was actually somewhat different, as Dennis explained in that lengthy letter of 9 January 1990:-

'Regarding the 7th deal, I let the chaps think I was a clot and the Dornier's gunners got me, but we had a new boy flying as my No 3; he was trying to get himself a squirt and as I turned to attack he let fly, taking out my controls plus half the dashboard instruments, and put bullets into the tank. Thank you! I met a very friendly farmer who insisted that I share a flask of brandy with him. Oh boy! Good old Kentish hospitality! When I arrived back at Hornchurch in a commandeered car, having sobered up, I had a quiet talk to this young man the next morning.'

Pilot Officer Dennis Adams (fifth from left) poses amongst other 611 Squadron pilots with the 'scoreboard' – a wing panel from the 2(F)/121 Do 215 he destroyed over North Wales on 21 September 1940.

There was a clever system now in place regarding replacements. Under the 'Stabilising Scheme', conceived on 7 September 1940, when things were critical, fighter squadrons were categorized A, B or C units. 'A' were those in the frontline, 11 Group, fully operational. 'B' were those being rested and part-way through refitting, but strong enough to be called upon if necessary. 'C' squadrons were re-forming after a tour in the frontline, devoting their time to providing further training for pilots direct from OTU. 'B' and 'C' squadrons were based in 12 and 13 Groups, away from the main combat zone. The places left in 611 Squadron by the departure of Pilot Officer Adams and friends, all experienced pilots posted to an 'A' squadron, were taken by Sergeants Sadler, Pattison and Scott. This was their opportunity to gain more flying hours on Spitfires and receive tactical instruction before being posted to an 'A' squadron. Initially, the three new pilots had gone from 7 OTU on 23 September to 266 Squadron at Wittering, a 'C' unit, then four days later to 611, a 'B' squadron. All being well, next stop would be to an 'A' squadron in the south-east.

Kenneth Clifton Pattison was a 27-year-old married man from Nottingham who joined the RAF Volunteer Reserve on 11 November 1938. Learning to fly at the weekends and studying ground-school subjects during the evenings, 'Pat' continued to work full-time at the city's John Player cigarette factory, until mobilised on 3 September 1939. His elementary flying training was then completed at Hanworth, before service flying training at Yatesbury and advanced flying training at Montrose. On 31 August 1940, Sergeant Pattison reported to Hawarden, converting to Spitfires. Two days after arriving at Ternhill, he made his first flight with 611 Squadron. On 8 October, Sergeant Pattison made his first operational flight in response to a suspected raid approaching Coventry and Leicester, and landed back safely without incident.

During the late afternoon of Friday 11 October, German reconnaissance aircraft were active over that night's proposed targets, including Liverpool. At 1730 hrs, 'A' Flight of 611 Squadron was scrambled from Ternhill, nearly an hour later intercepting three Do 17s, destroying two; the third struggled back to base badly damaged. At 1745 hrs, Blue Section of 611's 'B' Flight, comprising Flying Officer Barrie Heath (Blue Leader), Sergeant Ken Pattison (Blue 2) and Sergeant Robert Angus (Blue 3), was scrambled with orders to patrol the Point of Ayr at Angels 20. At 1830 hrs, while the section flew in line astern over Prestatyn, Blue Leader sighted two Do 17s approaching from the south-west, some 500 feet before the Spitfires and a quarter of a mile to port. The fighters, enjoying the advantages of height and sun, attacked. The Germans spotted the threat however, and the two raiders commenced a shallow dive towards Speke. As Heath closed in, both rear gunners opened fire.

Heath replied and the bombers separated, Heath's target turning right, the other left over Hoylake. After ordering Blue 2 and 3 to deal with the other Dornier, Heath attacked repeatedly, exhausting his ammunition, then watched the bomber gliding slowly towards Flint, dropping incendiary bombs as it went; a Hurricane appeared and made a fleeting beam attack before turning back towards Liverpool. Heath last saw the Do 17 turn into cloud near Denbigh, then, in rapidly fading light, set course for Ternhill.

When the action began, Blue 3, Sergeant Angus, went to head off the port enemy aircraft, which turned inland, firing a short burst from 400 yards. Bits flew off the bomber's underside. Angus pursued his victim towards the sea, getting in another burst, this time from 150 yards. The Do 17 pilot managed to control his dive and was last seen by Angus heading seawards. No German loss cross-references to either enemy machine attacked by Blue Section, so it must be assumed that both returned safely to base. Heath and Angus landed at Ternhill at 1850 hrs.

Blue 2, Sergeant Ken Pattison, flying Spitfire P7323 'FY-P', failed to return. Nothing had been seen of 'Pat' since the section turned into the attack, after which the other two pilots were totally committed to the job in hand.

Eventually word reached 611 Squadron that P7323 had crashed at the village of Cooksey Green, between Bromsgrove and Kidderminster, in north-west Worcestershire. In fading light, lost and with no ground-to-air direction-finding facilities in this area, the relatively inexperienced pilot had missed his Shropshire base at Ternhill and wandered south, into Worcestershire. Short of fuel and in rapidly failing light, Blue 2 needed to put down – fast. Harry Turner, the local blacksmith at Cooksey Green, saw the Spitfire circling with its navigation lights on and undercarriage down. Having selected a suitable field for a forced landing, 'Pat' was almost safely down when a herd of startled cows stampeded directly in his projected landing path. The pilot instinctively heaved back on the control column but failed to find either the power or lift for a second circuit and attempt. The Spitfire stalled, hitting a pear tree with a splintering crash, and screeched, inverted, half the field's length,

The unfortunate Sergeant Kenneth Pattison and his young wife Joan in happier times at Skegness.

58

bouncing fifteen feet into the air before coming to rest against an ancient tree stump. Mr Turner ran to the scene, finding the pilot hanging upside down by his straps. Cutting his safety harness with a pen-knife, the blacksmith gently slid the injured young man out of the cockpit and dragged him away from the smoking aircraft. Without delay, an ambulance arrived on the scene, conveying the gravely injured sergeant to Barnsley Hall Military Hospital, near Bromsgrove.

Mrs Joan Pattison rushed to the hospital, only to watch her husband suffer and linger on in this world until death became a peaceful release on 13 October 1940. Buried at Wilford Hill Cemetery in Nottingham, Ken Pattison never knew his daughter, Jean, born seven months after his death.

On 9 January 1990, Dennis Adams commented thus:-

'611 Squadron's Mk II Spitfires were transferred to us of 41 at Hornchurch. I asked what had happened to "P", and was told that it had crashed, killing the pilot attempting a wheels-down landing at dusk. I blame the Flight Commander and CO for not briefing the new boy that he and his training were worth more than an aircraft. In those days it was estimated that the cost

The Olympian Squadron Leader Don Finlay DFC, CO of 41 Squadron, with his pilots at Hornchurch – Pilot Officer Dennis Adams is second from left, standing on the Spitfire.

From the album of Squadron Leader Bob Beardsley, an enthusiastic 'snapper', pilots of 41 Squadron at Catterick during the winter of 1941; Flying Officer Dennis Adams is third from left. On the print's reverse is scribbled 'Terry, Wings, Fanny Adams, Briggs, Hoppers, Smokey, Bake'.

of pilot training up to ops standard was £40,000 – a Spit £8,000. If you could run to it, a donation of £5,000 gave you a Spit. Heath's father did just that.'

In an undated letter, Dennis added: 'Someone was at fault. If separated, what to do?! In the circumstances, my briefing would have been steer until you sight the "Mush", the coastline, or the rivers Dee or Mersey, easily visible from 10,000 feet most times of the year. There you have four aerodromes, Speke, Hooton Park, Sealand and Hawarden. Get me going on this one and I will say too much on what an "old school" outfit 611 was. Pattison should have landed wheels-up – that would have saved him, and the Spitfire would not have been written off.'

In 1993 I was pleased to send Dennis a copy of my book *Through Peril to the Stars*, which included the story of 'Blue Two'. There was no reply. Dennis's letters stopped arriving. On 31 July 1995, Mary Adams, Dennis's ex-wife, to whom he remained close, wrote explaining that Dennis's mental and physical condition had declined to such an extent by 1992, owing to Alzheimer's, that he had been admitted to the Bill Buchanan Home for the Aged. It was a depressing letter, observing that 'He is painfully thin and shuffles like an old, old man. His fishing life is long past.' Sadly, so too were Dennis's letter-writing days – and those heady, exciting, times when he flew Spitfires.

On 20 November 1995, Dennis Adams passed away. As Mary wrote when sending me the unwelcome news, 'I hope he has fun, wherever he is!'

Chapter Five

Group Captain 'Uncle'
George Denholm DFC

Spitfire Pilot

A proud Scot, George Lovell Denholm was a highly respected and accomplished individual in both war and peace. Born at Tidings Hill, Bo'ness, on the Forth in West Lothian, on 20 December 1908, into a wealthy business family, young George was educated at Cargilfield and Fettes before going up to Cambridge. There, at St John's, he read economics. This background was demonstrably privileged, the Denholms being part of Britain's socio-economic elite. The family, however, was insistent that young George should appreciate his opportunity at Cambridge and privileged status by gaining life experience. Consequently, he was sent to work in a 'tough Glasgow office'… 'to learn a thing or two'. It must have worked,

because it always seemed to me that, unlike many of the elite, George Denholm was very much a 'people person', as well as being a quiet but compelling leader similar in personality and style, perhaps, to 19 Squadron's Squadron Leader Brian Lane. The former MP Tam Dalyell, who knew George well, described him as 'quietly formidable'.

At Cambridge, George joined the University's Officer Cadet Corps, taking a great interest in the artillery section and desiring to fly more than study economics. In June 1933, he joined 603 'City of Edinburgh' Squadron of the Auxiliary Air Force (AAF). The AAF was another Trenchard initiative aimed at providing a trained reserve for use in an emergency. Based on a County Association similar to the Territorial Army (TA), the AAF comprised locally-raised units, part-time in nature, and was a social *corps d'élite*, many of its pilots being wealthy young men of independent means who flew their own aircraft privately for pleasure. So it was that Pilot Officer Denholm began flying training at MacMerry and East Fortune aerodromes, qualifying as a flying instructor in 1937. Called to full-time service on 23 August 1939, it would be over the Firth of Forth on 28 October 1939 that Flight Lieutenant Denholm, as he now was, shared with other pilots from 602 and 603 Squadrons the accolade of shooting down the first German aircraft to crash on British soil during the Second World War. This He 111, of *Stab*/KG26 based on the island of Sylt, was engaged on a long-range armed reconnaissance sortie when intercepted by the Spitfires; the intruder force-landed at Long Newton Farm, Humbie, near Edinburgh. The crew were captured and, needless to say, the incident and wrecked aircraft generated enormous interest.

After a course at the Air Fighting Development Unit (AFDU) at Northolt, George became commander of 603 Squadron's 'A' Flight. In January 1940, George and a section of 603 Squadron were deployed to Montrose, from there to fly the endless round of convoy protection patrols. This was the 'Phoney War' period, with enemy aerial activity largely confined to reconnaissance and attacks on shipping. Lone German bombers prowled over and around Britain, gathering intelligence. On 17 March 1940, Flight Lieutenant Denholm damaged one of these intruders, a Do 17, off Aberdeen. Soon afterwards he served a stint in the Operations Room at Turnhouse, returning on 5 June 1940, promoted to squadron leader and taking command of 603 Squadron. By that time, the Dunkirk evacuation was over, during which many other Spitfire squadrons had been properly blooded in action over the French coast – meeting the lethal Me 109 for the first time. While all that was ongoing, 603 Squadron kicked its heels around Dyce and Montrose, still stooging over convoys and chasing the odd lone raider. The position was unchanged when the Battle of Britain began on 10 July 1940. Four days previously, a particular replacement pilot had reported to Squadron Leader 'Uncle' George Denholm; the latter responded to my written enquiry on 27 May 1991:-

'Your letter has interested me very much and it would be rewarding to help you in the way of material for your proposed article about Richard Hillary.

'When he came to 603 with Pease and Pinckney, the Squadron's base was Turnhouse, and the two flights were detached separately to Dyce and Montrose for operational duty. My own contact with Richard Hillary was not so close as it might have been, for that reason.'

Who, though, was Richard Hillary, and why the interest?

Richard Hope Hillary was born in Sydney on 20 April 1919, the son of a British civil servant. Three years later, the family moved to London, Richard being educated at Shrewsbury and Trinity College, Oxford. Reading Modern Greats and History, the exceptional Hillary became President of the exalted University's rugby club and secretary of its world-famous rowing club. While at Oxford he joined the University Air Squadron (UAS), another initiative providing a (comparatively small) trained reserve. In June 1939, Hillary was commissioned into the RAFVR, which operated on the 'citizen volunteer' principle and was based around centres of population. Unlike the territorially-based AAF, with locally raised part-time squadrons, the VR trained young men to be pilots in their spare time; they remained in their civilian occupations until required. In time of emergency this substantial reserve was mobilised, and individuals, after 'square bashing' and service flying training, were posted to squadrons as much-needed replacements. This is how and why Pilot Officer Richard Hillary of the RAVR came

George Denholm painted by Eric Kennington while commanding 603 Squadron in 1940. (Via Edward McManus, BoBLM).

to be posted to 603 Squadron of the AAF on 6 July 1940. Unable to provide enough replacement pilots from within the AAF, the identity of these auxiliary squadrons was rapidly changing as personnel, such as volunteer reservist Richard Hillary, were posted in from other stables.

Pilot Officer Hillary joined 603 Squadron's 'B' Flight at Montrose, commanded by Flight Lieutenant 'Rusty' Rushmer. Flying Officer Laurie Cunningham led the six-strong flight's other section. Then there were Pilot Officers 'Raz' Berry, 'Bubble' Waterston, Boulter, and 'Broody' Benson, the latter apparently possessed, according to Hillary, of but one ambition: 'to shoot down Huns, more Huns, and then still more Huns!' Another pilot, Don MacDonald, typically in an auxiliary unit, had an older brother in 'A' Flight, and 23-year-old 'Pip' Cardell, the most recent addition to the squadron before Hillary and friends arriving, was 'still bewildered, excited, and a little lost'. The flight also had two pilots from overseas, Flying Officer Brian Carbury, a New Zealander, and Pilot Officer 'Stapme' Stapleton, from South Africa. With these young men, the 21-year-old Hillary would share a brotherhood – and soon go to war. The time at Montrose, however, provided an important opportunity for pilots like Richard Hillary to augment the meagre experience gained previously on Spitfires at OTU.

By mid-August 1940, the Battle of Britain was in full swing over south-east England, the *Luftwaffe* determinedly battering 11 Group's airfields, with heavy losses on both sides. Air Chief Marshal Dowding had sensibly not concentrated all or even most of the fighters at his disposal in the battle area, instead dispersing them throughout the land, observing the responsibility to defend the rest of Britain and maintain a robust reserve. This also meant that after a period in the frontline, depleted and exhausted squadrons could be rotated northwards and replaced by squadrons at full strength. On 20 August 1940, both of 603 Squadron's flights were recalled to the Sector Station at Turnhouse, meaning one thing: a move south was in the offing. There was great excitement amongst the pilots, 19-year-old Pilot Officer Benson beside himself, shouting, 'Now we'll show the bastards!' Nothing, however, happened. The squadron stood-by for further orders. As Hillary later wrote, 'We were like children promised a trip to the seaside, broken because of rain.' At last, on 27 August, a signal was received ordering 603 Squadron to Hornchurch to replace the Defiants of 264 Squadron which had been virtually annihilated. There, east of London, 603 Squadron found the tempo very different to what they were used to up in Scotland. Instead of lone reconnaissance and nuisance raiders, 'Uncle' George's pilots were now faced with the full fury of the German air assault, involving mass formations and, crucially, fighter escorts.

Shortly after arriving at Hornchurch, 603 Squadron was scrambled. By the end of that first day, Flight Lieutenant Cunningham and Pilot Officers MacDonald and Benson, the teenager who was 'going to show 'em', were all dead. In response, Squadron Leader Denholm destroyed an Me 109, and Flying Officer Waterstone probably destroyed another. There was no respite the following day. During the relentless action on this day, Hillary tacked himself onto Squadron Leader Peter Townsend's 85 Squadron, confusing the Hurricane pilots as to the identity of his aircraft and causing a fatal split-second delay in recognising an attack by 109s. In the ensuing ambush, 85 Squadron, to their CO's fury, lost a valuable Flight Commander killed, and Hillary himself was shot up, force-landing at Lympne. While Townsend commented (see Chapter One) that 'Hillary might have known better', Richard later described the incident as 'most amusing but painful'.

On 30 August 1940, 603 Squadron flew three sorties, meeting the enemy twice more. Squadron Leader Denholm was shot down and forced to bale out of Spitfire L1067, XT-D, which he wrote to me about, amongst other things, on 5 January 1989:-

'While my recollections of some personal experiences in 1940 is still quite vivid, sadly my log book was destroyed in a fire several years ago,

Squadron Leader Denholm, third from right, with other 603 Squadron pilots after the Battle of Britain. (Via Edward McManus, BoBLM).

and there is no means of pinning memories to any particular aircraft except L1067, which was my "personal" aircraft up to 30 August, when we parted company.

'N3026 could well have been in Red Section when a Heinkel was shot down off Kinnaird Head on 3 July. It is a matter of great regret to me that I landed N3026 at Montrose without ensuring that the wheels were properly down. I had collected the aircraft at Turnhouse, where a modification was being carried out, and arrived at Montrose at dusk with the landing area lights in operation and was confused. Shortly afterwards there was a warning of a hostile attack and the Station was blacked out.

'L1067, mentioned above, was recovered from a peat bog near Dungeness about ten years ago by supporters of the Brenzett Aeronautical Museum and I suspect that when it went in there was no petrol or ammunition. It was said that a local farmer dumped in the hole some explosives which he had for sabotage behind the German line – if it ever came to that.

'The painting of names and emblems on our aircraft was unofficial and purely personal. L1067 was the only "Blue Peter" and it surprises me to find that there is no special photograph to send you.'

On 20 July 1992, Group Captain Denholm explained that 'L1067 was called "Blue Peter" after the horse of that name which won the Derby in 1938/39. In their own classes they were both beautiful and superb performers, and worthy to be compared with each other.'

The day 'Uncle' baled out of 'Blue Peter', Hornchurch was heavily bombed in what was a day of bitter fighting. 603 Squadron were in action four times that day, claiming twelve Me 1098s destroyed and other enemy aircraft probably so or damaged. And so it went on. Relentlessly. In his letter of 25 July 1992, Group Captain Denholm explained:-

'We had to learn quickly when we arrived in 11 Group. I determined that we would never be "bounced" from above, which is to say taken by surprise by a high-flying enemy. I would therefore fly on a reciprocal course to that provided by the Ground Controller, until reaching 15,000 feet when I would turn the Squadron about, climbing all the time. That enabled us to usually see the enemy flying inland, beneath us, giving us the advantages of height and surprise. It was never possible to deliver more than one concerted attack as a Squadron, because after the initial contact we all split up, fighting our own individual battles. After action, the Squadron would return in ones and twos. I would then wait for an hour before chasing up the fates of any missing pilots.

Hornchurch, 1 September 1940, showing Spitfires of both 222 and 603 Squadrons. It was in XT-M that Pilot Officer Richard Hillary was shot down and badly burned two days later.

Sometimes we might receive a telephone call from a pilot who had landed at another aerodrome, for whatever reason, or force-landed a damaged aeroplane, or baled out. Other times we would receive notification from the police or army that a pilot was safe, perhaps in hospital. Or we would receive bad news. Or there would be no news at all, which was worse.'

Pilot Officer Richard Hillary wrote, 'At the time, the losing of pilots was somehow extremely impersonal; nobody, I think, felt any great emotion as there simply wasn't time for it.'

On 3 September 1940 – the first anniversary of war – 603 Squadron was scrambled at 0915 hrs – and to Squadron Leader Denholm's enormous credit, considering his many other duties and responsibilities, he led the squadron in the air on most sorties throughout the Battle of Britain. The main attack that day assembled over the Pas-de-Calais at 0830 hrs: 'Raid 45', comprising fifty-four Dornier bombers escorted by eighty Me 110s, crossed the Channel and headed up the Thames Estuary at 20,000 feet. By 0940 hrs, sixteen RAF fighter squadrons had been scrambled to patrol over Essex and Kent. Ground controllers were unsure whether the 'Valhalla' would continue towards London or turn north into Essex, continuing its assault on the sector stations north of the Thames. At 0945 hrs, the enemy turned north, slightly west of Southend, heading for North Weald. As more of 11 Group's fighters were scrambled, the bombers successfully attacked their target from 15,000 feet, causing extensive damage. It was only as the raiders turned for home that the defenders, having achieved the necessary height, attacked them. Eight Spitfires of 603 Squadron joined in the frantic mêlée of twisting, turning, firing aircraft, an enormous combat developing over the Thames Estuary and Channel as the Germans fought their way out.

Pilot Officer Richard Hillary:-

'At about 12,000 feet we came up through the clouds; I looked down and saw them spread out below me like layers of whipped cream. The sun was brilliant and it made it difficult to see the next plane when turning. I was peering anxiously ahead, for the Controller had warned us that at least fifty enemy fighters were approaching very high. When we sighted them, nobody shouted, as I think we all saw them at the same moment. They must have been 500-1,000 feet above us and coming straight on like a swarm of locusts. I remember cursing and going automatically into line astern; the next moment we were in among them and it was every man for himself. As soon as they saw us they spread out and dived, and the next ten minutes was a blur of twisting machines and tracer bullets. One Me 109 went down in a sheet of flame on my right, and a Spitfire hurtled past in a half-roll; I was weaving and turning in a desperate attempt to gain height, with the machine literally hanging on the airscrew. Then, just below me and to my left, I saw what I had been praying for – a *Messerschmitt* climbing and away from the sun. I closed in to 200 yards and from slightly to one side gave him a two-second burst. Fabric ripped off the wing and black smoke poured from the engine, but he did not go down. Like a fool, I did not break away, but put in a three-second burst. Red flames shot upwards and he spiralled out of sight.'

Unbeknown to Hillary, an Me 109 was astern, unseen, his Spitfire now filling the *Revi* gunsight of *Hauptmann* Eric Bode, *Kommandeur* of II/JG26 based at St Ingelvert. The German pilot opened up with cannon and machine gun, plastering the Spitfire with shot and shell. Immediately, Hillary, in fighter pilots' parlance, became a 'flamer':-

'At that moment I felt a terrific explosion which knocked the control column from my hand, and the whole machine quivered like a stricken animal. In a second, the cockpit was a mass of flames; instinctively I reached up to open the hood. It would not move. I tore off my straps and managed to force it back; but this took time, and when I dropped back in the seat and reached for the stick in an effort to turn the plane on its back, the heat was so intense that I could feel myself going. I remember a second of sharp agony, remember thinking "So this is it!" and putting both hands to my eyes. Then I passed out.'

Miraculously, Hillary was thrown clear of his blazing Spitfire, and, coming to, despite horrendous burns, managed to deploy his parachute. Landing in the Channel, two hours later he was rescued by the Margate lifeboat.

Minutes after despatching Hillary, Bode also caught Pilot Officer Dudley Stewart-Clark unawares, who was likewise soon floating earthwards beneath his life-saving silk canopy. On 27 May 1991, Group Captain Denholm wrote to me about Dudley:-

'I am glad to send you for copying the enclosed photo of him taken probably at an Edinburgh race meeting. The camera he is carrying would be perhaps one of two which were ex a German bomber and awarded to 603 Squadron as war trophies. Being damaged but capable of repair, we drew lots for the two together, marking a ticket to each pilot for each week he spent with us at Hornchurch in August/September. They were won by Dudley, who got both repaired and then gave one to me. Mine was recently sent in to the "Reach for The Sky Appeal".'

Dudley Stewart-Clark was wounded but not burnt when shot down that day, returning to operational flying only to be killed serving as a flight commander with 72 Squadron in 1941.

For Richard Hillary, being grievously burned was, unsurprisingly, a life-changing experience, physically and mentally. Under the expert care of the pioneering plastic surgeon Sir Archibald McIndoe, Hillary became one of the fabled 'Guinea Pigs' at East Grinstead's Burns Unit.

Above left: Richard Hillary pictured by Eric Kennington in 1942.

Above right: Pilot Officer Dudley Stewart-Clark, like Hillary shot down by *Hauptmann* Erich Bode, pictured at the Edinburgh Races early in 1940.

During his lengthy recovery, Hillary wrote his memoir, *The Last Enemy*, providing us with a deeply moving and superbly written account of his experiences as a fighter pilot. This is no gung-ho romp through derring-do however. On the contrary, it is a painfully honest dissection of Hillary's own character before being burned and the effect on him thereafter – a classic of literature, an essential text which should be read by many more than just those interested in the Second World War. This then explains my interest in this extraordinary young man, who, incredibly, after many operations and years recovering from his ordeal, returned to flying. While training to fly Blenheims and night-flying on 8 January 1943, Richard Hillary crashed and was killed with his navigator. Yet another senseless waste of a life overflowing with potential and talent. Appropriately, Hillary's ashes were scattered over the Channel – by George Denholm.

For 603 Squadron, while Richard Hillary lay in hospital, the fighting continued unabated – for Denholm's men remained in the frontline until December 1940. The Battle of Britain officially concluded on 31 October 1940 – by which time only eight of those who originally arrived at Hornchurch on 27 August remained alive. According to the research by John Alcorn, mentioned elsewhere, which revised the long-accepted ranking of Fighter Command's squadrons (using data based upon actual enemy losses, as opposed to unconfirmed RAF combat claims), 603 Squadron emerged as the top-scoring RAF fighter squadron, with 57.8 confirmed victories (against the 44 of the Polish 303 Squadron, which *claimed* 130 and remains officially the top-scoring squadron). Indeed, 603 Squadron claimed 67 victories, so had a very accurate claim/confirmed ratio of 86%. For this terrific achievement, much of the credit has to go to Squadron Leader 'Uncle' George Denholm for his leadership and inspirational personal example.

On 22 October 1940, George Denholm's DFC was gazetted: 'Since the commencement of hostilities, Squadron Leader Denholm has led his squadron, flight or section in innumerable operational patrols against the enemy. His magnificent leadership has contributed largely to the success of the squadron, which has destroyed fifty-four enemy aircraft in about six weeks; four of these aircraft were destroyed by Squadron Leader Denholm himself.'

In April 1941, upon promotion to wing commander, George left 603 Squadron after what was a long association, becoming a ground controller at Turnhouse. He was on duty there the day Rudolf Hess, Hitler's deputy, parachuted into Scotland in a misguided attempt to negotiate peace with the Duke of Hamilton – all of which is, as they say, another story.

GROUP CAPTAIN 'UNCLE' GEORGE DENHOLM DFC

Wing Commander Denholm returned to operational flying in December 1941, flying the peculiar Turbinlite Havoc, a twin-engined night-fighter on which a searchlight was mounted, and later took over 605 Squadron from Peter Townsend, again specialising in night interceptions on twin-engined Bostons. Later he destroyed his last enemy aircraft, flying Mosquito night-intruder operations over the Netherlands. Having survived the war, Group Captain G.L. Denholm DFC left the RAF in 1947. For the next thirty years he devoted himself to the long-established family business, J&J Denholm, exporting coal and importing timber, retiring as Managing Director in 1980. George passed away at Tidings Hill, the Bo'ness home in which he was born, on 15 June 1997; he was a man I admired and respected enormously, and wish I had got to know better. From our correspondence there was, perhaps, one most telling line:-

'Your request for information about those far off days depends entirely upon my memory, which has now become filled with pictures that half terrify me.'

Chapter Six

Squadron Leader Jack Stokoe DFC
Spitfire Pilot

Jack Stokoe, then a 20-year-old sergeant pilot, was one of 'Uncle' George Denholm's pilots on 603 Squadron during the Battle of Britain.

It was in August 1992 that I first met Jack, when I presented him with mounted items from Spitfire R6644, which, as previously explained, had been recovered by our former Malvern Spitfire Team in 1987. Jack's logbook confirmed that he had flown that Spitfire on 12 June 1940, practising aerobatics while a pupil at 5 OTU. Several years after we met, I probed a little deeper, leading to some lengthy letters from Jack and several more meetings.

Jack was born on 1 February 1920, the son of a miner in West Cornforth, Durham. After leaving school, he travelled south in search of work and a better life than depressed north-east England was likely to offer, finding an administrative position with Buckinghamshire County Council at Aylesbury. In June 1939 he joined the RAFVR, as he explained in a letter dated 7 July 1995:-

'Only a year before the Battle of Britain began, my contemporaries and I were pursuing our civilian careers whilst learning to fly with the RAFVR in our spare time. The majority of us were eighteen or nineteen years old and given the rank of sergeant on call-up, which at first caused much dismay amongst the ranks of professional sergeants, many of whom had taken twenty years to reach that exalted rank!

'Most of us had only fifty or sixty hours flying on elementary types like Tiger Moths and Magisters when we were called up. After a brief spell at ITW to instil some discipline into us, we had about 100 hours on Harvards at FTS, which included a few trips actually firing guns. We were then posted to an OTU, in my case Aston Down, before being posted to an operational fighter squadron with just ten to fifteen operational hours on combat aircraft.'

Afterwards, Jack was first posted to 263 Squadron flying Hurricanes, but when the unit converted to the twin-engined Westland Whirlwind, Sergeant Stokoe elected to remain on single-engined fighters. Jack continued:-

'I eventually joined 603 "City of Edinburgh" Squadron, an AAF squadron, and there were only three sergeant pilots, the remainder already being pilot officers. By 27 August 1940, the Squadron moved south to Hornchurch, by which time I had about seventy hours on Spits and had sighted, but not engaged, two *Heinkel* reconnaissance aircraft in the north of Scotland.

'On 29 August 1940, we flew four patrols, intercepting Me 109s on two of them. I claimed one damaged but the trimming wires of my own aircraft were shot away. On 30 August we made four more interceptions, during the course of which I was credited with one Me 109 confirmed and one damaged. My own aircraft was damaged, by a cannon-shell in the windscreen, and my hand slightly cut by splinters.

'On 1 September came three more interceptions of 20 plus bandits, one of which I shot down in flames in the Canterbury area.

'On 2 September, I was involved in two interceptions, during the course of which I damaged two enemy aircraft but was myself shot down in flames and baled out. On that occasion, as I was attacking an enemy aircraft I remember machine-gun bullets, or maybe cannon shells, hitting my Spitfire, followed by flames in the cockpit as the petrol tanks exploded. I thought "Christ! I've got to get out of here and *quick*!" I undid the straps and opened the hood, but this turned the flames into a blowtorch. I was not wearing gloves, as during our hasty scramble I had forgotten them, but had to put my hands back into the fire to invert the Spitfire so that I could drop out (no ejector seats in those days!). I remember seeing sheets of skin peeling off the backs of my hands before I fell out of the plane. I was then concerned regarding whether the parachute would function or whether it had been damaged by fire, but I pulled the ripcord and the chute opened.

'I landed in a field, but the Home Guard queried whether I was an enemy agent! A few choice words in English soon convinced them I was genuine,

Sergeant Jack Stokoe, tunic top button undone in true fighter pilot fashion.

and thereafter I was rushed into the emergency hospital at Leeds Castle, suffering from shock and severe burns to my hands, neck and face.

'I was in hospital for six weeks before returning to operational duties on 22 October 1940, with further combat successes. A second tour of duty with 54 Squadron followed, which included a second baling out, into the North Sea, before secondment to a training unit and night-fighter duties later in the war.

'The point about the incident when I was shot down over Kent on 2 September 1940 is that at the time 603 Squadron was suffering such heavy casualties that things got pretty chaotic, so for four days after baling out, I was reported "Missing in Action"!

'The Squadron records show that in the thirty days after arriving at Hornchurch the casualties were nine dead, nine wounded, one missing and one PoW! Not bad for a lot of amateurs, which we of the RAFVR and those of the AAF were!

'I hope this diatribe gives you the information you wanted, and if you run short of subjects for future publications, the exploits of the RAFVR, those enthusiastic amateurs, might have some interesting highlights.'

On 22 July 1995, Jack wrote again:-

'One other incident of which I was only aware after the war was that on 31 August 1940, 603 Squadron intercepted a raid over Woolwich, during which I shot down an Me 109E, apparently flown by a *Leutnant* Binder of I/JG3 – which, as it plummeted to the ground, collided with a 603 Squadron Spitfire flown by Flying Officer "Bubbles" Waterston, who was killed. The Spitfire fell on Woolwich and burnt out, the bulk of the 109 crashing into gardens at Plumstead.

'Another point which may be of some interest relates to Pilot Officer Richard Hillary, who was eventually killed in an accident whilst undergoing night-fighter training at East Fortune on 8 January 1943. I was at that time an instructor there on Blenheims and Beaufighter Mk IIs, and was on duty on 8 January 1943, but only during the day, and not in the ensuing night-flying when he was killed.

'You ask about Flight Lieutenant "Rusty" Rushmer, but I have no real knowledge and don't believe I actually met him. Before the Battle of Britain, I joined 603 Squadron's "A" Flight at Dyce, near Aberdeen, and Rushmer commanded "B" Flight at Montrose. When we moved to Hornchurch the flights remained rather separate, often at different states of readiness, and on the few occasions we operated as a Squadron there was little time for formal introductions. When Rushmer was killed on 5 September 1940, I was myself in hospital, suffering from burns.

'Hope this is of some help!'

On 1 August 1995, Jack sent me several photographs, 'plus one of me being fished out of the North Sea at the end of a rope from a minesweeper. There's a lot of sea and not much of me! Date 20 April 1941, when I was with 54 Squadron. The picture was taken by one of the crew which pulled me out.'

A letter was rapidly in the post requesting more details of that incident, to which Jack replied on 8 September 1995:-

'I have had some difficulty remembering the sequence of events just before and after being shot down – not entirely surprising as when I was admitted to hospital I was suffering from shock, concussion, exhaustion and hypothermia, aided and abetted by a generous helping of Navy rum, for which at the time I was extremely grateful!

'A lot of sea but not much of me' – Jack being rescued from the North Sea, having been shot down on 20 April 1941.

Jack pictured after the war, having returned to the RAFVR.

'As far as I remember we were patrolling about ten to twenty miles out in the North Sea, off Clacton, probably vectored there by Control reporting "bandits" in the area, then suddenly we were in a combat situation and I was firing at an enemy aircraft. Then – a blank! I was still in the air, but minus an aircraft, which had disappeared entirely (probably as a result of one or more direct hits from cannon shells behind the armour-plated seat).

'I had not opened the hood, or disconnected my oxygen supply or intercom, or unstrapped the seat harness, and I seemed not to be surprised or unduly worried that I was apparently flying without any visible means of support. Nor did I seem to have any sensation of falling! My helmet was missing, as were my gloves and one of my flying boots, and when I got around to looking, my parachute looked somewhat the worse for wear. However, I pulled the ripcord, the chute opened, and I landed in a very cold and somewhat wild sea.

'My hands did not seem to be functioning properly, and I was unable to free myself from the parachute (which remained attached to me and shows quite clearly in the photograph). I slowly recollected that I ought to have an inflatable dinghy, and after another struggle managed to inflate it, only to have it burst. Whether it was damaged, or whether I inflated it too quickly we will never know, but I certainly reached a new low in the survival stakes. However, I managed to hang on grimly to a certain amount of air in an undamaged corner of the deflated dinghy and struggled feebly to stay afloat.

'When I had just about given up hope, I heard voices, a ship was near me and ropes were thrown. I grabbed one and was hauled aboard. I remember little else, but was told the rest of the story by a couple of the crew members (possibly the Captain and his Mate) when they visited me in Harwich Hospital and presented me with the photograph you now have.

'Apparently, they wrapped me in blankets, gave me an unspecified hot drink, and laid me to rest in a bunk. An RAF Air Sea Rescue launch then arrived and wanted to take me back but fortunately the Skipper said I was comfortably resting aboard and he was returning to port anyway. So, I remained where I was. I say 'fortunately' because I was told that the launch overturned in rough sea outside the harbour, and I was in no state to face another struggle.

'They also reported seeing an enemy aircraft crash into the sea before fishing me out.

'I was in hospital for seven days and had seven days' leave, but strangely enough I have no recollection of whether I went home or not, although it is likely that I did. I returned to duty with 54 Squadron and was back in action again on 6 May 1941.'

On that day, 54 Squadron had taken off from Hornchurch at 1625 hrs to patrol Barrow Deep. On arrival, a *Staffel* of Me 109s was sighted above, one of which attacked the Spitfires head-on, passing above them before turning to assault 'A' Flight from astern. The squadron broke in all directions, after which Pilot Officer Colebrook was last seen heading seawards,

Squadron Leader Jack Stokoe DFC signing with Dilip Sarkar at the Biggin Hill Air Show, 1998.

streaming glycol. *Oberleutnant* Winfried Balfanz of *Stab*/JG51 claimed a Spitfire destroyed, that most likely being Colebrook's. The Royal Navy, however, claimed the destruction of two Me 109s, but there were, in fact, no such casualties. Given how Jack's aircraft dramatically disintegrated around him, it is likely that he was hit by anti-aircraft fire, not by a 109 – a victim of so-called 'friendly fire'. When I put this to Jack, his response was understandable: '"Friendly Fire"? Wasn't very bloody "friendly", you take it from me!'

During his time flying Spitfires in 1940 and '41, Jack destroyed seven enemy aircraft and was commissioned on 26 June 1941. After spells instructing, his DFC was gazetted on D-Day, 6 June 1944. In 1946, Jack was demobbed, going to work for Rochester County Council as a weights and measures inspector. Keen to fly again, in 1947 Jack re-joined the RAFVR, instructing in his spare time on Tiger Moths and Chipmunks until 1952. In 1998, Jack joined me for a book-signing at that year's Biggin Hill air show, at which we were joined by a German Battle of Britain ace who, Jack decided, was not his 'cup of tea'. Nonetheless, together with William Walker, whose story is also told in this book, a good day was had by all. Considering that he was such a successful ace, and such an aviation enthusiast, it always surprised me that when I found Jack back in the late 1980s he really was living in happy obscurity. Indeed, it was not until 1998 that he joined the Battle of Britain Fighter Association. Jack, though, was always surprised at the interest in his personal exploits – I was not, and his letters evidence why.

Squadron Leader Jack Stokoe DFC died on 1 October 1999, aged 79.

Chapter Seven

Group Captain Herbert 'Pinners' Pinfold

Hurricane Pilot

Herbert Moreton Pinfold ('Dilip, never known as "Herbert", always "Pinners"!') took a Short Service Commission in the RAF in September 1934. Having completed flying training, Pilot Officer Pinfold was posted to 6 Squadron at Ismalia, Egypt, flying Hawker Hart biplane light bombers in the army cooperation role. Some subterfuge then surrounded his next posting. In October 1935, Mussolini's Italy had invaded Abyssinia (Ethiopia). Given British imperial interests in the Middle East, there was naturally concern over Mussolini's aggressive and expansionist foreign policy – and a real concern that this might lead to war between Britain and

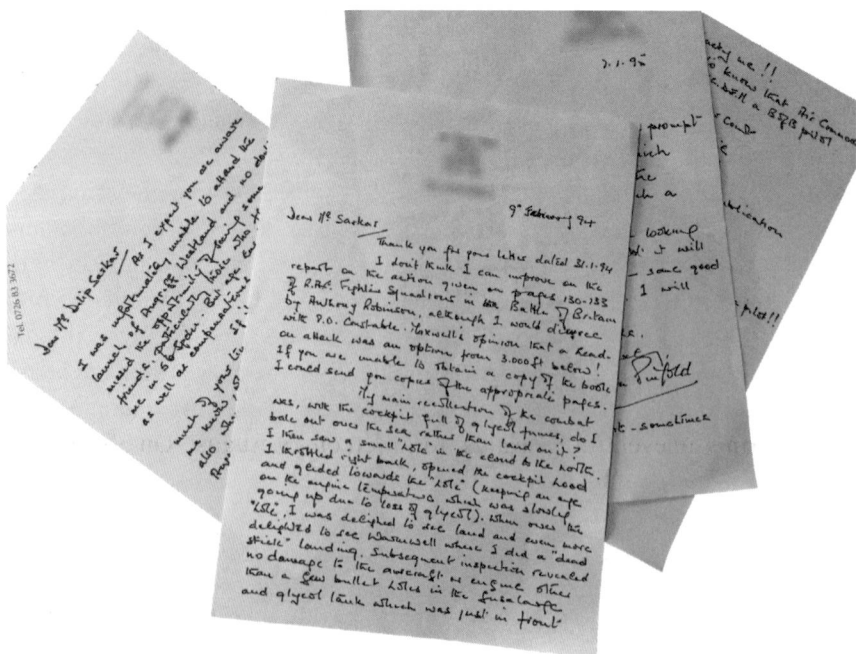

Italy. Consequently, Britain's forces in the area were quietly expanded. On 1 March 1936, 64 Squadron re-formed at Heliopolis in Egypt, equipped with the Hawker Demon two-seater fighter – but the official announcement stated that the unit was based at Henlow, in England. In the event of war between Britain and Italy, 64 Squadron would move west, to Mersa Matruh, from where it would attack Italian air bases and cover RAF bombers while refuelling. By June 1936, the Italians prevailed in Abyssinia, after which things settled down, so in August 1936, 64 Squadron returned to England, based at Martlesham Heath. Pilot Officer Pinfold had joined 64 Squadron on 19 March 1936, officially at Martlesham – but in reality only moved from Ismalia to Heliopolis to join his new unit. He would remain with 64 Squadron for over two years, when, as a flying officer, Pinners became an instructor on Hawker Hinds with 502 'Ulster' Squadron of the AAF, based at Aldergrove in Northern Ireland. From there, Flying Officer Pinfold was posted to become 603 Squadron's Adjutant at Turnhouse. On 2 July 1940 he became an instructor at 3 FTS, South Cerney, but after the Battle of Britain began, answered the call for volunteers to fly fighters. Having converted to Hurricanes during a shortened course at 5 OTU, Aston Down, on 25 August, Flight Lieutenant Pinfold, as he then was, reported to 56 Squadron at North Weald as 'supernumerary'.

56 Squadron had flown Hurricanes during the Battle of France and had been heavily engaged throughout the first half of the Battle of Britain. On 27 August, Pinners made his first flight with his new squadron, local flying of over an hour in Hurricane R4117, followed by an R/T test in the same aircraft later that morning. During the afternoon he joined Flight Lieutenant 'Jumbo' Gracie's 'B' Flight at Rochford, remaining at readiness there until returning to North Weald for tea. At 0840 hrs the following morning, Pinners scrambled with 'B' Flight in response to an 'X-Raid', but the hour-long patrol was uneventful. The flight landed and stood-by at Rochford, from where it was scrambled at 1230 hrs to intercept a formation of German bombers, escorted by fighters, over the Thames Estuary. This would have been Pinners' first sight of the enemy – and what a sight it must have been! Several of 56 Squadron's pilots made claims, but Pinners was not amongst them. Further uneventful 'X Raids' followed on 29 August. On 30 August, Gracie was shot down, force-landing at Halstead and breaking his neck in the process – he survived but was out of the battle from then on. Surprisingly, given his lack of combat experience, on that day Pinners was promoted to acting squadron leader and given command of 56 Squadron, the CO of which up to that point, 'Minnie' Manton, being promoted to wing commander and posted to command RAF Station Hawkinge. The commander of 'A' Flight,

however, Flight Lieutenant Percy 'Steve' Weaver, was an experienced fighter pilot, and possibly, therefore, better suited to command a fighter squadron on active operations. Weaver was slightly junior to Pinners on the Air Force List, which may explain the choice, or it could possibly have been because Weaver was considered tour-expired and plans were afoot to move 56 out of the frontline. Either way, the gallant Weaver was reported Missing in Action the next day – on which date his DFC was gazetted.

A day later, 56 Squadron was withdrawn from North Weald in 11 Group to Boscombe Down in 10 Group, providing an opportunity, downgraded as a 'B' squadron, to absorb and train replacement pilots in the quieter West Country. As previously explained, a 'B' squadron was still considered strong enough to undertake operational duties and be called upon when required, which was just as well because there was a surprising amount of fighting over the 10 Group area. Indeed, it was from Boscombe Down on 16 August 1940 that 249 Squadron's Flight Lieutenant James Brindley Nicolson scrambled to perform his 'signal act of valour' over Southampton – earning Fighter Command's only VC of the Second World War. The West Country also included other priority targets, including the ports at Bristol, Cardiff and Swansea, and a number of aircraft factories, such as Gloster's at Brockworth, Bristol's at Filton, and Westland's at Yeovil. It was unlikely, therefore, to be an uneventful sojourn, and so it would prove.

Herbert 'Pinners' Pinfold pictured shortly before the Battle of Britain. (Via Edward McManus, BoBLM).

Over the 11 Group area, the battle continued to intensify, especially from 7 September 1940 onwards, when, in an attempt to force the British government to surrender and to draw Fighter Command into the air for destruction *en masse*, the Germans began bombing London round-the-clock. By the end of September, this strategy too had failed, and by then the German bomber force was unable to continue sustaining such heavy losses. Indeed, the final straw came over the West Country. During the third week of September, the *Luftwaffe* changed tack yet again, focussing on targets connected with the British aircraft industry. On 24 September, the Supermarine factory producing Spitfires at Southampton was attacked; the next day, a highly successful raid was made on Filton; on 26 September, KG55 destroyed Supermarine's, causing great loss of life. A return to Filton the next day, however, was well-met by Fighter Command, and the Germans suffered a beating. Three days later, they were back, KG55's He 111s bound for Westland Aircraft at Yeovil.

Having taken off at 1524 hrs, forty-three He 111s of KG55 rendezvoused over Cherbourg with forty-seven Me 109s of JG2, five of JG53, and forty Me 110s of ZG26. While this formation ponderously made its way across the Channel, a diversionary attack was made on Southampton by eleven Ju 88s of KG51. As the main raid approached Portland, the Hurricanes of 238 Squadron were scrambled from Chilbolton at 1600 hrs. Over the sea, fifteen to twenty miles south of Portland, the Hurricanes intercepted and battle was joined. At 1608 hrs, twelve Spitfires of 152 Squadron were scrambled, followed two minutes later by Pinners leading five other 56 Squadron Hurricanes. Both RAF fighter squadrons arrived over Portland and Lyme Bay at 1630 hrs.

Pinners climbed 56 Squadron slightly to the west of Portland Bill to gain the advantage of sun. When flying due south at 16,000 feet, sighted 'God knows how many Do 215s and Me 110s', the bombers reported at 19,000 feet, the enemy fighters 5,000 feet above and behind. All of the He 111s appeared to open fire simultaneously on 56 Squadron, which put up an impressive defensive barrage. Pinners climbed his Hurricanes to 19,000 feet, and as 56 Squadron attacked the bombers from astern, inevitably the fighter escort rained down. Pinners attacked a He 111, but a bullet from the *Gruppenkeil*'s combined firepower hit his Hurricane. On 9 February 1994, Pinners wrote to me, recording his memory of that engagement:-

'My main recollection of the combat was, with the cockpit full of glycol fumes, do I bale out over the sea, rather than land on it? I then saw a small "hole" in the cloud to the north. I throttled right back, opened the cockpit hood and glided towards the "hole" (keeping an eye on the engine temperature, which was slowly going up due to loss of glycol). When over the "hole" I was delighted to see land and even more delighted to see Warmwell, where I did a "dead stick" landing. Subsequent inspection revealed no damage to the aircraft or engine other than a few bullet holes in the fuselage and glycol tank, which was just in front of the cockpit. Lucky me!!'

Pilot Officer 'Taffy' Higginson reported seeing the He 111 Pinners had fired at 'going downwards with both engines streaming black smoke'.

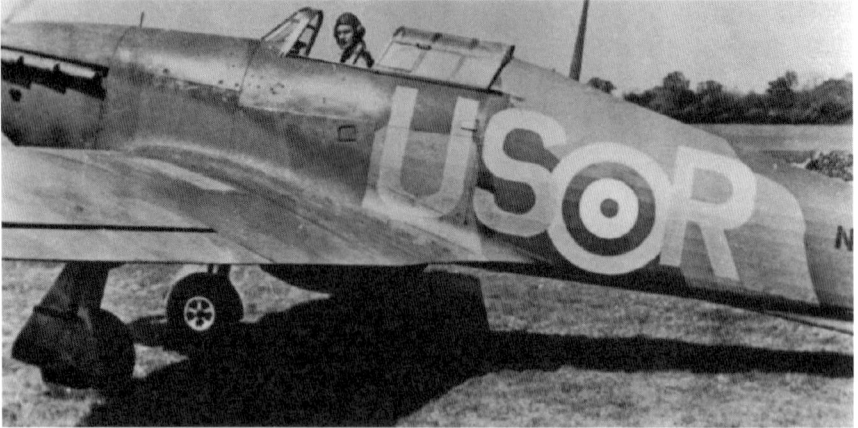

Pilot Officer Peter Down taxying his 56 Squadron Hurricane at North Weald during the Battle of Britain – 'Pinners' succeeded 'Minnie' Manton in command and led the squadron in action over the West Country.

Back at Warmwell, Pinners claimed the enemy aircraft as a 'Do 215' destroyed. Flight Lieutenant R.E.P. Brooker and Sergeant P.E.M. Robinson both damaged another 'Do 215', and Higginson shared a 110 destroyed with Pilot Officer W.D. Williams of 152 Squadron. 56 Squadron, however, lost two Hurricanes destroyed, both pilots baling out safely, and, in addition to Pinners, two other pilots force-landed with damaged machines. Nonetheless, for the enemy, the raid was not a great success. The target area was found to be covered by 10/10ths cloud, frustrating the bomber crews who had fought their way so far inland. Wheeling about, the formation leader spotted, through a gap in the cloud, a town of similar size to Yeovil, which likewise straddled a railway line. The decision was made to bomb it. The He 111s changed formation into *Ketten* in line astern, travelling north-east to south-west. At 1640 hrs, bombs rained down. The problem was that this was not Yeovil, nor indeed Westland Aircraft beneath the bombers, but the picturesque and peaceful West Country town of Sherborne. Fifty bombs fell on the town in a line from Bedmill Copse to Crackmore. Gas and water mains were seriously damaged and the electricity supply failed. UXBs lay about, the railway line was hit, as was the cemetery, where coffins were blown out of the ground. Incredibly, Sherborne Abbey, standing in the centre of the destruction, was unscathed. Thirty-one properties were destroyed and 776 damaged. Eighteen people were killed, ironically including a London evacuee who had only arrived the previous day, and thirty-two were injured. Percy Coaker, a well-known character, immediately placed a sign in what remained of his furniture shop window in the devastated town centre: 'We have been bombed, buggered and bewildered, but business as usual'!

High above, the fighting continued, the enemy harried nearly all the way back to France. This day saw one of the last great daylight battles of summer 1940, during which the *Luftwaffe* lost forty-six aircraft destroyed against Fighter Command's twenty. After this, the OKW was forced to withdraw the He 111 from daylight operations. The emphasis of the enemy air attack, as previously explained, switched to bombing at night, presenting both sides with a whole new set of problems. Of course, British propaganda made hay with the raid, declaring it a deliberate 'terror attack' against a non-military target, but in truth the tragedy of Sherborne arose due to a genuine navigation error. Indeed, the infamous traitor William Joyce, better-known as 'Lord Haw-Haw', who opened his radio show with 'Germany calling, Germany calling', broadcast an apology to Sherborne – while predicting that Yeovil's turn was yet to come.

I received other letters from Pinners, concerning publication of my book *Angriff Westland*, the reason I contacted him about the events of 30 September 1940, but the best extract was that single paragraph regarding his forced landing at Warmwell.

Sometimes, less is more.

Chapter Eight

Warrant Officer Peter Fox
Hurricane Pilot

Peter Hutton Fox was born on 23 January 1921 at 'Silverdale', Summerfield Road, Hildenthorpe, Bridlington, Yorkshire, the son of Frederick Hutton Fox, a 'seed crusher's salesman', and his wife Ethel. The young Fox joined the RAFVR in June 1939, learning to fly at Kidlington. Mobilised on 1 September 1939, after 'square-bashing' at 1 ITW, Cambridge, Peter successfully completed his service training at Yatesbury and Montrose. On 8 February 1994, Peter wrote to me, and takes up the story:-

'I was a "sprog" pilot, as Denis [Nichols] and I joined 56 Squadron [at Boscombe Down] from 5 OTU Aston Down [on 17 September 1940],

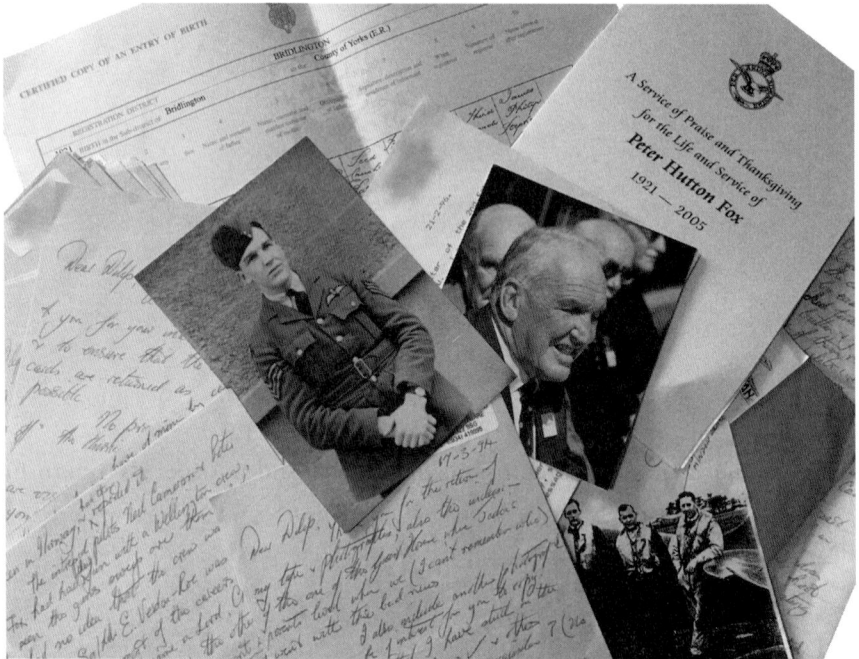

and I think it was the day after joining that he and I acted as coffin-bearers to a pilot of 56 Squadron killed in action… We were just "also rans", having become operational late in the Battle of Britain.'

As previously related, 56 Squadron had been relieved at North Weald by 249 Squadron, whose Hurricanes the former unit took over. Consequently Peter's logbooks recorded many flights in 'GN' coded Hurricanes, as opposed to 56 Squadron's 'US' identification letters. On 22 February 1994, Peter continued:-

'On 20 September 1940, in GN-I, I was flying for 1.30 hours on a "height test", and have entered in my log book "32,800 feet". I remember well the way I had to fight in nursing the Hurricane up the last few hundred feet, and kept falling out of the sky in stalls… I remember that a Polish pilot was lost as he and I were both weaving as "tail-end Charlies", and I did not even see him hit.'

Like his CO, 'Pinners', I had actually contacted Peter regarding his experiences of the raid on 30 September 1940, which he also provided, at length, in that same letter:-

'Saga! I was nineteen-years-old, had flown Hurricanes for twenty hours, and just didn't believe it when I saw the enemy, which I understood to be a 60+ raid of *Heinkels* and fighter escorts of Me 109s and 110s. I had never seen so many aircraft together before, and as far as I knew, we of 56 Squadron would be attacking the bombers – I doubt if we were up to the full Squadron strength of 12 – and a Spitfire squadron would be engaging the enemy fighters. Tally Ho!!

'I do know my mouth felt very dirty-tasting with apprehension. We gained height, going out to sea, and then curved down and round and into attack the *Heinkels*, which were going towards the English coastline. One or more of ours went into attack the leaders of the enemy, and others to the rear. I selected one at the rear, pressed the button and aimed firstly at one engine and then sprayed across to the other. I did not see any return fire from the gunner, but suddenly the *Heinkel* seemed to slow down and slowly peel off to port. I started to follow him down, still firing, when there was an explosion and I saw that there was little left of my instrument panel! I had been advised by an "old-timer" to fly with my hood open when in full action, as bullets could damage the hood so it would not open. Luckily, on this day, I had followed that advice, otherwise my head would have been blown off as the shell hit the canopy. I peeled off starboard, pulling upwards and away, with all controls seemingly working correctly.

'I got over land at 3,000 feet and was wondering whether I could make the coastal airfield at Warmwell (near Weymouth), when I saw flames coming up between my legs. I don't think that I even thought about my next action, which was to instinctively roll the kite upside down and release my harness. I then saw my feet still above me and the Hurricane above my feet, presumably stalled. Where was the rip cord? I told myself to calm down, and pulled the "D" ring straightaway. I had never before pulled a rip cord, never seen one pulled, never seen a parachute packed, and never had any instruction! The "D" ring was flung into the air, followed by some wire. Obviously, I had broken it! I then felt the tug of the pilot chute followed almost immediately by the wrench of the main parachute. I was safe! The next second, I was aware of an "enemy", which I assumed was going to shoot me. It was, however, my flaming Hurricane, which literally missed me by inches! The kite slowly screwed round, going into a steeper and steeper dive until almost vertical, and aimed directly at the cross-hedges of four fields to the northeast of a wood towards which I was drifting. The aircraft hit the cross-hedges spot on, a short pause then a huge explosion followed by another pause before flames shot up to a great height. I'm glad that I wasn't in it!

Sergeant Peter Hutton Fox.

'I was safe again but didn't feel it as the sea looked rather close and I didn't want to end up swimming. I then recalled a film about a German parachutist, which had shown how if you pulled the parachute lines on one side or the other, the direction was slipped off accordingly. I tried, but which side I don't know as I could not see which way I was drifting. I certainly could not think aerodynamically at that moment! Leave well alone, I thought! I was safe again, then, blood! Trickling down my right leg. I tried to lift my right leg to see, but couldn't. I'd met aircrew who had lost limbs but could still feel extremities that were no longer there. My leg must have been shot off and would crumble beneath me upon landing! I was getting close to the ground and worried about my 'shot off' leg when I remembered the story of a pilot being shot in the foot by the Home Guard. "BRITISH!" I shouted at the top of my voice. I pulled hard as my parachute clipped a tree on the edge of a wood. Upon landing I just fell over gently, when the wind pulled the chute sideways, and I shouted "BRITISH!" again. As no one came I started to roll up my parachute when a farm labourer climbed over a nearby fence and requested confirmation that I was okay.

'My "shot off" leg was not, in fact, "shot off". It was just a tiny wound on my knee where a small piece of shrapnel had entered, and another the same size half an inch away where it had come out. A lady on horseback then came along and I draped my parachute over the animal. Off we went on foot until a van took me to Lyme Regis Police Station. I was then entertained in the local pub while I awaited transport back to Warmwell. Someone from Air Sea Rescue arrived and I told him that I was pretty sure that "my" *Heinkel* had gone into the drink.'

Sergeant Fox's Hurricane, N2434, US-H, crashed at 1630 hrs, 800 yards north of the Wootton Fitzpaine to Monkton Wyld Road, at Wootton Fitzpaine, near Lyme Regis on the Dorset coast. Without doubt the teenage pilot had been hit by 20mm cannon-fire from an escorting Me 109 or 110. After recuperating, Peter returned to 56 Squadron, later joining 234 Squadron, flying Spitfires at Warmwell during Fighter Command's so-called 'Non-stop Offensive' – which Peter described for me not by letter but in a cassette recording in 1994:-

'It was not long after the CO of 234 Squadron, Squadron Leader H.M. Stephen DSO, told me he would hold back his recommendation for my commission by two weeks (because in a fortnight my Flight Sergeant's Crown would be due, meaning that if I was commissioned thereafter, I would be a flying, not pilot, officer) that things started to go wrong. The prospect of a commission was about time! I had first missed being commissioned at No 1 ITW, Cambridge, due to a posting; then, at No 8 FTS Montrose, a post with telephone wires interfered with the process, and then, in 1940, while serving with 56 Squadron at Boscombe Down, I was flown into a haystack. One may think that a haystack would be soft enough, but it was 3½ days later that I woke up again with a broken back. Meanwhile the commission passed by again!

'However, it was a lovely morning on 20 October 1941 at Warmwell airfield in Dorset, and everything seemed to be going well – my back had mended, I was 20 years of age, my commission was on the boil again, and I was poised to go home to Oxford on leave.

'In one pocket of my best uniform was a signed leave pass, and in another a snapshot of some of the pilots, including myself, standing round the Squadron Transport with "234" painted on the windscreen. My parents would have been interested to see it in a few hours time after I had flown to Kidlington in the station Magister. I was also intending to show my parents the identity disc with "rissole" on one side and "234 Squadron. F/Lt Mortimer-Rose" on the reverse. My Flight Commander, "Morty", had only recently given me the dog. There was also my invention! I had drilled a small hole in the lever of the CO_2 bottle which when pulled inflated the Mae West. A piece of cord was then passed through the hole and was tied with a bow to the buoyancy cushion which, on top of a parachute, formed a seat for the pilot. This would give automatic inflation of the Mae West, whether or not the pilot was conscious, having baled out over the "drink". It was just necessary to remember to untie the bow before getting out of the plane at base.

'It was lunchtime and the Squadron was about to be "stood down". "It won't count off your leave!" was the CO's response to me volunteering for a nuisance raid over France. Sergeant Sapsed volunteered as my No 2. The sortie was to locate and blow up an ammunition dump sited just inland and to the east of Cherbourg. Another volunteer pair were to strafe an aerodrome to the west of Cherbourg.

'Wind blowing from west, so a course was calculated from Portland Bill to a bay east of Cherbourg. All four Spitfire Mk VBs, each armed with two 20mm cannon and four machine-guns, were ready to go. Take-off on Warmwell's grass runway, with wind from the west, meant taxying away from dispersal, the full length of the aerodrome and then turning into wind. I applied my brakes to turn into wind for take-off and a tyre burst! Undo harness, undo bow to CO_2 bottle and out; run the length of the aerodrome and into another Spitfire, AZ-H, AD203, in place of AZ-C, AD726, which I usually flew and which was now standing empty at the far end of the field with its burst tyre. No revolver or Verey pistol in the pocket of the new Spitfire!

'Over Portland Bill course set, and no sign of the other pair, just "Sappy" following me, flying just above sea-level across the Channel. What appears to be the correctly-shaped bay appears in just under half an hour; cross the coastline and what seems to be a single machine-gun opens up – a thud and the oil pressure gauge drops to zero; I tell Sappy over the R/T "I've had it",

Spitfire pilots of 234 Squadron at Warmwell, summer 1941. Sergeant Fox is third from right, standing.

but the R/T doesn't work, probably damaged by the same bullet. No revolver or Verey pistol with which to destroy the Spitfire, so must turn back to sea to dump it, hoping to then swim back to land. Engine now objecting to running without oil, and sounding very rough. I fired a short burst of my guns in anger until I noted the poor cows scattering in the field ahead. Coast in sight, engine stops, speed drops, and I hit a telegraph pole with one wing. The aircraft slews round and gently tips on its nose and then settles back. Quite a gentle crash, really. Must try and escape – undo harness, jump up – up blows Mae West, can't get out! Bags of fumbling, a great raspberry as the Mae West pressure drops, out I get, run across a couple of fields and dive under a hedge, where the cover is good and thick.

'I was in the hedge quite deep, at the junction of hedgerows, and had time to take off my Mae West, undo my escape kit, take off right shoe and sock and place money, maps and compass under the instep before replacing sock and shoe. Voices come closer, a male French voice shouts "Come out, boy. He see you or he shoot." Two shots rang out, although I do not know whether fired into the hedge or air. After some quick thinking I decide that discretion is the better part of valour and crawl out, hands up, to face a small crowd of civilians and a German soldier armed with a rifle on the farther side of a fence to another field. Mae West thrown over fence, two hands on top of fence, a great leap and I am in their field. I well remember the civilians'

89

applause for my athletic prowess! In an endeavour to convey my sadness at not having been able to destroy my plane, and my knowledge of the German language being schoolboyish in the extreme, I point to my Spitfire, klaxon blaring, in the centre of the adjacent field. I placed my hand on the German's rifle. Our conversation in German must have been absorbing, because he let go of it! A moment later a couple of German officers appeared – one slapped the soldier's face, snatched the rifle from me and returned it to the soldier. Life returned to "normal". Salutes having been exchanged, we all walked across the field to a road. There a soldier ran out of a building to take my photograph. I will never know why on earth I raised my arm over my face to prevent the photograph being taken, as such a photograph could have been used to show an "ashamed *Terror-Flieger*".

'Then we went off to Maupertus airfield near Cherbourg, where I met some Me 109 pilots of I and II/JG2. Most of them spoke English but I considered it wise not to tell them that on 26 August my Squadron had strafed this airfield – I had blown up a petrol bowser! We enjoyed considerable good-humoured banter, but they would not let me fly a Me 109 to formulate a comparison! While playing table tennis with one of the pilots a very different kind of uniformed officer abruptly stopped the game and it was a hard bed in a small cell for me for the rest of the night.'

In 1993, Peter Fox, left, was returned to the scene by the author and met eyewitnesses to his bale-out and crash at Wootton Fitzpaine on 30 September 1940.

During the excavation of Hurricane N2434, Peter was the most enthusiastic digger, rewarded with the biggest find – a piece of reduction gearing.

Peter Fox is unique amongst the Few as he became the legal owner, as this chapter relates, of his Battle of Britain Hurricane – conserved parts of which were presented to the former pilot by the author in 1995.

For Flight Sergeant Fox, there followed years in the 'bag', all of which is another story:-

'Five main PoW camps plus three working party camps and three-and-a-half years later elapsed before I was home again in England and able to read in my log book the entry "20 October 1941, Spitfire H203 Missing – shot down by flak over La Mazerie". I never did get that commission! I left the RAF in 1946 as a Warrant Officer, and later became a surveyor.'

Before leaving the service, Peter met Beryl, a WAAF serving at RAF Cosford, the couple enjoying married life together, retiring to Weston-super-Mare in the West Country.

In 1994, after the release of *Angriff Westland*, my book which brought us together, I decided upon a cunning plan. We knew where Peter's Hurricane had crashed on 30 September 1940, and obtained the landowner's permission to excavate the crash site – with Peter present. To do so required a licence from the MoD, which was applied for and issued in Peter's name. In November 1994, the dig went ahead, Peter being very clear regarding where his Hurricane impacted, and joining us for the occasion with Beryl and our great friend, based in nearby Poole, former *Luftwaffe* fighter and bomber pilot and prisoner of war *Leutnant* Hans 'Peter' Wulff. There was little of

Peter Fox (centre) went through flying training with Ken Wilkinson (left) and Denis Nichols (right). All flew fighters during the Battle of Britain. The 'Three Musketeers' are pictured here at a Lakenheath reunion. Sadly all are now deceased.

the aircraft to be found, mostly fragments, but enough was recovered to keep the regional television news cameras happy and justify submission of the necessary 'Returns Form', listing finds, to the MoD – which then assigned rights of ownership from the Crown to the Licence Holder: Peter Hutton Fox. A number of the Few have attended recoveries of 'their' crashed aircraft since aviation archaeology became popular in the 1970s, amongst whom Peter is unique as the only one to actually own his Battle of Britain fighter – even if it was in a million pieces! It gave me great pleasure to make Peter a framed presentation of conserved items from Hurricane N2434 at the launch of *A Few of the Many*, in which Peter's story was included, at Worcester Guildhall on 8 May 1995.

Peter Fox was a tremendously positive, enthusiastic and friendly man, which I always thought must have sustained him during those long years in captivity. He left us on 10 June 2005.

Peter and Denis Nichols also trained with 19 Squadron Battle of Britain Spitfire pilot Ken Wilkinson, the 'Three Musketeers', all great friends and popular guests at our book-signings, lectures and other events. On 21 June 2005, I attended Peter's funeral at St Paul's Church, Kewstoke, with Ken; a 56 Squadron Tornado beat up the church in style, eventually going vertical over the church with such power that the ground shook and all the car alarms within quite some radius went off.

As Ken said: 'Peter would have loved that.'

Chapter Nine

Flight Lieutenant Denis 'Nick' Nichols
Hurricane Pilot

Denis Hugh ('I am better known as "Nick"') Nichols was a railway clerk and another young man who benefited from the creation of the RAFVR, with which he learned to fly at Sywell before being mobilised on 1 September 1939. Along with pals Peter Fox and Kenneth Anstill Wilkinson, Nick completed his service flying training and pre-fighter course at Montrose. Then Sergeant Wilkinson was sent to train on Spitfires at 7 OTU, Hawarden, while Sergeants Fox and Nichols converted to Hurricanes at 5 OTU, Aston Down. Wilkinson then first went to 616 Squadron at Kirton on 1 October 1940, before joining 19 Squadron at Fowlmere on 17 October. Sergeants Fox and Nichols, both aged 19, were posted to 56 Squadron at Boscombe

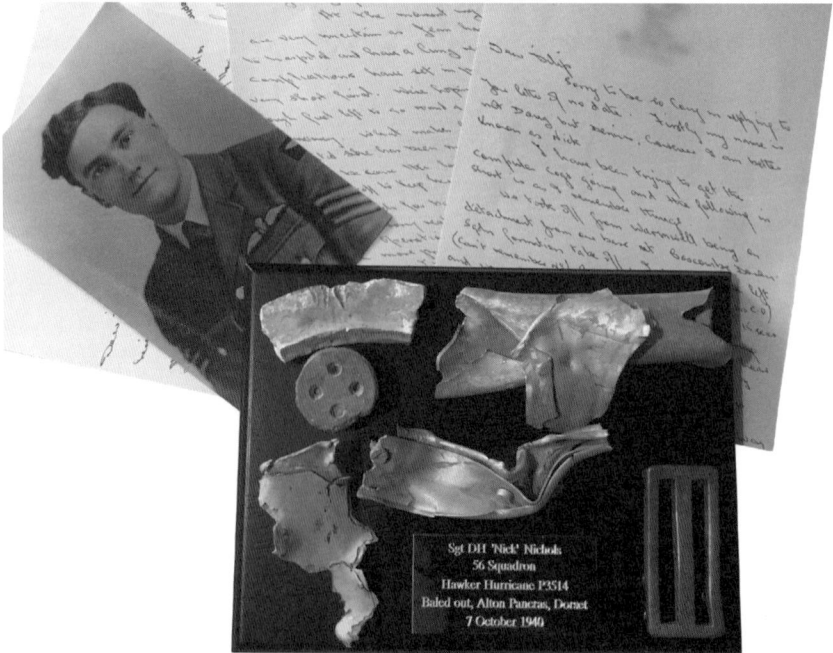

Sgt DH 'Nick' Nichols
56 Squadron
Hawker Hurricane P3514
Baled out, Alton Pancras, Dorset
7 October 1940

Down on 15 September. As we have seen, on the last day of the month, Sergeant Fox was shot down and baled out, wounded, over Lyme Regis, during what was the last day of the great daylight battles. For Sergeant Nichols, a similar experience awaited a week later.

Having withdrawn the He 111 from daylight operations, while still prioritising targets connected with the British aircraft industry, the *Luftwaffe* began attacking during daylight hours with heavily escorted formations of Ju 88s, their best bomber, up to *Gruppe* strength. Having failed to hit Westland Aircraft at Yeovil on 30 September 1940, on 7 October a return visit was planned by twenty Ju 88s of II/KG51, based at Paris-Orly. Escort was provided by thirty-nine Me 110s of ZG26 and fifty-nine Me 109s of JG2 and 53. The enemy formation rendezvoused over Cherbourg and headed north across the Channel towards Portland. British radar detected the raid approaching, which was designated Raid 139. Immediately, 10 Group fighter squadrons were scrambled, including five Hurricanes of 56 Squadron, at 1530 hrs. On 25 October 1992, Nick wrote to me about the events of that day:-

'We took off from Warmwell, being on detachment from our base at Boscombe Down. Squadron formation take-off. I was on the left of the leader, Flight Lieutenant Brooker, and I was "Pip-squeak" man, my radio being blocked every 15 seconds. I can't remember hearing any R/T transmissions so perhaps the wireless was on the blink. I did not even hear the "Tally Ho!". Flying in tight formation, the first I saw was tracer coming from our leader's guns. Quick glimpse and I saw a Ju 88 and fired, still in formation, but had to break away to avoid collision with the Flight Lieutenant. I then lost the Squadron and pulled up, searching for the enemy. No sign of the bombers but 110s in a defensive spiral above. I pulled the "tit" for maximum power and went to intercept.

'A Spitfire was attacking the top of the spiral so I went head-on for the bottom. I fired but, perhaps not surprisingly in view of their heavy forward firing armament that I must have overlooked, was hit. Flames poured from the nose of my aircraft and the windscreen was black with oil, so I broke away as I could not see out. I turned the aircraft on its back to bale out at 25,000 feet. First time a slow roll but I remained seated. Second time I tumbled out, spinning. I told myself not to panic and gave the rip cord a steady pull. When the parachute deployed, the lanyards on one side were twisted. I tried to untangle them without success but relaxed, as at about 15,000 feet I appeared to be coming down reasonably slowly. I did not see the ground ultimately rush up at me and crumpled in a heap upon landing.

Above left: Denis 'Nick' Nichols upon joining the RAFVR before the war.

Above right: Sergeant Nichols pictured with newly awarded 'wings'.

Denis Nichols having been commissioned after the Battle of Britain.

'The Home Guard then appeared on the scene and told me to stick my hands up. They thought I was German but I just laughed at them between groans as I had actually broken my back. There was a Jerry parachutist stuck up a nearby tree, from the Ju 88, but the locals refused to get him down until they had seen to me.'

Nick had landed near the village of Alton Pancras on the Dorset Downs. At about 1600 hrs, Charlie Callaway, another 19-year-old, was ploughing in the 'Vernall' when he saw the Hurricane 'coming down hard and well on fire!' His younger brother Sam, 17, was rabbiting nearby and he too saw the doomed British fighter 'descending at a shallow angle but all ablaze and travelling sharpish like. It was so close that I could have reached out and touched it. There were several parachutes in the sky at the same time.' Nick's Hurricane, P3154, impacted at Austral Farm, nine miles north of Dorchester.

Despite Nick's back injury, both he and Peter Fox were lucky: both had met the enemy on their first operational patrol, had been shot down, and survived.

The crash site of Hurricane P3154 at Alton Pancras, Dorset, with the site investigation underway in November 1993.

Nick recovered from his broken back and returned to operational flying. Instead of single-engine fighters, however, he found himself patrolling nocturnal skies over North Africa and later the Mediterranean in a 255 Squadron Bristol Beaufighter. He was not to meet the enemy again, and was more fortunate than Peter given that Nick was commissioned in March 1942. After the war he became an airline pilot and so flew throughout his working life.

It was from talking to Nick, who lived near me at the time, that I first became particularly interested in the raids against Westlands on 30 September 1940 – when, as it happened, Nick's friend Peter Fox had been shot down – and 7 October 1940, when Nick also baled out over Dorset. This research ultimately led to publication of my *Angriff Westland: Three Battle of Britain Air Raids Through the Looking Glass* in 1994. At the time, I was actively involved with aviation archaeology, and so was naturally keen to return Nick and Peter to their crash sites and recover any remaining artefacts. When I explained this to Nick, however, his reaction was 'I threw it [his Hurricane] away in 1940, and don't want it back now!' In time, though, Nick warmed to the project and eagerly accepted our invitation to join our (former) Malvern Spitfire Team's site investigation in November 1993.

Denis Nichols, left, in conversation at his Hurricane's crash site with our great friend Hans 'Peter' Wulff – a former *Luftwaffe* fighter pilot who was captured and who made his home in England after the war.

At Austral Farm we received a warm and kindly welcome from the Ralphs, although we were not the first enthusiasts to have examined the site. The villagers treated Nick like a king. He was both surprised and moved by this exhibition of respect and appreciation. Many smashed components of the Hurricane were found, including a piece of armoured glass windscreen through which Nick had last peered over fifty years before at the wrong end of an Me 110. Another Battle of Britain pilot,

Squadron Leader Iain Hutchinson, who had flown Spitfires with 222 Squadron, and our German fighter pilot friend Hans 'Peter' Wulff joined us at the site. The latter was formerly a *Luftwaffe Leutnant* who had flown He 111s against the Russians, and Me 410s and FW 190s against the west until shot down and captured on Operation *Bodenplatte*, New Year's Day 1945. Peter had made his home in England after the war and was a true aviation enthusiast, having flown every year of his life, excepting 1946, since learning to glide with the Hitler Youth. It was tremendous that Peter was welcomed by the two British veterans, not as an enemy but as a fellow enthusiast and combat pilot who shared their common bond. Television cameras and reporters swarmed over the site, and with pilots and eyewitnesses present the events of 7 October 1940 were vividly brought back to life as all remembered that dramatic day.

Nick was always good company and another welcome guest at our events, the Fox, Wilkinson Nichols trio being quite a handful on occasions! Denis was the first of the three friends to pass away, on 23 August 2001, followed by Peter in 2005. Ken, whose story I last told in *The Final Few*, left us on 31 July 2017, aged 99. It was a privilege to have counted the 'Three Musketeers' amongst my friends.

Leutnant Wulff in his II/ZG26 Me 410 in 1944. Peter was shot down flying a FW 190 by a Tempest on Operation *Bodenplatte*, New Year's Day 1945, and captured; he died in 1997.

Perspex and plates recovered from the crash site of Hurricane P3154.

Denis Nichols, a lifelong pilot, pictured at one of the author's signings with fellow Battle of Britain pilots William Walker (right), Bernard Jennings (extreme left) and George Unwin.

Chapter Ten

Wing Commander Frederick 'Taffy' Higginson OBE DFC DFM
Hurricane Pilot

Frederick William ('Call me "Taffy", everybody does!') Higginson was a remarkable man, an aviator through and through. It is a great pity that Taffy never wrote a memoir. Indeed, his wartime service and life in aviation generally is worthy of several books, including, as it did, extensive combat experience, escape and evasion, staff appointments and senior roles in civil aviation. With his handlebar moustache, he was the very epitome of the fighter pilot's public image – but he was not from a privileged background.

Taffy, born in Swansea on 17 February 1913, was a policeman's son (as was Air Vice-Marshal Johnnie Johnson, officially the RAF's top-scoring fighter pilot of the Second World War). After leaving Gowerton County Intermediate School, the young Welshman opted for a career in the RAF, signing up as an Aircraft Apprentice in January 1929. In December 1931 he passed out of the RAF's technical school at Halton as a skilled metal rigger, and posted to 7 Squadron as a mechanic/air gunner. Initially it was envisioned that all RAF pilots would be officers, but it became apparent that not all officers automatically possessed the ability to fly. It therefore became necessary to open the doors of flying training schools to non-commissioned personnel in an effort to increase the service's establishment of trained pilots. Taffy was amongst the regular pre-war NCOs who benefited from this scheme, applying for and successfully completing flying training. On 1 July 1936, Taffy joined 19 Squadron at Duxford, flying the Gloster Gauntlet, having made what was a quantum leap, from mechanic to fighter pilot.

Having served with 66 Squadron and Anti-Aircraft Cooperation Unit, on 20 October 1937 Taffy joined 56 Squadron at North Weald, with which he was serving as a flight sergeant, flying the Hurricane Mk I, on 3 September 1939. In May 1940, Flight Sergeant Higginson and 56 Squadron's 'B' Flight was deployed to Vitry-en-Artois, and during the Battle of France Taffy destroyed a number of enemy aircraft. On 27 May 1940, his DFM was gazetted, the citation of which significantly reads that 'Despite being an airman pilot,

Exhaustion: Flight Sergeant 'Taffy' Higginson DFM at North Weald during the Battle of Britain.

he led a section of 56 Squadron during all operations, his determination in the face of the enemy and his cool and courageous leadership being an example to his squadron.' At this time, British society remained strictly hierarchical, on the basis of socio-economic-educational status, the three services reflecting this. In those early days, the RAF had no definition of the qualities required to be a leader; it was simply assumed that attendance at a public school, along with a School Certificate 'A' and a letter signed by any colonel, was sufficient endorsement of a candidate's suitability to bear arms and lead men into battle. It was soon discovered, however, that in combat in the air, it was experience that counted, not rank or social class, and hence Taffy found himself leading a section of Hurricanes which included officer pilots. This, as Johnnie Johnson always emphasised, was an example that the RAF was forward-thinking and became more of a meritocracy, advancement and responsibility based more upon a man's abilities than social class. How many other airmen would have made excellent fighter pilots and leaders is anyone's guess. Men like Higginson definitely proved the point.

As a key member of 56 Squadron, Taffy was constantly in action during the Battle of Britain, scoring more combat successes and surviving being shot down twice. It was in 1993 that I wrote to him, enquiring of his experiences on 30 September and 7 October 1940. Soon an undated written response arrived, together with copies of Taffy's logbook for the squadron's period at Boscombe down, some entries making great reading:-

12 September: Flap. Failed to catch an 88. He got away in cloud 10/10.

14 September: Engaged Do 17 who went into cloud, stalked him for 40 miles out to sea, got him in a clear patch and he dived into drink "WHOOSH".

27 September: Attacked 110 Jaguars. Bunch of 'em. Got port engine streaming glycol. Seen by F/Lt Edwards.

28 September: 109s started to Blitz us but lost their nerve and shot off home.

30 September (two separate engagements):-

Attacked by 110s and 109s. "Fouzens" of 'em. Got engine of one. Seen by Sgt Smythe. Also blitzed by a 109/no result. Landed Boscombe Down.

Attacked large force of Do's escorted by lots of 110s and 109s. Got one 110 both engines. This time seen to crash by P/O Williams, 152 Squadron, Spit.

7 October: Flap. No luck. Landed Boscombe.

56 Squadron line-up just after the Battle of Britain, including Pilot Officer Higginson (second left, sitting).

Taffy's letter continued:-

'Incidentally, I was commissioned from F/Sgt to Pilot Officer while at Boscombe in September 1940, and in late December took over "B" Flight.

'The main recollection I have of that period is that we were a somewhat disorganised lot. I don't know whether that is the correct word, but we had taken a beating in the preceding months at North Weald and France, and needed re-equipping and receiving new pilots.

'The Station Commander at Boscombe was Group Captain Ramsbottom Isherwood, who, I believe, later took a unit to Russia and was killed. He was a first-class chap, good rugger player and much-liked by us all. During the early part of that period I remember thinking that morale would perhaps be boosted if we had a Squadron mascot, so I went to the local town and bought a small monkey, which we named '109'. He was a great success and kept in a cage, on a lead. Anyway, the Group Captain gave a cocktail party for the Squadron and requested 109's presence. 109 went down very well, until, that is, he started to undertake enthusiastic sexual self-gratification! Morals being what they were in those days we had to remove him quickly!!'

Most of our communication was by telephone, rather than correspondence, leading me to make an appointment to see Taffy at his Tenby home. Traffic held me up, so I arrived a few minutes later and, not known to ever be late, a little stressed and very apologetic. I found Taffy up to his armpits in onions in his vegetable patch.

'What are you late for?' said the Wing Commander.

'Well, we have an appointment, you are kindly helping me with my book.'

'Oh, do we? Am I? Great! You'd better come in.'

We then spent an afternoon going through this Battle of Britain legend's logbook and photographs, throughout which Taffy was extremely charming and helpful. I left a couple of hours later, still uncertain as to whether the penny had dropped regarding who I was and the arrangement we had made a few days before, and Taffy happily returned to his garden. It was a memorable afternoon's research!

Ten years after my visit, Taffy died on 12 February 2003, five days before his 90th birthday. I am pleased I made that trip.

Chapter Eleven

Flight Lieutenant Reg 'Johnny' Johnson
Spitfire Pilot

'I will try to reply to your correspondence in January. I was flying alongside P/O Whitbread in tight formation when he was blasted out of the sky. I can add to your information.'

So read a postcard received from Flight Lieutenant Reg Johnson, in response to my letter of 23 November 1991 asking whether he remembered Pilot Officer Herbert Laurence Whitbread, in whom I had a particular interest. Further correspondence was awaited with great interest. When it arrived, the contents of the envelope were illuminating and shocking in equal measure.

The first document was a letter from Reg, dated 18 January 1992, explaining that he had 'done my best to be helpful' and concluding: 'It is encouraging to know that there are still people about who wish to

know about P/O Whitbread.' The first handwritten paper was entitled '222 Squadron (Spitfires) Battle of Britain, 1940':-

'I was awarded my wings in January 1940. After finishing training, I was posted to 222 Squadron in April 1940 at RAF Duxford. I arrived there only to be told that the Squadron had moved to Digby. I arrived there to learn that 222 had moved to Kirton, such was the level of administration in 1940. On joining the Squadron no-one was unkind to me but I was the first RAFVR pilot (recognisable by my badges) to join this regular squadron. After about a week I was shown the 'knobs and things' by Sergeant J.I. Johnson (an ex-Halton boy), and sent solo. After successfully landing my engine failed and I was picked up in a green MG sports car by Flight Lieutenant Douglas Bader, who was Flight Commander of "A" Flight.

'I was a member of "B" Flight. I soon learned that 222 Squadron was addicted to tight formation flying, for which I had no training whatsoever. A study of the pre-war career of our CO, Squadron Leader Mermagen, might explain this addiction, particularly in flying so tight that our wings overlapped. From Kirton he led us off in squadron formation; three behind three, we even looped in formation. We even rolled as a squadron on one occasion! Mermagen was an exceptional pilot but such training was to prove unsuitable for the Battle of Britain yet to come.

'Our Squadron went south to Hornchurch on 28 August 1940. In the first 48 hours we had lost eight to ten aircraft and a number of pilots. We proceeded to go into action in tight formation and our losses were heavy. Eventually we evolved a weaving "Tail-end Charlie" section – above and below – behind the Squadron (still in tight formation), and it helped. I was made a permanent member of Green Section, given that job to do.

'It was a great privilege for me to be a member of 222 Squadron in which I completed 101 operational sorties; was shot down twice; parachuted twice; and wounded once. From being the junior reserve pilot, I soon became the senior NCO pilot due to my incredibly good fortune. Relationships between NCO pilots and officer pilots in our Squadron were formal, based mainly upon respect for each other's abilities and commitments. Of course, many friendships did not last for long due to our heavy losses.

'I am very glad that so many records were kept – have survived – and been written up in so many books. Bearing in mind the chaotic conditions of the time it is understandable that small errors of detail creep in, and for a blow-by-blow account not all particulars can be trusted in detail.

'In Mason's book *Battle Over Britain*, it is recorded that Sergeant Pilot J.I. Johnson (a personal friend of mine) was shot down and killed on

29 August 1940. He was, but later it is recorded that he was shot down and wounded on 14 September. He was not – it was me. My wife was informed by official letter that it happened to me on 15 September. I did not fly on the 15th, with my left foot – ankle – and calf damaged by minute pieces of shrapnel from the previous day.

'In *The Battle of Britain Then & Now* it states that on 3 September I landed by parachute slightly hurt. I wasn't. On 14 September I landed slightly wounded by parachute, of which no mention of being wounded is made. These are only minor errors but when applied to me such errors must also relate to other happenings.

'Pilot Officer Laurie Whitbread was an established Squadron member when I joined in April 1940. When I write his account, other errors will come to light.'

The second paper's title was 'Pilot Officer L Whitbread, 222 Squadron (Spitfires), 1939/40':-

'Pilot Officer Whitbread was an established member of the Squadron when I joined it in April 1940. During the following weeks and months, he proved himself to be a pleasant and friendly young man. We spent many hours together in conversation at Dispersal Point and I enclose a poor photograph of him beside "my" Spitfire at Dawn Readiness (about 4 a.m.) on a June morning at Kirton-in-Lindsey. We each took each other's. The light at that early hour was poor, but it had to be done secretly because we were not allowed cameras.

'He was also a very good hockey player and spent long periods with his hockey stick dribbling around the aircraft and running around bouncing a ball on the shaft of his stick. I think he had County Colours for Shropshire.

'We spent many hours together flying in Squadron training, often wing tip to wing tip. He was much more skilled at tight formation flying than I was at that time.

'There was definitely in our Squadron and RAF a social barrier between officer and NCO pilots. Pilot Officer Whitbread, whom I never knew as "Laurie", overcame this with natural charm, at ease with all ranks. He never lost face because of it and we became firm friends. We "enjoyed" a number of Squadron flying adventures together at Kirton and of course suffered a number in the first three weeks of September at Hornchurch, until the fateful day of 20 September.

'My vivid memory is that this sortie was a "B" Flight commitment only, led by Pilot Officer Broadhurst in Blue Section, followed by Pilot Officer

Sergeant Reg Johnson pictured with Spitfire in a snapshot taken clandestinely at first light by Pilot Officer Laurie Whitbread, June 1940.

Whitbread, myself and another in Green Section. We climbed to the suicidal height of 14,000 feet and stooged around in tight formation with only one pair of eyes available to scan the sky in front, perhaps over 200°. I do not think that we deserved to be "jumped upon", but we were certainly inviting it. We were banking gently to the left, which allowed me at No 3 to look over the top of No 1, and I shouted the warning "Bandits! 2 o'clock above – attacking!" I turned over and dived straight down. There is no way that Pilot Officer Whitbread could even have seen the enemy, formating as he was on the aircraft to his left and with three-quarters of his head and back to the attackers. When I left it was his right side facing the 109s, which were already in firing range. I have always been puzzled by the fact that later records stated that he was badly wounded down his left side. I can only assume that having received my warning he too rolled to his right, thus exposing his left side to the enemy and was hit before his dive down. It was a tragedy.

'I would ask for it to be remembered that the keeping of accurate records at the time was impossible. Often we took off from Hornchurch and had to land at Rochford, with all our administrative staff at Hornchurch, including the Intelligence Officer. And Hornchurch was bombed, and bombed, and bombed.

'From my now very senior years I remember the Pilot Officer as a brave young man of the highest quality. Naturally courageous, he was always prepared to give his life for his country, but it was taken away from him due to the practice of unsatisfactory tactics.'

This was, of course, excellent first-hand material.

Herbert Laurence Whitbread was born on 21 August 1914 in the picturesque and fortified Shropshire town of Ludlow. Laurie lived with his parents and sister at 4 Linney View, attending the local primary and grammar schools, where he was a popular pupil, excelling at sport. In 1933 he became house captain of Wright's; a master, George Merchant, later described Laurie in the house photograph as 'sprawling in his majesty, flanked by his henchmen and surrounded by his minions'. At Ludlow Grammar School Whitbread's name became synonymous with boxing and rugby, and our hero also represented Shropshire at hockey.

On 12 January 1939, Laurie successfully passed an interview at the Air Ministry and was awarded a Short Service Commission. By 26 November, Pilot Officer Whitbread's service flying training was complete and he was posted to 222 'Natal' Squadron, a new unit based at Duxford. 222 Squadron was commanded by Squadron Leader H.W. 'Tubby' Mermagen, a Cranwell graduate who had led the Inverted Flying Formation at the 1937 Hendon Air Pageant and performed solo aerobatics for His Majesty the King. Initially 222 Squadron was equipped with twin-engined Blenheims, but soon converted to Spitfires and participated in the Dunkirk air fighting. Pilot Officer Whitbread flew on virtually all of the squadron's operational sorties. Then came the Battle of Britain, in which 222 Squadron, now commanded by Squadron Leader Johnnie Hill, was heavily engaged, Pilot Officer Whitbread personally destroying two Me 109s and damaging another, and probably destroying a Do 17.

Reg returned the favour: Pilot Officer Whitbread at Spitfire, Kirton, June 1940.

FLIGHT LIEUTENANT REG 'JOHNNY' JOHNSON

On 14 September 1940, Laurie wrote to his mother from the Officers' Mess at RAF Hornchurch:-

Dear Mother

Thank you for your letter, received this morning. How nice to have Rex and Doris, and Colin at home together. I am disappointed that I won't be there too. Fancy Ludlow having some bombs!

Everything is going fine down here. We get far less to do now that the weather has broken. There is no sign of us leaving this station yet, so I doubt that I will get any leave until things quieten down again.

I am keeping fit – except that I got a touch of frostbite in the left hand last week. Its better now except for a large blister on the thumb.

Mother, would you see if I've left my RAF navy blue blazer at home? I don't want it but can't find it here. Please tell me in the next letter. I do hope I haven't lost it.

Love to all, Cheerio, Laurie.

As for 'getting far less to do', the next day, 15 September, has gone down in history as 'Battle of Britain Day', the whole fury and might of the enemy being thrown repeatedly at London. On that great day however, Pilot Officer Whitbread's Spitfire, N3023, ZD-R, was unserviceable, necessitating him flying it from Rochford to Hornchurch for repair.

On Friday 20 September 1940, for the first time, twenty-two Me 109 fighter-bombers of II/LG 2, protected by numerous fighters, took off from their Pas-de-Calais bases, London bound. Between Calais and Dover, the Germans climbed to 25,000 feet before swooping down on the capital. Believing the enemy fighter sweep to be no threat, Fighter Command's squadrons were kept on the ground, permitting the fighter-bombers to reach London unmolested. Attacking from 22,000 feet, the fighter-bomber pilots had already turned for home when their bombs exploded in the City of London and on a rail terminus west of the Thames's great bend. Listening to the British radio frequencies, German intelligence reported a great confusion of orders and counter-orders after the 'fighters' had dropped their bombs.

After the first wave of raiders had caused confusion, a second was reported incoming over the Kent coast at 14,000 feet. Unbeknown to the RAF controllers, there were no fighter-bombers in this formation, so the Biggin Hill and Hornchurch Spitfire squadrons were scrambled. 222 and 603 Squadrons were up from Hornchurch at 1055 hrs, but as they desperately

Left: Pilot Officer H.L. 'Laurie' Whitbread, killed in action, 20 September 1940.

Below: Reg Johnson while instructing after the Battle of Britain at 52 OTU.

climbed for height over the Thames Estuary, the 109s fell on them. The first Spitfire pilot to fall in action that day was Pilot Officer Whitbread, whose aircraft crashed at 1115 hrs in the garden of Pond Cottage, Hermitage Road, Higham, near Rochester, Kent. That day, Me 109 pilots claimed eight Spitfires destroyed. Back in 1993, with less information available, I suggested that *Oberleutnant* Hans 'Assi' Hahn of 4/JG2 was responsible, who claimed a Spitfire over 'London'. Today I do not believe that to be the case. Historical research is an evolving process, interpretations often shifting and changing over time as more information and sources become available. I now know, for example, that Major Adolf Galland, *Kommodore* of JG26, claimed a Spitfire specifically 'South of Hornchurch'. It is highly likely, therefore, that Pilot Officer Whitbread was actually killed by that great German ace.

The final document in the package received from Reg 'Johnny' Johnson was an undated letter from his wife, Nora:-

'It is with great pride that I send you this, and with sadness too, as my husband died on Sunday evening.

'On and off he had been working on this last week and we were due to post on Monday. Under the circumstances, I have kept it a few more days to be photocopied.

'My brother-in-law, a Lancaster pilot, will be here shortly, and my immediate neighbour, an ex-helicopter pilot. Both will have copies and see your letter.

'I know there is great tension when Johnny goes over these events, but how fitting that it should be Laurie's memorial. I did not meet him, though of course lost many 222 pilot friends and dance-partners from the Kirton days.

'After lunch on Sunday, Johnny went as we do in our age group to sleep. About four, he called me and was staggery. I settled him in his chair and sat opposite, reading, knitting, and no doubt nodding off. In the dim light I let him sleep on, until I felt that it would be more sense to waken him, to settle more comfortable in bed. It was then that I felt how cold he was, and I knew.

'He hadn't been very coherent as he settled in his chair, yet quite clearly his last words were "Get those two aircraft trimmed!"

'How very rewarding to us all.'

Further words would be superfluous.

Chapter Twelve

Air Commodore Herbert 'Tubby' Mermagen CB AFC
Spitfire Pilot

On 14 December 1931, a headstrong but exceptionally talented pilot called Douglas Bader crashed at Woodley airfield while attempting a slow roll. Miraculously the 23 Squadron pilot officer remained alive within the mangled wreckage of his Bristol Bulldog biplane. Bader, the sporting and aerobatic legend, subsequently suffered amputation of both legs – and with iron willpower learned to walk again on what at the time were comparatively primitive, heavy, 'tin' legs. King's Regulations however did not provide for limbless pilots, and so it proved impossible for Bader to return to flying fighters. Unable to accept a chairborne role, Bader left the service he loved

Flight Lieutenant Douglas Bader (centre) pictured at Hornchurch during the Dunkirk air fighting while serving as a Flight Commander in Squadron Leader Mermagen's 222 Squadron. Also pictured is another ace: Flight Lieutenant Bob Stanford Tuck of 92 Squadron (with cap).

so much, in 1933, going to work for the Asiatic Petroleum Company. That year, Hitler came to power in Germany, and from then the countdown towards war began. After Munich in 1938, Bader was beside himself, and constantly harangued the Air Ministry to take him back, arguing that trained pilots would soon be badly needed. Eventually the air marshals acquiesced, agreeing that Bader could return to the RAF in a flying capacity in the event of war actually being declared and providing he passed a flying test. Both events came to pass, and on 7 February 1940 Flying Officer Bader reported for duty at Duxford, there to fly Spitfires with 19 Squadron, commanded by his old Cranwell and 23 Squadron chum Geoffrey Stephenson.

The 30-year-old Bader found things much changed however – mainly his fellow pilots, who were so young. According to Paul Brickhill, author of the globally best-selling yarn about Bader's extraordinary life, *Reach for the Sky*, 'His only cheerful moment in the Mess that evening was meeting again with Tubby Mermagen. Years ago, he had known Mermagen as a pilot officer, but Mermagen now commanded the other squadron at Duxford, 222… It was fun to talk over old times, but when he took off his legs to go to bed he felt again a comparatively elderly flying officer.' I read Brickhill's book when I was 10 years old, and for some reason Mermagen's name stuck in my mind. I next encountered reference to Tubby in *Spitfire!*

The Experiences of a Fighter Pilot, written by Squadron Leader Brian Lane under the pseudonym 'B.J. Ellan':-

'Back in the Mess it was still too early for breakfast, so we sat about in the anteroom swapping yarns. Tubby Mermagen, who had been responsible for shooting down the first 110, told us a really *stirring* tale. Literally, I mean, for Tubby volunteered the information that the miracle had been achieved by use of his *stirring* attack. By stirring it was discovered that he meant stirring the stick around the cockpit once his sights were on, thereby getting a hosepipe effect from his guns. This, then, was the secret of how to shoot down a Hun when at 1,200 yards range! ... any patrol that Tubby was on invariably turned out to be an amusing one, at any rate in retrospect when he got back to the Mess. He was a great humorist, and now he improved the shining hour before breakfast by giving an exhibition of his actions and reactions on a previous patrol when he had found himself short of oxygen. He had us all rocking in our seats with laughter. It was the first time I ever remember being convulsed with mirth at such an early hour in the morning!'

Many years after Brian wrote those words about the Dunkirk air-fighting, my interest in Pilot Officer Laurie Whitbread eventually led to me confirming that Air Commodore Mermagen was still alive; a letter was soon in the post.

Herbert Waldemar Mermagen was born on 1 February 1912 in Southsea, taking a short service commission after leaving Brighton College in June 1930. Becoming a fighter pilot, flying Gamecocks with 43 Squadron at Tangmere, Mermagen was found to be a pilot of exceptional ability and became a flying instructor in 1934. Having been permanently commissioned in 1936 as a staff-member of the Central Flying School in 1937, Flight Lieutenant Mermagen led the Inverted Flying Formation at the Hendon Air Pageant. The following year, promoted to squadron leader, Tubby performed solo aerobatics for His Majesty the King. On 2 December 1991 he replied to my inquiry:-

'I formed 222 Squadron in October 1939 at RAF Duxford – as a night-fighter unit equipped with Blenheim aircraft – it was a unit of 12(F) Group, AOC AVM Leigh-Mallory. I was supplied with a dual Blenheim to convert pilots to this type (I had been on the staff of the Central Flying School, a qualified A1 flying instructor).

'Whitbread was one of the earliest postings to the new squadron, I think he came straight from FTS. I can just remember him as a pleasant, well-mannered, quiet individual, a shortish, stocky, cheerful character whom I instantly liked – a good mixer.

'My flying log book records that on 12 December 1939, at 1200 hrs, I took him up in the dual Blenheim, L6712, for a test/conversion to Blenheim Mk Is. The flight lasted twenty-five minutes and I must have been suitably impressed since, so far as my log book shows, Whitbread had no further instruction and went solo immediately afterwards. I understand that he had trained on twin engined Oxfords, but even so he displayed a good standard of flying. The Squadron subsequently conducted a very large number of

Air Commodore Herbert 'Tubby' Mermagen – of the 'stirring technique'!

flying hours and we were soon operational, with no accidents.

'To our delight the AOC, Air Vice-Marshal Leigh-Mallory, decided to re-equip us with Spitfires. The already enthusiastic pilots faced this conversion with great excitement (from twins to singles!). To help me with the conversion of all pilots, I was supplied with a Miles Master dual training aircraft, N7570. My log book then records that on 18 March at 1600 hrs Whitbread went up for forty minutes conversion-to-type flying. I did the same the following day for another thirty minutes and he must have then satisfied me completely because he went solo on a Spitfire with no further instruction immediately afterwards.

'I can confirm that I led the Squadron and wing over the Dunkirk beaches on 28 May 1940, at 0630 hrs, duration of sortie 2.45 hours, a long sortie for a Spitfire. The Squadron carried out several further sorties, ending 3 June, when the wretched evacuation appeared completed – no life on the beaches or country behind. I lost four pilots killed and one missing during that period. Pilot Officer Whitbread must have taken part in most if not all of these sorties. I know that I had already recognised him as a good, reliable and sound Spitfire pilot.

'I left the Squadron in late July, on promotion, but temporarily commanded 266 Squadron at RAF Wittering, their CO, Wilkinson, a good friend of CFS days, had been killed – his burnt parachute had been left in the CO's office – and I didn't much like seeing it on arrival.

'Coincidentally, I led 266 Squadron at 1030 hrs on 20 September 1940, 25,000 feet London area, just about the same time as my old Squadron, 222, was operating in the same district. Whitbread must have crashed with fatal results near Rochester when I was flying near him.

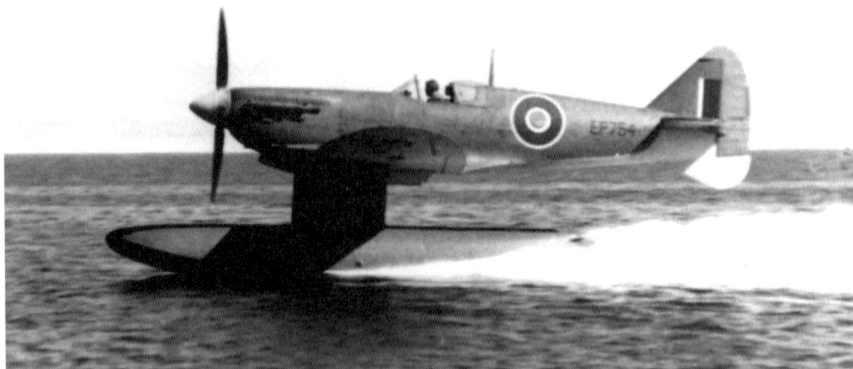

Tubby taking off from Lake Nassau in a Spitfire floatplane.

'This is all I can say about him, one of the many very nice chaps who lost their lives in the Battle of Britain. It always seemed to be the decent types who got killed, leaving some peculiar characters behind – I survived, just! Hope you can read this scribble and that it will help you a little.'

26 January 1991:-

'The comments about me in Brian Lane's book amused me very much. I didn't know that my "stirring" technique had been recorded; anyway it worked then and I tried it again on a very dark night against a *Heinkel* over Hull. But never claimed. I did not like claiming unless definitely confirmed by witnesses. There was, as I've said before, too much claiming by pilots – even by the aces.

'Lane I well remember from Duxford days. He was a quiet type, almost studious, and a person to be respected. I regarded him as the best of all the flight commanders I had met, except possibly for Oxspring… We (222) were so new at Duxford and made to feel so – but we could formate as a full squadron better than most. Take-off in four sections of three in formation and land back, without breaking. Duxford was then a large grass airfield, which helped.'

9 December 1991:-

'Regarding 266 Squadron, I handed over that Squadron on 23 September 1940 on posting to RAF Speke, to command as Wing Commander. I have noted from my log book that the date 20 September 1940 lists several sorties in which I was involved. Public Records Office may hold extracts from Squadron Intelligence Officers – but these people were not always on the ball. The one I had in 222 Squadron seemed quite aged to us and not always present on our return from early morning sorties – he did not impress me. The 266 chap I can't ever remember meeting!'

We exchanged letters over a number of years, about this and that. During the mid-1990s I was hoovering up first-hand recollections of pilots and supporting personnel who had served with Group Captain Sir Douglas Bader; on 23 January 1996 Tubby wrote:-

'Here is a bit of info for you about Bader.

'When I was commanding 222 Squadron at RAF Duxford 1939/40, Bader, a personal friend from the early thirties, asked me to ask my AOC, Leigh-Mallory, for him to be posted to 222. He knew I had a flight commander suspected to be "lacking moral fibre" who I wished to get rid of. Bader was then serving with 19 Squadron, alongside 222 at Duxford, commanded by one Geoffrey Stephenson, an old buddy of his when they were serving with 23 Squadron at Kenley 1931/32. Bader now found it difficult serving under him after all these years. The AOC agreed to his posting to 222. He was easy to "keep in order" and proved an excellent flight commander. He carried out several operational sorties under my command, displayed unusual leadership qualities and was a fine Spitfire pilot. Soon after I left, he was posted to command 242 Squadron at Coltishall. Hurricane-equipped, a Canadian squadron suffering from poor morale. Douglas was known to the AOC and knew of his record, crash, amputations etc. I had spoken to the AOC on more than one occasion and confirmed that he was an 'above average' Spitfire pilot and a most mature character, quite outstanding as a flight commander. I feel pretty certain that it was because of my high opinion that "DB" achieved such rapid promotion. He thoroughly deserved the promotion, as it proved when he led the "Bader Wing". I knew DB very well; our wives were good friends.'

Group Captain Mermagen while serving in the Middle East.

Tubby certainly had an interesting war. In June 1941 he was posted to the Middle East, commanding the fighter base at Port Said, and later joined

119

Above: Air Commodore Mermagen with the CO and a Flight Commander of a Tempest squadron at RAF Gatow, Germany, in 1945.

Left: Tubby Mermagen, a keen golfer, pictured in retirement.

Supreme Headquarters Allied Expeditionary Force (SHAEF). While with SHAEF, Group Captain Mermagen was responsible for arresting certain senior German officers, including *Feldmarschall* Keitel, General Jodl and Admiral Dönitz. Retiring from the post-war RAF as an air commodore in 1960, after a variety of command appointments, Tubby became a director of the bullion brokers Sharps Pixley, settling in Painswick, Gloucestershire. It was there that I visited him in 1993, and I distinctly recall being very much in awe of this living link with so much of the RAF's wartime and pre-war past. Tubby died in January 1998 – and were he still with us now, there is so much more I would like to ask him about those 'stirring' days.

Chapter Thirteen

Wing Commander Frank 'Fanny' Brinsden

Spitfire Pilot

In September 1940, the official Air Ministry photographer, Stanley Devon, visited Fowlmere airfield, the Duxford satellite in 12 Group, there photographing the Spitfires and personnel of 19 and 616 Squadrons. These professionally-taken pictures provide a superb record of a fighter squadron at war in 1940, although, inevitably, many of the photographs were posed and therefore lack a certain authenticity. One that was not posed, however, is literally a one-in-a-million image of Spitfire pilots freshly landed from a patrol over London. Central is the haunting image of 23-year-old Squadron Leader Brian Lane DFC, the CO of 19 Squadron, his face clearly showing the strain of combat flying. Over the years, this iconic snap has been used to illustrate countless publications, often with a generic caption not identifying the pilots concerned. As a child, I always wondered who the dark-haired young squadron leader was, so striking was his likeness, and was sad to later discover that he was reported Missing in Action on 13 December 1942. By chance, I also found that the book *Spitfire! The Experiences of a Fighter Pilot*, written by a 'Squadron Leader B.J. Ellan', was actually written by Brian Lane. Heavily censored in respect of locations and identities, I resolved to unravel these riddles. As my research progressed, I became inexorably drawn in by the young CO's story, and that of 19 Squadron during that early war period. By the late 1980s, I decided that to raise awareness of the inspirational Lane's story, I should write a book – and via the Battle of Britain Fighter Association and other sources set about tracing and communicating with survivors. One such was Frank Brinsden, with whom I came to enjoy both protracted correspondence and friendship.

Francis Noel Brinsden was born in Auckland, New Zealand, on 27 March 1919, and after attending Takapuna Grammar School worked as a bank clerk. In 1936, however, the RAF began expanding, albeit late in the day, one initiative to increase the establishment of officers being the Short Service Commission. Hitherto, officers had been 'permanently' commissioned, which is to say they signed on for the duration of their working lives. Flying, however, is a young man's game, and so the short service commission provided an opportunity for young men of ability to serve for four years before resuming their civilian lives as a trained reserve, eligible for call-up in time of emergency. 'Frank' was one of those many young men from the dominions to answer the call, and was accepted for a short service commission in 1937, sailing for Britain in the RMS *Arawa* that summer. On 9 October 1938, his flying training completed, Pilot Officer Brinsden joined 19 Squadron at Duxford.

On 19 March 1989, Wing Commander Brinsden replied from his home in Gooseberry Hill, Western Australia, to my inquiry regarding his former CO:-

'How pleased I am that Brian Lane is to receive public exposure and recognition at last. Being the Commander of a squadron based on the fringe of the battle area, which was not allowed to be used to its potential because of personality frictions, he was barred from showing his skills and did not, therefore, excite the acclaim afforded to the commanders of squadrons based in the Southern Counties. I have digressed a bit but I feel very strongly about the under-use of 19 Squadron during those vital few months.

'My recollections of Brian. He was received politely but coolly as "Sandy" Lane when he arrived from Wittering… because the residents of 19 Squadron

WING COMMANDER FRANK 'FANNY' BRINSDEN

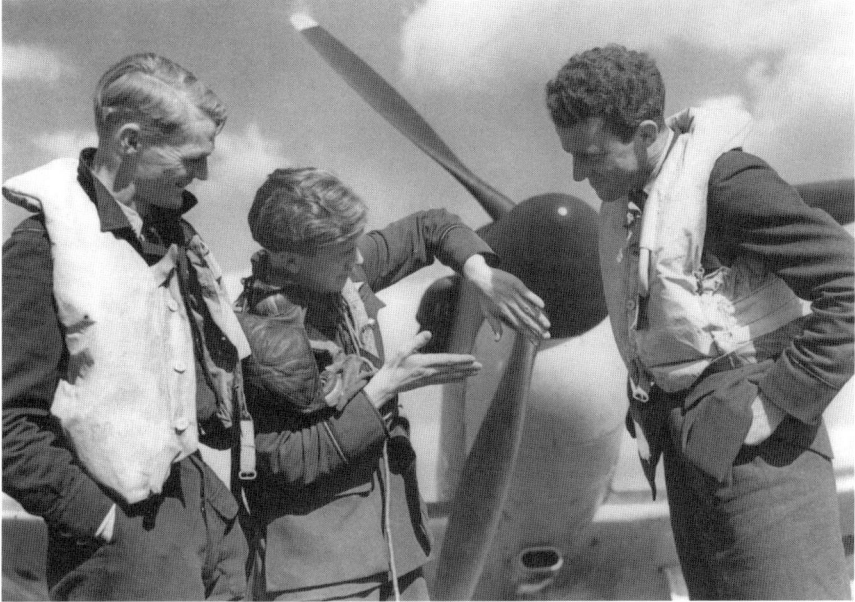

Flying Officer Frank Brinsden (left) and the American Pilot Officer 'Uncle Sam' Leckrone listening to Pilot Officer Leonard 'Ace' Haines DFC explain how it's done!

thought a number of them could have filled the bill without calling in an outsider who, despite the small number of officer pilots in Fighter Command at that time, was unknown to us. However, within a week or two Brian's calm dignity and professional skill showed through and the sobriquet "Sandy" was never used again within the Squadron: he became "Brian". The somewhat derogatory tag of "Sandy" was quite incongruous. His dignity was not a pose and he enjoyed Squadron sorties to the local as much as we all did – and all were equal to him. However, I recall a formal dressing down I received from him after which my respect for him was enhanced. In later years as a CO I used the same technique with, I hope, a comparable result.'

Our correspondence developed apace, so here Frank's letters tell their own stories.

3 May 1989:-

'The original Squadron pilots I remember well but not many of the new recruits who arrived with a rush to make up the War Establishment. Also, at one time we had a surfeit of newly "winged" pilots on strength for training preparatory to posting to squadrons newly forming. Fellows like the

A snapshot by Pilot Officer Peter Howard-Williams outside 19 Squadron's modest Fowlmere HQ in September 1940; from left: Pilot Officer Wallace Cunningham, Sub-Lieutenant Giles Blake, the Czech Pilot Officer Frantisezk Dolezal, and New Zealander Flying Officer Frank Brinsden.

"Admiral" Blake; Burgoyne, Aeberhardt, and in particular Leonard Haines I remember well. Leonard was a most self-confident and aggressive pilot and at the time he impressed me more than any of the other new pilots as the one most likely to become an "ace". I believe that overconfidence killed him after he left 19.

'Although I enjoyed my thirty years in the Royal Air Force, I did not have a particularly noteworthy career, and apart from a few unusual postings went through the usual mill of appointments as seniority, promotion and experience grew. I passed the RAF Selection Board in Auckland, NZ, and was posted to the Reid & Siegrist Civil Flying School at Desford in Leicestershire in late September 1937. Thence to No 3 Flying Training School at South Cerney, by now in uniform as a commissioned officer. There, service flying training began in Hawker Hart and Fury biplanes, in November 1937. After a short Pilot's Navigation Course at Brough in Yorkshire, I joined 19 Squadron for flying duties in October 1938, although I had been shown on the Squadron strength since July of that year.

'I was with 19 Squadron until November 1940 when posted to 303 (Polish) Squadron, then resting at Leconfield, as RAF Flight Commander/

Liaison Officer. It was such a capable and well-led Squadron that it soon became obvious that I was surplus to their needs and so I applied for transfer to 485 (NZ) Squadron, then forming on Spitfires at Driffield, this being in March 1941. After about four months with 485 at Redhill, I was posted to the staff of the Merchant Ship Fighter Unit at Speke. This was the Unit which catapulted Hurricanes off merchant ships. I managed to ease my way back into operational flying through a year in command of 3 Aircraft Delivery Flight, followed by a night-fighter conversion course and a posting to 25 Squadron, equipped with Mosquitos, as a flight commander. Our sector at Church Fenton was very quiet at the time and so we persuaded our Group to let us do a few intruder sorties, which is just what I was doing on the night of the Peenemunde raid by Bomber Command, when I finished up in the sea off Sylt.

'On return after the Armistice, I was posted to command the Missing Research & Enquiry Service fossicking around Denmark, Norway, and in fact NW Europe, for Allied aircrew buried in unmarked graves and whom we exhumed in the hope that we could identify them. Thence some months in NZ visiting relatives and on return to the UK a posting to a Night Fighter Refresher Course, leading to command of 141 NF Mosquito Squadron in June 1948. Following this, a tour in Malaya, manning an Ops Room in support of Army Units fighting the Bandit War, and a posting to the Staff of Air HQs Malaya at Changi, as Air Staff Plans. On return to England in September 1952, a short spell of command of a small unit of three American P2V5s, examining the possibility of using their complex radar fitments as early warning low-level radars. Then a spell of about four years in radar sites, either in command or as Wing Commander Ops, before being posted to West Malling in command or as Wg Cdr Admin when the Station enjoyed a short rejuvenation as an Operational Station. Following this, a Guided Weapons Course in January 1961, leading to a posting to M of A with an attachment to Melbourne and on return to UK a staff job writing up an evaluation of Red Top, leading then to retirement. In between these postings I had of course done most of the lesser training or briefing courses General Duties officers were subject to. So, not a particularly distinguished career but I had fun and enjoyed it.

'I remember how "chuffed" we were to learn that we were to re-equip with cannons. This led to certain disappointment when they did not function well in practice and I personally got into several scraps when both jammed after firing only a few rounds. Distortion somewhere under "G" forces was suspected and I proved this on several practice sorties over the Wash when both cannons jammed when "G" forces similar to those in combat were built up. I also felt a bit cheated sometimes when for random reasons I was late off the ground, too late to take part in whatever was going on; or having a day off when the Squadron got into combat; or arriving with the Squadron over the battle zone to find all gone home. This latter I sheet home to the tactics of our 12 Group Commander and the ponderous progressions of the Bader Balbos. Even our traditional vics of three aircraft proved too restrictive, and when these gave way to the much more nippy "finger" formations, which freed up eyes for searching and space for manoeuvre, we had a new efficiency and independence. Then the constraints of mass formations. Disaster, a retrograde step. Nothing was achieved by arriving *en masse* because the Wing disintegrated almost immediately battle was joined. In fact, time, and therefore advantage, was lost during assembly and this compounded the effect of scramble orders. These observations on tactics are, of course, in retrospect but I do recall at the time feeling some unease or dissatisfaction at 19 Squadron's inability to do better. I don't believe many of us at pilot level realized that we were engaged in a full-scale battle, nor how important the outcome would be if lost. Again, in retrospect intelligence briefing was sadly lacking in its scope.'

15 June 1989:-

'James Coward is a natural raconteur and I am sure will fill in a lot of gaps and provide a mass of "gen", both serious and funny. He was very good at sketching. He was always prepared to be a little different to the rest of us and whereas we all had dogs, James, with tongue firmly in cheek, sported a cat in the Crew Room.

'See if you can track down Group Captain Johnnie Petre, badly burned before the Battle of Britain started but spent a lot of his convalescence leave with 19 Squadron at Fowlmere. I should elaborate on "badly burned". Operating from Duxford one night in early 1940, he attacked a He 111 somewhere east of Duxford. Searchlights unfortunately illuminated his Spitfire during the engagement and gave the German gunner a pot shot. John's aircraft literally blew up in his face and he suffered terribly disfiguring burns, which, I am pleased to say, have become less obvious with the passage of time. It's terrible to think that I have lost touch with him, because he officiated as Best Man at our wedding.

'Jack Strang of 485 I remember very well as a quieter member of the Squadron. But particularly I remember his very pretty young wife who was terrified whenever he flew from Redhill, where 485 was based at the time. My own young wife was perhaps a bit more hardened or philosophical

Flying Officer Frank Brinsden, Manor Farm, Fowlmere, September 1940.

about a fighter pilot's life expectancy having lost her only brother in a flying accident at Catterick (with 41 Squadron), and spent a deal of time trying to comfort her. There were two quite exceptional fighter pilots in 485 at that time, and they had been in 11 Group squadrons during the Battle of Britain and have gone down as aces. One was Flying Officer "Hawkeye" Wells and the other "Billy" Crawford-Compton, a Sergeant Pilot. Both were fearless, aggressive and very good pilots. Both finished the war with multiple decorations. What am I doing rambling on about 485 Squadron?'

25 July 1989:-

'Further to your note about Eileen Lane's pre-war hobby of motor-racing, I thought this bit of trivia might be of interest: The captain of the He 111 "Johnnie" Petre shot down was at first detained in our Mess and Ladies Room. Eileen Lane called at the Mess to see Brian, who was absent, and shown unwittingly to the Ladies Room by the Duty Officer.

On her entry, the German officer rose to his feet and greeted Eileen as an old acquaintance – they had known each other on the motor racing circuits of Europe!

'I well remember Brian (Lane) always using a cigarette case without affectation. He was always so much more elegant than the rest of us. His fine old Armstrong-Siddeley car, black and always polished, whereas our old Morrises, Standards, Fords etc battered and in need of loving care and attention.

'Douglas Bader: I feel free to elaborate on this comment as Douglas raised the matter and I was there. Any "young pilot officer with little experience" on 19 Squadron assigned to brief Douglas Bader would actually have been flying Spitfires since October 1938. By early February 1940, when Bader came on the scene, that pilot officer would have been qualified to fly operationally by both day and night. Is such a pilot officer therefore likely to have omitted from the briefing the rather important matter of raising the undercarriage? In any case the crew room had an ample supply of Pilot's Handling Notes and anyone who embarked upon his first solo in such a (for its time) radical aircraft without fully understanding its controls was a complete bloody fool!

'You have my views on the Bader Balbos, and being cynical I believe that leading these was an ego-trip when the quick response and rapier-thrust of "finger fours" would have been more telling. As a folk-lore idol so necessary in war his contribution to morale was immeasurable. His sheer guts in overcoming his disability an example to all.

Flying Officer Frank Brinsden and Spitfire, Fowlmere, September 1940.

I would probably have sat around and moaned in similar circumstances. And we should never forget his untiring efforts in encouraging the limbless, post war.'

7 September 1989:-

'Since George "Grumpy" Unwin doesn't mind the use of his Squadron nickname, although incongruous because he was a most cheerful cove, I should confess that thanks to Wilf Clouston I was known as "Fanny". Whether he implied the Yankee meaning or British, or neither, I will now never know. We then had "Grannie" Withall, a delightful Tasmanian, quiet and meticulous in everything he did. "Ace" Pace was a buff on First World War fighter aces and an avid reader of flying comics, fictional, of course, and glorifying the stupendous exploits of mythical aces.

'Now, a little bit about my experience on 31 August 1940. Myself leading, Jennings (always known as "Jimmy"), Roden, Blake and Potter "scrambled" before breakfast to intercept a large raid heading west at the mouth of the Thames. Our next radio briefing had it turning north-west, towards Debden, which turned us south-east, then easterly in the still rising sun and striving for altitude. During this scrabble for height, Jennings dropped out owing to a technical fault, and the "Admiral" and Jack Potter lost Roden and me in the glare. Struggling for height and travelling towards the sun put us in the worst possible tactical position. Probably at about 15,000 feet, while still climbing and controls therefore still sluggish, I was attacked head-on and from up-sun by a 110 – which I then noticed was part of a large formation. Followed a mighty bang, loss of control – and out. I was lucky not to have caught fire because I reeked of petrol and was violently ill during the parachute descent, possibly because of the parachute's motion. I landed at Starling Green, near Saffron Waldon, and my Spitfire, R6958, at Brent Pelham.'

In May 1990, my first book, *Spitfire Squadron*, was published, concerning Brian Lane's and 19 Squadron's story, which was launched at the RAF Museum Hendon in the presence of the majority of the squadron's surviving Battle of Britain pilots. In September, in that fiftieth anniversary year, Frank and Cynthia Brinsden travelled from Australia for the commemorations, visiting me at my Worcestershire home. At Worcester's Tudor House Museum I was pleased to reunite Frank with fellow 19 Squadron Spitfire pilot Ken Wilkinson, together with former groundcrew members Fred Roberts and John Milne. At our Battle of Britain exhibition there, Frank was able to once more see the cigarette case that he remembered the 'sophisticated' Brian Lane using 'without affectation'. And in that trinket lies another tale.

After the Second World War, Brian's widow, Eileen, did not remarry, but buddied up as a travelling companion with wealthy landowner and fellow motor-racing enthusiast Owen Fargus. Having travelled extensively, in South Africa especially, the pair lived on the Channel Islands – where sadly Eileen died prematurely of cancer in 1971. In 1989 I traced Owen, who told me that during the 1950s he had accompanied Eileen to a nursing home in north London, and there gave most of Brian's personal possessions to his aged mother. What became of them after Mrs Lane died, nobody knew, but in his possession, from Eileen's estate, Owen had… Brian's silver cigarette case. This he generously loaned me for our Tudor House exhibition, but then I was shocked to learn that soon afterwards Owen had died suddenly, having been overcome by carbon monoxide fumes while working on his Daimler. I hastened to communicate with his estate's executors to explain the historical significance of this sole and very personal tangible connection

Wing Commander Brinsden (second right) visited the author from Australia in 1990 and is pictured here with Dilip's first ever book, *Spitfire Squadron*, fellow 19 Squadron Spitfire pilot Ken Wilkinson, and armourer Fred Roberts.

with the exceptional fighter pilot and leader Squadron Leader Brian Lane DFC. Owen's heir, Henry Fargus, agreed that I should remain curator of the item, which I have been proud to do these past thirty years. In 2019, my massively updated and completely rewritten history of 19 Squadron 1938-41, *Spitfire!*, produced with the survivors' full cooperation and majoring on the tragic story of Brian Lane, was published. Launched at Bentley Priory Museum in July 2019, my feeling was afterwards that there was little else I could personally do beyond that to raise awareness of Brian's story. Consequently it was agreed with Henry that the case should be gifted to the Imperial War Museum Duxford – and returned to 19 Squadron's spiritual home. This I was proud to do at a major event on, appropriately, 19 October 2019. Today, in this eightieth anniversary year, this unique artefact can be seen by all in the newly refurbished Duxford Battle of Britain Operations Room.

Sadly, none of 19 Squadron's Battle of Britain survivors lived to see publication of *Spitfire!* or their beloved Chief's cigarette case go on show at their former base.

Wing Commander Frank Brinsden died at Auckland, New Zealand, just three miles from where he was born, on 16 November 1994. Following a military funeral, Cynthia, together with the couple's four sons, observed Frank's dying wish and scattered his ashes over Auckland Harbour. With Frank, like so many others, died a treasure-trove of memories.

Chapter Fourteen

Wing Commander George 'Grumpy' Unwin DSO DFM

Spitfire Pilot

In the famous photograph of Squadron Leader Brian Lane DFC taken at Fowlmere in September 1940 by Stanley Devon (see Chapter Eleven), two other pilots are pictured. At left is Flight Lieutenant Jack 'Farmer' Lawson DFC, Commander of 'A' Flight; the other is Flight Sergeant George 'Grumpy' Unwin DFM, the latter described by fellow 19 Squadron Battle of Britain pilot Ken Wilkinson as 'The "ace", the High Priest of 19, all-powerful and looking down from on high'. Of the three, only the 'High Priest' survived the war.

George Cecil Unwin was born a miner's son at Bolton-on-Deane, Yorkshire, on 18 January 1913. Fortunate to attend the local grammar

school, in April 1929 George joined the RAF as an apprentice clerk, his first posting being to RAF Records at Ruislip. Two years later he was a Leading Aircraftman (LAC) and serving as a clerk at HQ Fighting Area, Uxbridge. Anyone who knew this tough man of action though, would be fully aware that such a role was hardly his ideal. In 1921 however, contrary to his original elitist vision for officer pilots, Trenchard, to both achieve the number of pilots he needed and create a trained reserve, began training a small number of NCOs as pilots. The concept was that these men would fly for five years before resuming their original trades, whilst eligible for recall to flying duties in the event of an emergency. The initiative was both popular and economic, but numbers remained small: in 1925, 13.9% of pilots were NCOs, rising to 17.1% in 1935. That year, George successfully applied for and completed flying training at Woodley and Wittering before joining 19 Squadron at Duxford on 1 January 1937. Sergeant Unwin now found himself flying Gloster Gauntlet biplane fighters – a far cry from pushing a pen at Uxbridge. George and his great friend and fellow northerner Sergeant Harry Steere, both professional airmen and NCOs, would become the solid core of 19 Squadron.

On 4 August 1938, 19 Squadron became the RAF's first Spitfire squadron, and Sergeant Unwin was the first NCO pilot to fly one of the new fighters. By the time of Dunkirk, George was a most experienced pilot, and throughout Operation Dynamo and the subsequent Battle of Britain well demonstrated his courage, skill and aggressive spirit – claiming the destruction of twelve enemy aircraft, along with three 'probables', another damaged and one shared. By the end of the Battle of Britain, Flight Sergeant Unwin DFM was fourteenth on Fighter Command's list of top-scoring pilots – and unlike certain others, his claims can be considered largely accurate. After the Battle of Britain he recorded further combat successes before being posted away, aged 27 and elderly by fighter pilot standards, as an instructor. Eventually George and Harry argued their way back on 'Ops', flying Mosquitoes. After the war George served with distinction in command of a Brigand squadron during the Malayan Emergency, for which he was appointed to the DSO. In 1961, Wing Commander Unwin retired from the RAF, working in the charitable sector, and settling in Ferndown, Dorset, where he pursued his passion for golf with the same fervour he flew a Spitfire in 1940. It was there, in Golf Links Road, that I first wrote to and visited George in 1988. A great friendship and protracted correspondence ensued, as George enthusiastically supported my research, especially concerning my first ever book, *Spitfire Squadron*. Again, extracts from some of George's letters tell their own story…

7 October 1988:-

'If my memory serves me well, the Spitfire Mk I had a fixed-pitch-two-bladed airscrew. I'm sure all were replaced by a three-bladed variable pitch prop and became the Mk IA before the outbreak of war… R6623 we received (new) in June 1940, followed by R6633. These "R" numbered aircraft were part of a batch of eighteen fitted with two 20mm guns and nothing else. The guns didn't work properly and we got rid of them at the end of August 1940.'

13 October 1988:-

'I can be of real assistance regarding Spitfire P9546. As you know, 19 Squadron was given the only Spit Mk IBs to be built – these were the aircraft with the two 20mm cannons and no .303 guns. Due to a faulty feed mechanism these guns did not work, and after weeks of frustration they were taken from us and replaced by Mk IA aircraft, with eight .303 guns. P9546 was one of those replacements and became my own aircraft, QV-H. We only had these replacements for a very short time as they were from an OTU and very much worn out. I flew P9546 on the following dates: Sept 3, 4, 5, 6, 7 and 11. During this period I claimed two Me 109s and shared in one Me 110. On 11 September, I attacked a Dornier over London and was stupid enough to get shot down by the gunner they carried in the "dustbin" below the fuselage. I landed in a field near Brentwood in Essex, without further damage, and was taken to RAF North Weald by army jeep. With the aid of a fitter plus spares, the aircraft was repaired and I flew it back to Duxford on 13 September. One bullet had penetrated the bullet-proof part of the windscreen and this could not be repaired on the Station. It was flown to a Maintenance Unit for repair. In any case, on 14 September we were equipped with the Spitfire Mk II. As you will see, P9546 was with 19 Squadron from 3 September to 13 September 1940.'

3 November 1988:-

'Brian Lane was a first-class pilot and leader. He joined 19 Squadron shortly after the outbreak of war, from 213 Squadron, and was firstly my Flight Commander, then my CO. Completely unflappable, he instilled confidence in all who flew with him. Despite the difference in rank we were good friends and flew together for over a year. It was a sad loss when he was killed.

'So far as the Fairey Battle is concerned, I reckon anyone who flew one of these abortions and lived deserved a VC. We were given one as a dual for new pilots prior to flying the Spitfire. After one flight test it was pushed into a remote corner of a hangar and never appeared again.'

19 November 1988:-

'Although I flew with Brian Lane for more than a year, and we were in complete accord in the air, he was an officer and I was a NCO, so we did not associate off-duty. My very last flight in 19 Squadron was formation aerobatics with Brian leading and my very great pal Harry Steere making up the three. Harry and I had trained together and been together from 1935 to December 1940. We were both leaving 19 Squadron to go on an instructor's course, after which we joined forces again in February 1942, as CFS instructors. He was killed in 1944 on Mosquito Pathfinders, at the time I was on Mosquito V1 intruders.

'You ask me what was the Battle of Britain like? At the time, I felt nothing out of the ordinary. I had been trained for the job and luckily had a lot of experience and was most disappointed if the Squadron got into a scrap when I was off-duty – this applied to all of the pilots I knew. It was only after the event that I began to realise how serious defeat would have been – but then, without being big-headed, we never, ever, considered being beaten, it just wasn't possible in our eyes. I hope this doesn't sound stupid but it simply was our outlook. As we lost pilots and aircraft, replacements were forthcoming – we were never much below full strength. Of course, the new pilots were inexperienced – but so were the German replacements, and it was clear by the end of 1940 that these pilots had not the stomach for a scrap with a Spitfire. The foregoing is my view of 1940, but as you suggested the question you raised would bring forth many different answers.

Squadron Leader Brian Lane DFC (centre), the 23-year-old CO of 19 Squadron, in a haunting, un-posed, photograph taken at Fowlmere at the Battle of Britain's height by Air Ministry photographer Stanley Devon. Both Brian and Flight Lieutenant Jack Lawson DFC (left) were later reported missing, making Flight Sergeant George Unwin DFM the one-time only living link to this classic image.

All I can say is that I was first of all lucky to have the finest fighter ever built, together with four years' experience on fighters. Secondly, being in this advantageous situation. I was privileged to have taken part in such a historic event.'

6 June 1989:-

'The forced landing was at Sudbury, Essex, on 9 March 1939, in K9797. A coolant pipe had broken causing the engine to partially seize up. I decided to land on a large playing field and was doing fine with undercarriage down until the schoolchildren who were playing on the various pitches saw me descending (I was apparently on fire and trailing smoke). They ran towards me and onto the path I had selected for a landing. I was then at less than 100 feet and decided to stuff the Spitfire into the thick hawthorn hedge just in front of me. The impact broke my straps and I gashed my right eyebrow on the windscreen but was otherwise unhurt. For this I received an AOC's Commendation.

Flight Sergeant George Unwin DFM and his Alsatian, 'Flash', at Fowlmere in September 1940.

WING COMMANDER GEORGE 'GRUMPY' UNWIN DSO DFM

'In early March 1940, three aircraft were sent daily to Horsham St Faith (Norwich), which was in process of construction. The area for landing and taking off was very small. On this occasion my numbers 2 and 3 were Sergeant Potter and Flying Officer Douglas Bader, the latter picking up procedures etc after his return to the RAF. On this occasion I decided that if we were scrambled he would lead the Section. We were scrambled, but he forgot to put his engine into fine pitch for take-off and failed to get airborne, crashing the aircraft which was a write-off. The only damage he sustained was that both his tin legs were smashed. It was again at Horsham some time later with Bader that he was filing his new legs to get them in perfect working order, that I remonstrated with him scratching and scraping whilst I was trying to sleep. The film *Snow White and the Seven Dwarfs* was the rage then and Bader replied "Shut up, 'Grumpy'". From then on, that was my nickname.'

26 June 1989:-

'Keep up the good work – as far as the proposed figurine of a Battle of Britain pilot is concerned, I do not mind so long as I do not have to do any posing – I can't imagine myself as a "male model" at seventy-six!'

9 August 1989:-

'On the day Coward and Brinsden were shot down (31 August 1940), I was taking cover in a slit trench at Fowlmere, due to the fact that my aircraft was on a routine inspection. I therefore took no part in that engagement.'

8 September 1989:-

'At least I can answer your request about 16 August 1940… I was Red 3 with Flight Lieutenant Lane and Sergeant Roden. We left Coltishall at 1715 hrs and were ordered to 15,000 feet, which was altered to 12,000 feet. After twenty minutes a large formation of E/A were spotted, escorted by Me 110s in the rear and Me 109s above. As we went in to attack the bombers, the 110s spotted us and attacked. I attacked one of the Me 110s and gave him a short burst. He half-rolled and went down almost vertically. I could not see what happened to him as I was attacked by another 110. I out-turned him and found myself with a perfect target at close range. My starboard cannon had a stoppage but I fired the remainder of my ammo into the 10. Bits fell off the E/A and he went into a steep dive, during which the tail came off. I followed him down and when I came out of cloud I saw the end of a splash in the sea.'

18 October 1989:-

'As to my views on Wing fighting… Quite simply, they were a huge success from our point of view at Duxford in that not only did we destroy more E/A, but the casualties among the three Hurricane squadrons were greatly reduced. Further, from the morale point of view it must have been quite a shock to the *Luftwaffe* to be met by sixty fighters when their propaganda was telling them we were licked. On the other hand, large wings of five squadrons were out of the question when operating from the aerodromes around London. You just could not get them in position in time to intercept. We at Duxford and Fowlmere (only three miles apart) had forty or fifty miles to cover before arriving over the London area and this was sufficient time for us to form up. I have always thought that the so-called row between the two commanders (11 and 12 Group) was (if it even existed) pointless. They were both right in so far as the circumstances under which they were operating were totally different.

'As far as your idea of a 19 Squadron reunion is concerned, you can count me in. When the time comes, just let me know what you have arranged and I will be there. How about getting Jennings along also? All success to your scribbling – if future chapters are as good as chapter two, you should be on a winner.'

26 May 1988:-

'I have read your 19 Squadron and first book, *Spitfire Squadron*, and so have a couple of my golfing pals interested in WWII. They both agree with me that it was really professional. For myself I found it did bring back memories. I couldn't fault it on facts or presentation and it held one's interest from start to finish. Congratulations on a job well done.'

20 September 1991:-

'Many thanks for your letter, which I found most interesting. P9546 seems to be having a big influence on your efforts as an author and historian. You can count me in to help you any way I can, and I am sure the other survivors will feel the same. You can also use my name to endorse the project.

My health seems to be OK now, after one or two minor setbacks, and I am back on the golf course five or six days a week. The news regarding P9546 seems promising – let's hope final agreement is given for its excavation.'

Our correspondence regarding P9546 arose because, coincidentally, this Spitfire ultimately came to grief, crashing and killing the Canadian pilot at Dymock, Gloucestershire, while serving with a training unit. In 1993 our former Malvern Spitfire Team gained permission to investigate the site, recovering a number of small items, in which Pilot Officer Jock Cunningham DFC also scored a victory during the Battle of Britain. On 8 May 1995 – the fiftieth anniversary of D-Day, I was able to present both George and Jock with mounted items from their old Spitfire.

George was always so enthusiastic, the interesting thing being that he had disappeared into obscurity until we became friends. On 13 May 1990, George met many of his former 19 Squadron comrades at the launch of *Spitfire Squadron* at the RAF Museum Hendon, and subsequently attended many of my book launches and other events at Duxford and elsewhere. I remember standing with George and Wing Commander Bernard 'Jimmy' Jennings at Westland Aircraft in Yeovil for the launch of *Angriff Westland* during September 1994, when Andy Sephton beat up the airfield for us in the Shuttleworth Collection's Spitfire Mk V, AR501; 'My goodness,' said George, 'I didn't know you could fly a Spitfire *that* low!' – which must surely be a great compliment to Andy's skill. Always eager to share George's story, in 2006 I arranged for the die-cast model manufacturer Corgi to produce a 1/32 model of Spitfire P9546, complete with figures of George and his beloved Alsatian, 'Flash'. The presentation of George's model at his Ferndown flat made the national papers and my old friend was delighted with the model. On 28 June 2006, George passed away, aged 93. It was a great honour but sad duty to speak at the funeral – after

Wing Commander George Unwin DSO DFM pictured at home by the author in 1989.

which George's brother returned to me the mounted items of P9546, as a souvenir of our close friendship.

Thirty years after, as an amateur would-be historian, I researched and wrote *Spitfire Squadron*. In 2019 my complete rewrite and update, *Spitfire!*, was published, a weighty and profusely illustrated tome, benefiting from all those extra years of research and communication with the survivors. Sadly, neither George, the 'High Priest', nor any of the other 19 Squadron survivors were around to see it, but the book is my tribute to all of them.

Every time I visit IWM Duxford, usually to enthuse about some aspect of the Battle of Britain and sign books there, I have a curious feeling of walking with ghosts…

Left: Wing Commander Unwin pictured with Corgi's diecast model of his Spitfire, P9546; sadly he passed away soon afterwards, aged 96.

Below: After the author spoke at George's funeral, the Unwin family kindly returned to him the mounted items from P9456 recovered and presented to George in 1993.

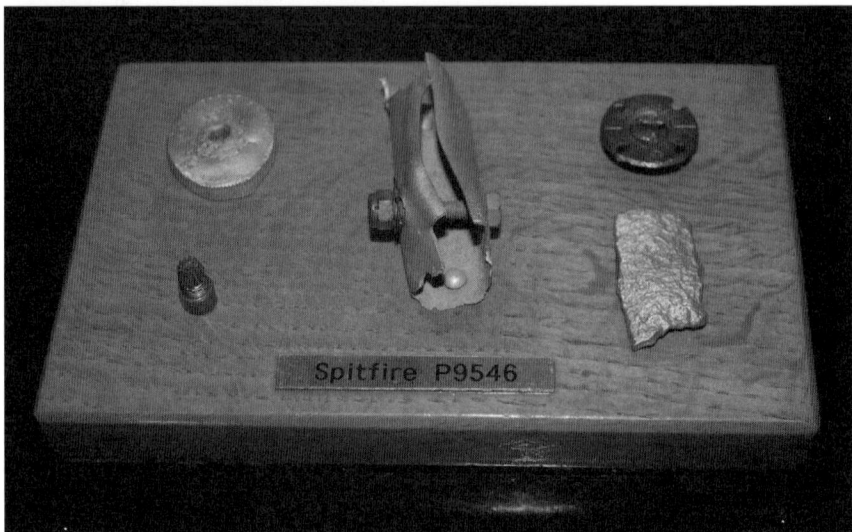

Spitfire P9546

Chapter Fifteen

Air Vice-Marshal David Scott-Malden CB DSO DFC

Spitfire Pilot

Francis David Stephen Scott-Malden was an impressive individual by any standards. Born on Boxing Day 1919, at Portslade, Sussex, his father taught at a preparatory school. After Winchester College, David went up to Cambridge, there to read Classics. Achieving a First, the scholar also won the Sir William Browne Medal for Greek Verse. An academic career poring over Latin texts, however, was not for David – who, in November 1938, had joined the Cambridge University Air Squadron. Having learned to fly, he was transferred to the RAFVR before the Second World War broke out, and mobilised soon afterwards. Commissioned, Pilot Officer Scott-Malden

completed his service flying training at Cranwell before reporting to Old Sarum for an Army Cooperation course. Pilot Officer Richard Hillary, author of *The Last Enemy*, was also at Old Sarum, his friend Peter Pease gloomily describing the Lysanders, which they were being trained to fly operationally, as 'flying coffins'. According to Hillary, 'We studied detailed map reading, aerial photography, air-to-ground Morse, artillery shoots, and long-distance reconnaissance. The Lysander proved to be a ponderous old gentleman's plane, heavy on the controls but easy to handle. It was almost impossible to stall it.'

Across the Channel, the BEF had been beaten back to and evacuated from the flat beaches around Dunkirk. As General Weygand said, 'The Battle of France is over – I expect that the Battle of Britain is about to begin.' It was not army cooperation pilots that were needed now but fighter pilots, to replace those men lost, wounded or worn out after the desperate fighting in France and over the French coast. Consequently Pilot Officer David Scott-Malden, and Richard Hillary soon after him, found himself posted from Old Sarum not to a Lysander squadron – but to fly every young man's dream: the Supermarine Spitfire. On 10 June 1940, Pilot Officer Scott-Malden therefore arrived at 5 OTU, Aston Down, for conversion to Spitfires. Many years later I developed a great interest in a particular Spitfire, R6644, which was ultimately destroyed when a Polish Battle of Britain pilot, Flying Officer Franek Surma, abandoned the aircraft over Malvern due to an engine fire on 11 May 1941. Cutting a very long story short, our former Malvern Spitfire Team recovered the meagre remains of

Prosser Hanks pictured during the Battle of France with 1 Squadron – who later 'owned' an illicitly obtained Gloster Gladiator when instructing at 5 OTU!

this Spitfire in September 1987, hence my efforts to collate details of flights made by individual pilots in this machine. From the aircraft's Form 78, or Movement Card, I knew that R6644 had previously been on charge with 5 OUT, and from the unit's Operations Record Book I had researched a list of pilots who had passed through Aston Down between those dates. Sadly, a number were killed during either the subsequent Battle of Britain or wider war. One whose name I recognised as a survivor, however, was David Scott-Malden – who had eventually retired as an Air Vice-Marshal and to whom a letter was soon on its way.

The following extracts are from our correspondence regarding David's time training at 5 OTU:-

25 August 1987:-

'It might amuse you to know that while searching for photograph I came across a short-lived diary scribbled in pencil, which covered the period at 5 OTU Aston Down. The entry for 19 June 1940 – the day on which my log book says I flew R6644 – does not mention the flight but reads as follows:-

Wed. 19th. Orderly Officer. Talked to the AA posts, who look forward to some work at last. The "Battle of Britain" starts with an air raid on the East Coast.

Some other entries are:-

Wed. 12th. Had a test at 1.15 on Harvard and passed successfully into Spitfire flight. First solo an indescribable thrill. Felt a pretty king man.

Fri. 14th. Paris falls. Astonishing to think of it in the hands of the Germans. Reynaud declares "Will fight on even if driven out of France". Marvellous days doing aerobatics in Spitfires.

Mon. 17th. The French give up hostilities. Cannot yet conceive the enormity of it. I suppose it will not be long before we start defending England in earnest.

Thur. 20th. Reports of another air raid, on South Wales. Fired eight Brownings for the first time, into the Severn. This getting up at 0430 am is beginning to tell.

(The last sentence about starting at 4.30 is repeated in several other entries. Can't think how I did it!).'

3 September 1987:-

'I remember very clearly that we treated flying under the Severn Bridge rather as a parting gesture when already safely posted to a squadron and reasonably safe from any complaints to the authorities.

'There are several large arches in the Severn railway bridge, and two smaller ones on the Welsh side. I had long arguments with my great friend George Barclay (sadly killed in the Desert) about whether a Spitfire could get through one of the smaller arches. He decided that it could get through on the diagonal, i.e. with the wings at 45° to the horizontal, and we watched while he did so, with some relief at seeing him emerge safely the other side. Personally, I played safe and used one of the larger arches. I'm afraid you will never discover if R6644 was used for that purpose, as it would not be recorded in anyone's log book, if they were wise.'

17 November 1987:-

'I'm afraid I can't answer your query about markings on 5 OTU Spitfires, but as I cannot remember any, and as subsequently I always recorded the aircraft letter in my log book, my guess is that they did not have any lettering.'

27 January 1988:-

'I'm afraid it is too much to expect me to remember the camouflage of Spitfires at 5 OTU. It is difficult enough to remember that I was there!!'

3 October 1988:-

'George Barclay and Tommy Lund were my close friends (at Aston Down), and I expect we were a bit clique-y (if that is a word).

'I wonder if you saw on Sunday the first episode on the television of *A Piece of Cake*, the television version of a recent book about fighter pilots in the Battle of Britain? Believe me, it is a load of rubbish.'

12 January 1990:-

'I was interested to hear that Prosser Hanks flew R6644 at Aston Down. I remember that he had his own Gladiator there, smuggled in surreptitiously from some previous unit, and those of us among his pupils who were considered "good boys" were allowed to fly it as a great treat. I flew it for thirty minutes on 21 June 1940. It is strange what recollections a small log book entry can summon out of the mists of time.'

After Aston Down, David was first posted to 611 Squadron at Digby, with which he served for most of the Battle of Britain before joining 603 Squadron as a flying officer at Hornchurch on 4 October 1940. His first combat claim, an Me 109 probably destroyed, came on 12 October 1940. Two damaged Italian CR42s were added to the list on 23 November 1940, and a Do 17 shared on 29. Still at Hornchurch, David was made Commander of 'A' Flight in May 1941, and that year added many more German fighters to his tally. A DFC was gazetted in August 1941, and in September 1941 'FDS' was promoted to Squadron Leader and given command of 54 Squadron. After a tour as a staff officer, in March 1942, Wing Commander Scott-Malden was appointed leader of the Norwegian Wing based at North Weald. And so the air-fighting continued, with the Wing Leader's score increasing further still. A Bar to the DFC followed, along with appointment to the DSO. After various staff appointments by August 1944, David was a Group Captain and given command of 126 Wing in Normandy. His final personal score stood at five destroyed, three 'probables', twelve damaged and three shared. This can only be considered a very accurate assessment of those combats' outcomes.

David Scott-Malden was a quiet man, I felt, thoughtful, intellectual, as his academic record confirms. We met once, when the Air Vice-Marshal signed an edition of prints in support of our one-time charity,

David Scott-Malden pictured after the Battle of Britain, by which time he was a highly accomplished and decorated wing leader.

In 1992, the author presented Air Vice-Marshal Scott-Malden with conserved items from Spitfire R6644 – which he had flown just once at Aston Down in 1940.

The Surma Memorial Trust For Youth. On that occasion, I was able to give this inveterate pipe-smoker a mounted souvenir from R6644, a Spitfire he flew so long ago. The brief entries from David's diary, that he so kindly shared with me, have real atmosphere and impact. Moreover, his stories about George Barclay and the Severn Bridge, and Prosser Hanks's Gladiator, are the kind of minute personal details impossible to glean from official records. This level of detail, the human touch, is only obtainable from those who were there. David, like so many others, distinguished though he was as a fighter ace and wing leader, never wrote a memoir – and sadly died in 2000. Both facts increase the importance of those hastily scribbled notes sent to me, now over thirty years ago.

Chapter Sixteen

Group Captain Alec Ingle DFC AFC AE
Hurricane Pilot

On 18 September 1993, I attended the annual reunion dinner of the 605 Squadron Association with Group Captain Gerry Edge, a pre-war auxiliary member of this fine old squadron, a flight which he commanded, flying Hurricanes during the Battle of France and early part of the Battle of Britain. We dined with Lord Harvington and the astonishing raconteur that was Air Chief Marshal Sir Denis 'Splinters' Smallwood. Afterwards I was introduced to Group Captain Alec Ingle, like Gerry one of the Few, leading to the subsequent provision of some interesting experiences.

605 'County of Warwick' Squadron was an Auxiliary Air Force unit and, like all such squadrons pre-war, flying personnel were drawn from the socio-economic elite. After war broke out, and especially after the Battle

of France, in which 605 fought, casualties from amongst the original establishment, many of whom were friends and family, and the need for replacements, changed the identity of these auxiliary squadrons. The volume of replacements required dictated that the AAF squadrons became similar to any other, taking in new pilots from all the different options available. So it was that during the Battle of Britain auxiliaries, regular airmen, whether Direct Entrants, Short Service Commissions or professional NCOs, volunteer reservists and foreign nationals, including men from the Commonwealth and occupied lands, all fought shoulder-to-shoulder, regardless of social class (albeit NCOs and officers being segregated on the ground) in the same squadrons. Amongst 605 Squadron's replacement pilots after the Fall of France was Pilot Officer Alec Ingle – of the RAFVR.

Born on 8 February 1916, Alec joined the VR before the war, training at Brough, and was mobilised when the Second World War began. On 19 June 1940, service flying training complete, Pilot Officer Ingle joined 605 Squadron at Drem, there to receive operational training and convert to Hurricanes. Three days later, France signed the Armistice. General Weygand's prediction that the Battle of France was over and the Battle of Britain about to start proved true: it did, on 10 July 1940. By 7 September, 111 Squadron at Croydon required relief, and so was replaced at that station by 605, which flew down from Drem where it had hitherto chased lone German bombers about. In 11 Group the tempo of combat was entirely different, mainly due to the Me 109's presence, the transition from the quieter north to the violent south being described to me by 41 Squadron Spitfire pilot Peter Brown as 'traumatic'. That day, 'Black Saturday', the *Luftwaffe* began the round-the-clock bombing of London, in order to bring Fighter Command to battle for destruction *en masse*, and in the mistaken belief that by so bombing of the capital's civilian population, the British government would be forced to sue for peace. 605 Squadron touched down at 1930 hrs that evening, the squadron diary reporting 'Heavy bombing of London and Docks in particular, commencing in the evening and continuing all night. Large fires from Dock and Peckham gas works could be seen from Croydon.' A greater contrast between peaceful Drem and war-torn London would be more difficult to imagine.

The following morning, 605 Squadron was scrambled at 1150 hrs, reinforced by eight Hurricanes of 253 Squadron, commanded by Flight Lieutenant Gerry Edge, and intercepted 'fifty Do 215s preceded by three Ju 88s and protected by twenty Me 110s at same level with fifty Me 109s behind and above, with twenty more Me 109s below the bombers' (ORB). The battle was joined between Maidstone and Tunbridge Wells, the enemy formation being 'turned completely', disappearing eastwards 'without dropping bombs'. Pilot Officer Ingle was amongst the successful 605 Squadron pilots, claiming a 'Do 215' probably destroyed:-

'I was Yellow 1 of "A" Flight… the Squadron was flying in sections vic echelon port, stepped-up. Yellow Section was guarding the tail at 17,000 feet. The enemy formation turned towards us and "B" Flight prepared to attack. A large formation of Me 109s appeared out of a thin haze or layer of cloud above us and a number dived on Yellow Section. Yellow 2 and myself turned to meet them but Yellow 3 (Pilot Officer Fleming) was shot down in flames. In the subsequent dogfight one Me 109 dived vertically to earth in a thick cloud of black smoke having been the target of Yellow 2's guns. Whilst searching for my formation I met two Do 215s which turned to meet me. I got a short deflection shot at one which poured out black smoke and dived through the clouds steeply. I subsequently fired a quick burst at another Me 109, which I observed attacking a Hurricane, no result observed.'

And so it went on, with 605 Squadron heavily engaged on a daily basis. To provide a strong escort to the bombers, however, Me 109s had moved in great numbers to the Pas-de-Calais and Cherbourg areas. When not tied to the close escort role, the fighters flew sweeps at high altitude, but when these incursions failed to lure 11 Group's fighters to battle, fighter-bombers were included in the enemy formation. Although the damage caused was negligible, albeit causing loss of life, after bombs rained down on London from what was believed to be a harmless fighter sweep on 20 September 1940, no German formation thereafter could be ignored. Of all the questionable tactics the *Luftwaffe* used to bring Fighter Command to battle, this was arguably successful. The 109s always had the height advantage, choosing the time and place for battle. Only the Spitfire could take on the 109 just beneath the stratosphere; the Hurricanes deployed to attack bombers lower down while the Spitfires fought off the fighter escort. The problem was, of course, that the 109s had climbed to height while assembling over France and crossing the Channel, whereas the Spitfire squadrons either faced exhausting standing patrols awaiting the enemy's next move or rapid climbs when scrambled – with the 109s enjoying the full advantage of height, sun and surprise. On 28 September 1940, the 605 Squadron diary makes a telling comment on this situation:-

'The Squadron was up in the air four times today, twice encountering Me 109s above them and each time being jumped on from superior height.

Feeling is growing rather strong about being sent up against the Me 109s without bombers at an inferior height, and complaints continue to be made to Control.'

By 12 October 1940, with the daylight bomber offensive having been defeated by the end of September, the high-flying German fighter and fighter-bomber incursions were a real problem. Indeed, on 1 December 1991, Squadron Leader Geoffrey Wellum DFC, a Spitfire pilot with 92 Squadron at Biggin Hill, wrote to me that 'during the months of September/October 1940, Me 109s were always in the Biggin Hill Sector airspace in numbers and caused problems. I recall that they were always above us as we never seemed to be scrambled in time to get height in time. Our climb was always a desperate full throttle affair, but we never quite got up to them. I did manage to get a crack at two Me 109s on one patrol but although I saw strikes

Alec Ingle pictured after the Battle of Britain, when leading the Typhoon-equipped 124 Wing.

I could only claim damaged.' According to the 605 Squadron diarist, by 1 October 1940 the Hurricanes were 'patrolling at 30,000 feet, if sufficient time is given, so as to avoid being jumped by Me 109s'.

On 12 October 1940, 605 Squadron patrolled twice as part of a wing with 615 Squadron. Pilot Officer Ingle, Green 1, was in action again at 1315 hrs over Dungeness:-

'...the Squadron was in sections, vic astern. At 25,000 feet the Squadron paired into six sections, staggered line astern.' This is interesting. Clearly the squadron had travelled from 'A' to 'B' in the usual vics of three, in line astern, but once in the battle area changed into fighting pairs, leader and wingman, in a stepped-up line astern formation. Alec's combat report continues:-

'After patrolling on various vectors, the Squadron was heading SE at 23,000 feet towards Dungeness, when three small formations of Me 109s passed about 1,500 yards ahead, heading NW. We held formation in a SE direction for about one minute, when four enemy aircraft appeared out of the sun ahead and above us. The leading sections, not already engaged, did a diving turn to the right and engaged the enemy aircraft below them, who were at that time being engaged by 615 Squadron. Various enemy aircraft broke out of the engagement and headed SE. I picked an isolated and unengaged one and chased it towards the coast. I expended all my ammunition on it in five equal bursts, in astern attacks, and after the third one saw oil come out of the starboard side. When about four miles out from the coast off Dungeness at 1,500 feet, I broke off the engagement and watched the enemy aircraft descend into the sea in a shallow dive some ten to fifteen miles East of Dungeness. Whilst chasing this aircraft I saw another enemy aircraft plunge into the sea about two miles off Dungeness. I returned to base at 1340 hrs.'

The combat was typical of the fighter clashes that autumn. 605 Squadron's Sergeant Peter McIntosh, a Croydon lad, was reported missing from this engagement. Later, his crash site was located through the efforts of his father and brother at Littlestone Golf Course, the pilot's remains being recovered for burial (another tragic tale told in *Battle of Britain 1940: The Finest Hour's Human Cost*).

On 26 October 1940, on 605 Squadron's second patrol of the day, Pilot Officer Ingle claimed another Me 109 'probable':-

'I was flying Blue 1. We left Croydon at 1134 hrs. Whilst on patrol at 23,000 feet, encountered about sixteen Me 109s. I engaged one, with no results observed. Engaged another, diving in a southerly direction, gave a two second burst from 150 yards to point blank range. I saw the greater part of the starboard wing root and starboard side of the fuselage disappear and petrol and glycol steam out. Enemy aircraft broke down to the right in a vertical dive as I broke up to the left. It disappeared into cloud at about 8,000 feet, as far as I can estimate, five miles North of Eastbourne. I subsequently returned to Croydon at 1245 hrs.'

The next day would prove significant for Alec Ingle, for a variety of reasons. On that day, 27 October 1940, Pilot Officer Ingle reported of the first patrol that day:-

'I was Blue 1. We left Croydon at 0850 hrs. Whilst on patrol above cloud approximately over base at 28,000 feet, we received information that four enemy aircraft were ahead and below. I received instructions from Red 1 (Squadron Leader McKellar) to engage these bandits, if sighted, under his protective cover. We were flying in pairs, loose line astern but I was flying to the left of the formation, guarding the flank exposed to the sun, we were heading north-east. I saw the four enemy aircraft ahead at approximately the same height, heading north-west, to the left of which, about 3,000 feet below, was another loose formation of about forty to sixty Me 109s. These turned left underneath the leader of our formation and attempted to head south – south-east. I led onto them until Red 1 saw them, upon which he took the Squadron into attack. I remained at 28,000 feet, until I saw that the four Me 109s at the same height did not attempt to attack the rear of the formation. I attacked two machines on the beam with no result. I therefore joined up behind the formation of Me 109s heading south-east in the hope that I would not be identified, this was the case and I closed right up behind a 109. The enemy aircraft at this time were in a loose formation, mainly abreast, stretching over a distance of about ten miles at 25,000 feet. I observed one machine peel off from the right to attack two Hurricanes flying 4,000 feet below in close formation. When a second machine peeled off I followed him and attacked from ¾ astern, diving, a two second burst had no visible result. I closed to 100-150 yards, during which time he alternately climbed and dived, violently and frequently. I gave him a five second burst from directly astern and he pulled out of the dive at 20,000 feet, glycol and petrol streamed out of him followed by dense black smoke, rapidly gathering in intensity. I decided to follow him to the ground but at that moment a cannon shell hit my port wing root and machine-gun bullets my starboard wing root and put out of action my aileron control, ASI, hydraulic gear and fractured my oil pipeline. I force-landed the machine at 0940 hrs at Barcombe, it was a complete write-off.'

Clearly Alec Ingle was an experienced fighter pilot – and on the way to becoming a successful one. Certainly the foregoing combat reports provide a detailed and exciting record of aerial combat. On 23 July 1995, Alec wrote to me:-

'You ask me to record how I was shot down on 27 October 1940. I cannot recall what we were about that day other than we were over Kent, so I can only recall the event itself, not what led up to it, in the attached note. Both times I was shot down in 1940 were whilst returning to base so I must have been out of ammo and not being as observant as I should have been.'

Alec's 'attached note' read:-

Shootings Down!
27 October 1940. Hurricane V7599 – Barcombe.
'I was returning to base from an engagement, flying at about 12,000 feet when I was hit from an unexpected quarter by quite heavy fire.

'I dived into cloud below me, whereupon the engine seized and black oil covered the screen. When I came out of cloud I looked for a suitable field on which to land but most were heavily obstructed. However, I sighted a field within which I estimated I could make a wheels-up landing and headed towards it by peering around the windscreen. To do this I had to release the shoulder lock on my Sutton Harness.

'At about 800 feet I decided to turn into the field but there was no response to the ailerons, so had to proceed straight ahead. On looking at the starboard wing I noticed a large hole with two jagged ends of wire protruding through it. I then saw a row of large trees ahead and by jinking, saw that there appeared to be a gap between them ahead. I was low, had no ASI and could not turn. I tried the flaps but got no result and suddenly a railway cutting appeared – but I just managed to jump the aircraft over it and arrived somewhat heavily on the other side among the trees.

'My head was obviously impinged on the gunsight because I could not lock my harness, and, somewhat dazed, I was surprised to see a number of people around me, including the District Nurse. She stuck a plaster on my head and the next thing I knew I was back at Croydon. I vaguely remembered that I should recover the radio crystals, as they were in short supply, but whether I did or not I cannot recall.

'The aircraft had been hit by cannon shell and machine-gun bullets from below; the aileron controls were severed, airspeed indicator damaged, the oil and hydraulic pipelines fractured and, of course, engine seizure.'

The following day, back at Croydon, Alec was promoted to flight lieutenant and took over 'B' Flight. Although the Battle of Britain officially concluded on 31 October 1940, as previously explained, the daylight bomber offensive had actually been defeated by the end of September, by which time Hitler had already postponed the proposed seaborne invasion of south-east England. The enemy's focus had shifted to night attacks, and by day the opposing fighter forces continued clashing at high altitude, the 'sunlit silence' shattered by the roar of their engines, the rattle of machine guns and thump of cannon, beyond the official British end-date of 31 October 1940. In a whirling mass of fighters over Kent on 8 November 1940, Flight Lieutenant Ingle claimed another Me 109 damaged. Two days later he destroyed an Me 109 over Rye, East Sussex, this being *Oberleutnant* J. Volk of 9/JG53, who baled out and was captured. A few days later, on 1 December, it was Flight Lieutenant Ingle who was forced to take to his parachute, when shot down in Hurricane V7609. The pilot was only slightly wounded, in the leg, Alec soon returning to operations. During the summer of 1941, he was rested as an instructor, later taking command of 609 Squadron, flying

A 605 Squadron Hurricane being refuelled and rearmed in a hurry at Croydon in September 1940. On 15 September 1940 – Battle of Britain Day – Pilot Officer T.P.M. Cooper-Slipper 'rammed' (his words) a Do 17 of 5/KG3 in this aircraft, L2012, over Marden.

Spitfires, until becoming leader of the Typhoon-equipped 124 Wing – by which time he had been awarded both the AFC and DFC. On 11 September 1943 he was shot down by a FW 190 during a low-level attack on a German airfield in northern France, baling out perilously low. Lucky to escape with his life, Alec suffered burns when the 'Tiffie' literally blew up in his face. Captured, he spent the remainder of the war as a prisoner. After repatriation, Alec remained in the RAF, retiring in 1966.

In that letter dated 23 July 1995, Alec also wrote that 'I did not keep a diary and dealt with the situation day-to-day, not, of course, expecting that the event would become historic. My clearest recollections are what the enemy did to me, rather than vice-versa! In any event, our Intelligence Officer did not appear to be particularly interested in my activities. One of these days I must look at the combat reports and Squadron diary, to refresh my memory if possible.' This is so typical of the Few, in my experience, often eager to talk about when they were shot down, or, in the words of Wing Commander Jimmy Jennings of 19 Squadron, 'did something daft', but rarely when the enemy was on the receiving end of their bullets. God forbid, of course, that anyone should be seen to 'Shoot a line'!

Although our correspondence did not develop owing to the pressure of other projects, I am pleased to have met Group Captain Alec Ingle and at least obtained an account from him of the first time he was shot down.

Chapter Seventeen

Air Commodore
Peter Brothers CBE DSO DFC*
Hurricane Pilot

Peter Malam Brothers – an RAF legend, fighter ace and one-time Chairman of the Battle of Britain Fighter Association – was another early correspondent who became a valued friend.

Born at Westerham in Kent on 30 September 1917, being a young man of means, Peter learnt to fly privately at the age of 16. In 1936, like many other air-minded, fit, well-educated and intelligent young men, he took a Short Service Commission in the RAF. Posted to fly fighters with 32 Squadron at Biggin Hill, by late 1938 Peter was a flight commander, a position he still

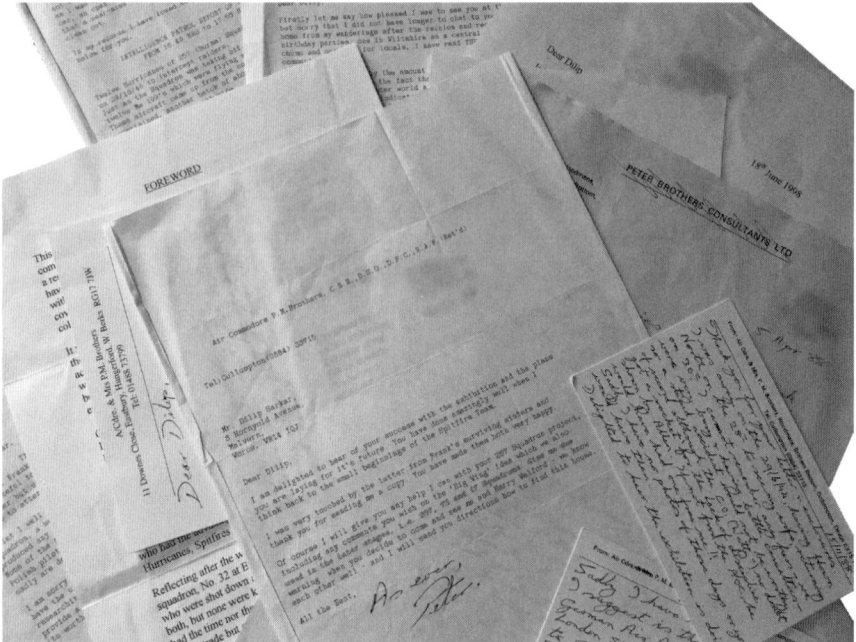

occupied when war broke out. In May 1940, 32 Squadron fought in France, and Flight Lieutenant Brothers opened his account as a fighter pilot when he destroyed an Me 109 on 19 May.

Having survived the Battle of France and the opening shots of the Battle of Britain, Peter was transferred to command a flight in 257 Squadron at Debden on 9 September 1940. There he served under Squadron Leader Bob Stanford Tuck and continued his success against the enemy. On 13 September he was awarded the DFC. It was that period of Peter's wartime service that first prompted a letter from me. Back then, in 1987, I was heavily involved with researching the story of Flying Officer Franek Surma, a Pole, who served with 257 Squadron between

Fighter pilot: Flight Lieutenant Peter Brothers, 32 Squadron, during the Battle of Britain.

22 October and 16 December 1940. In Larry Forrester's 1956 book telling Tuck's story, *Fly for Your Life*, a story is recounted of Surma being shot down on 29 October 1940, baling out and being mistaken for a German airman on account of his accent and his penchant for wearing a *Luftwaffe* flying jacket allegedly taken as a prize from a German bomber he had destroyed over Poland in 1939. Only Tuck's timely arrival on the scene in a pub garden near Matching in Essex, according to Forrester, saved Surma from being lynched by angry Free French troops. Of course, the obvious person to contact for an account of this was Wing Commander Stanford Tuck DSO DFC himself, which indeed I did. On 13 February 1987, Wing Commander Tuck responded, telling me, 'Of course I knew Franek Surma very well and there are many stories I could tell you of him. He was a wonderful little chap – but wild! He was a loyal and thoroughly trusty wingman! Franek and myself were birthday chums, 1 July 1916.' Unfortunately no mention was made of the Matching incident, and nor was it in further correspondence. From this I suspected that, as in so many other books published about war heroes in the immediate post-war period, written not by historians but by journalists, the incident was embellished

by Forrester. Nonetheless, Franek Surma was certainly shot down that day – and hence my letter to Peter regarding those events. On 23 March 1988, Peter replied:-

'I was not flying on 29 October 1940 but I vividly remember the bombing of North Weald as I was having tea in the Mess and we all dived under the table! My car, an open 3-litre Bentley, was parked outside and I was livid to find a near-miss bomb had filled it with soil, which took forever to clean out. In my records I have found the official report of the event, which I copy below for you.'

The Intelligence Report reads:-

'Twelve Hurricanes of 257 (Burma) Squadron left North Weald at 1640 hrs on 29/10/40 to intercept raiders.
    'Just as the Squadron was taking off, the aerodrome was bombed by about twelve Me 109s, which were flying at about 3,000-5,000 feet. These aircraft came up from the south-east. As far as can be ascertained, another batch of about twelve enemy aircraft attacked the aerodrome from the north side.

Peter's snapshot of the Gauntlet-equipped 32 Squadron 'scrambling' from Biggin Hill during the 1937 Annual Air Exercise.

A briefing during the 1937 Air Exercise.

'Just after Yellow 2, Sergeant Girdwood, had left the ground, a bomb exploded by him and threw his aircraft into the air, hitting it with splinters. The aircraft crashed in flames just outside the north-west perimeter of the aerodrome. Sergeant Girdwood was burned to death.

'Red 1, Flight Lieutenant Blatchford (Acting Squadron Leader), chased after an Me 109 which had just bombed the aerodrome. He got behind a cloud, hoping to catch the E/A, but was there too soon, and the Me 109 fired at him head-on with cannon, making a big hole in his fuselage, piercing the oil tank and damaging the tail unit of his Hurricane. Green 4, Sergeant Nutter, went below the cloud and made a short beam attack on the Me 109 but did not observe result.

'Red 2, Pilot Officer Surma (Polish) saw the bombs falling as he was taxying over the aerodrome. A bomb exploded on his left-hand side as his aircraft was running up. The explosion jerked him, but he took off satisfactorily. He noticed four of the enemy aircraft flying over the hangar between 4,000 and 5,000 feet. He also saw many planes to his right which he took to be Hurricanes.

'When he had climbed to about 3,000 feet, he heard an explosion in his cockpit, which filled with white smoke. His plane went into a spiral dive

159

and he felt that he had no control over the steering gear. He opened the Perspex. After a moment the plane appeared to come out of its dive and level out. However, it began to dive again to starboard. After trying to bring it out of the dive for the second time without result, he attempted to bale out. By this time, he had lost height to 1,500 feet and made a successful parachute descent. He landed in a tree-top by an Inn near Matching. After quickly convincing a Home Guard that he was a Pole and not a German, he was given two whiskies and driven back to the aerodrome. He had lost both flying boots on jumping out of the plane, and received a black eye, but was otherwise unhurt.'

So, there we have it: a rather more accurate account of the events following Pilot Officer Surma's parachute landing. The attack on North Weald that day had been brilliantly executed by Me 109 fighter-bombers of II/LG2, escorted by Me 109s of JG26. Pilot Officer Surma had been shot down by a leading *Experte*, the *Kommandeur* of III/JG26, *Hauptman* Gerhard Schöpfel, who safely back at Caffiers was credited with his twenty-first victory.

Air Commodore Peter Brothers, his wife Annette and three-legged dog Spindle, thereafter often visited me in Malvern, where I lived then, usually unannounced, as they passed by on their travels to and from their home in Devon. Our meetings were always enjoyable, the diminutive Peter enthusiastically puffing away on a cigar nearly as big as he! He was a marvel, a very, very experienced fighter pilot and leader – an ace decorated with the coveted 'double' of DSO and DFC. After the Battle of Britain, Peter had formed and commanded an Australian Spitfire squadron, 457, and later led the wings at Tangmere, Exeter, Culmhead and Milfield. After the war, he left the RAF and joined the colonial service in Kenya for a couple of years before coming home and re-joining the air force. Following a number of important appointments and commands, and having been made a CBE, Peter retired as an Air Commodore.

Pilot Officer Brothers during the 1937 Air Exercise – sporting privately purchased goggles.

An enduring personal memory of time spent in the company of the Few is when I was honoured to be the Battle of Britain

Fighter Association's guest at the annual reunion dinner on 20 September 1997. Every year a Battle of Britain Memorial Flight Spitfire from Coningsby provided a nostalgic display for the Few over Bentley Priory, Fighter Command's Headquarters in 1940, and, appropriately, the reunion venue. At the appointed time, we all awaited the Spitfire's arrival with growing anticipation. Peter and I stood chatting with other friends, until our conversation was lost in the roar of a Merlin! As ever, Squadron Leader Paul Day provided an excellent display, which brought smiles and applause all round.

Although an ace, it was, typically, virtually impossible to persuade Peter Brothers to discuss his own august exploits. We did, however, often discuss combat losses and claims, and especially my great interest in the 'Big Wing'. In that regard, Peter wrote to me on 24 October 1997, regarding my book *Bader's Duxford Fighters: The Big Wing Controversy*:-

'I am most impressed by the thoroughness of your researches. You have highlighted the fact that Leigh-Mallory, unlike Park, lacked experience in the fighter world and also was very ambitious. You have, correctly in my view, indicated that, because Douglas Bader was a pushy, newsworthy, character, "L-M" used him and his operational experience to draw attention to himself and cover his ignorance.

'I applaud your handling of claims made at the time. In the confusion which occurred during battle, it was inevitable that claims made proved later to be duplicated or worse. Apart from the few would-be aces, one of whom

Peter's 32 Squadron Hurricane Mk I at Gravesend in March 1940. This aircraft was later converted to become a Sea Hurricane.

Peter was another keen 'snapper' who often took his camera into the air. Here we see, during the actual Battle of Britain, Flight Lieutenant J.B.W. Humpherson DFC – who later lost his life flying B-17s.

Pilot Officer Franek Surma at readiness. On 29 October 1940 he was shot down and baled out while serving with Pete Brothers in 257 Squadron.

later in the war fired at and claimed me as an Me 109 destroyed, without even hitting me, I believe everyone reported what they honestly thought had happened. As a formation leader I found one could give a "new boy" a great boost in confidence when you had both fired at and hit a bomber by saying "I missed, you got it. It's your first. Well done!" After all, the name of the game was to build up and operate as a team. Douglas put the whole business in its proper context after the war, though, when he said "What does it matter? We won, didn't we?"

'Re-checking my log book I see that in early June when 32 Squadron did sweeps of the French coast after the hiatus of Dunkirk, we were on occasions in company with another squadron. Was Park perhaps ahead of the game in Wing use? This, of course, was planned, not a reaction. You have well drawn attention to his later problem of lack of time to react by comparison to that of 12 Group.

'I congratulate you on such an authoritative work and one which grips the attention, so difficult to achieve both. It is a first-class effort.'

What historian would not be delighted with such a review?

During the late 1990s, I produced a series of very popular photographic books based upon the Battle of Britain-related photographs I had collated from survivors and the families of casualties. At that time, Peter was Deputy Chairman of the Battle of Britain Fighter Association, and kindly accepted my invitation to contribute the foreword to *Battle of Britain:*

Oberleutnant Gerhard Schöpfel – another of the author's one-time correspondents – responsible for shooting Pilot Officer Surma down as the Pole took off from North Weald.

163

Pete snapped this Hurricane at Acklington just after the Battle of Britain, damaged in a taxying collision.

On promotion, Squadron Leader Brothers was given command of 457 (Australian) Squadron and is seen here in his personal Spitfire at that time, complete with swastikas representing 'kills' and his squadron leader's rank pennant.

The Photographic Kaleidoscope, Volume III, which marked the 60th anniversary. This read, in part, as follows:-

'It was inevitable, of course, that not all of the pilots who fought in the Battle of Britain achieved the mystic figure of five enemy aircraft shot down, thereby confirming ace status. Indeed, these were the majority who played a valiant part and without whom the Battle of Britain could not have been won.

'Generally speaking, these were the gallant youngsters who joined the RAFVR pre-war. When called up, by having already learned to fly, they were ready to convert to and gain some experience of the Hurricane or Spitfire, the aircraft that they were to operate in battle. Or they were the ones who joined in the outbreak of war and were rushed through flying training, followed by considerably less experience of the aircraft they were to fly in combat.

'The remaining non-regular element were the members of the then Auxiliary Air Force, later becoming the "Royal", the so-called "Weekend Flyers" who had the advantage in most cases of already being equipped with Hurricanes and Spitfires, or other operational types.

'Reflecting after the war on our losses during the Battle of Britain, I noted that in my squadron, 32 at Biggin Hill, of our pre-war pilots there were some who had been shot down and baled out unhurt, or burnt, or wounded, or both, but none were killed. Our losses were the new boys who

Spitfires of 457 Squadron snapped by the CO over the Isle of Man in 1941.

Air Commodore Peter Brothers pictured at home by the author in 1999.

never had the time or opportunity not only to learn or be taught the tricks of the trade, but also to know the performance advantages and limits of their aircraft and how to exploit them. Tragically, they paid the ultimate penalty for their inexperience.

'An example springs to mind. Prior to the Battle of Britain, operating over France as a flight commander, I naturally took our latest 'new boy' under my wing to fly as my Number Two. Suddenly I had that feeling we all experience at some time that I was being watched. Glancing in my rear-view mirror I was startled to see, immediately behind me and between my Number Two and me, the biggest and fattest Me 109 – ever! As I instantly took evasive action his front end lit up as he fired. I escaped unscathed, he climbed and vanished as I was doing a tight turn, looking for my Number Two. There he was, good man, cutting the corner to get back into position, as I thought, until he opened fire – at me! Suggesting on the radio that his action was unpopular, as there were no other aircraft in sight we wended our way home. Not only had he not warned me of the 109's presence or fired at it, he had had an easy shot at me but missed! I dealt a blow to his jauntiness by removing him from operations for two days intensive gunnery training. Sadly, it failed to help him survive.

166

AIR COMMODORE PETER BROTHERS CBE DSO DFC*

'As so much time has now elapsed since this country's last major war, and the key to victory provided by the Battle of Britain, I am constantly being surprised by the interest shown in it by people from all walks of life and from so many different countries throughout the world. The interest of historians and military men I can understand, but they are the few, not the many, whose demands for information seem insatiable. Fortunately, there are books like this to provide not merely information but also fascinating reading.'

Accompanying those lines was an undated postcard: 'Hope this is adequate. Short, maybe, but I teased a chum by asking him why his foreword was longer than the book; he was not amused!'

Air Commodore Peter Brothers died on 18 December 2008. In his obituary, the *Telegraph* accurately described my old friend as 'An inveterate cigar smoker and a connoisseur of malt whisky... a keen golfer, sailor and fisherman, and a great raconteur.' Shortly before he died, Peter was a staunch supporter of the campaign to save Bentley Priory, which was being sold off by the MoD: 'This,' he said, 'is the RAF's home, as HMS *Victory* is for the Navy.' The building was saved and is now home to the excellent Bentley Priory Museum. Appropriately, on the lawn outside this beautiful building is a replica Hurricane painted in Peter's 32 Squadron colours.

The replica of Peter Brother's Hurricane outside Bentley Priory – formerly Fighter Command HQ. The development now includes an excellent museum.

Chapter Eighteen

Flight Lieutenant Reg Nutter DFC
Hurricane Pilot

Another 257 Squadron pilot who had flown with Peter Brothers and Franek Surma was Reginald Charles Nutter, then a Sergeant Pilot, to whom I wrote at his home in Medicine Hat, Alberta, Canada. Born on 5 January 1921, in 1986, two years before my letter landed on Reg's doorstep, he had retired from teaching, so our correspondence provided the first opportunity for him to record some of his wartime memories. On 18 April 1988, Reg replied to my initial inquiry:-

'As you are probably well aware, time and age tend to dim one's memory but I will do my best to recall events which happened during those very hectic days in 1940.

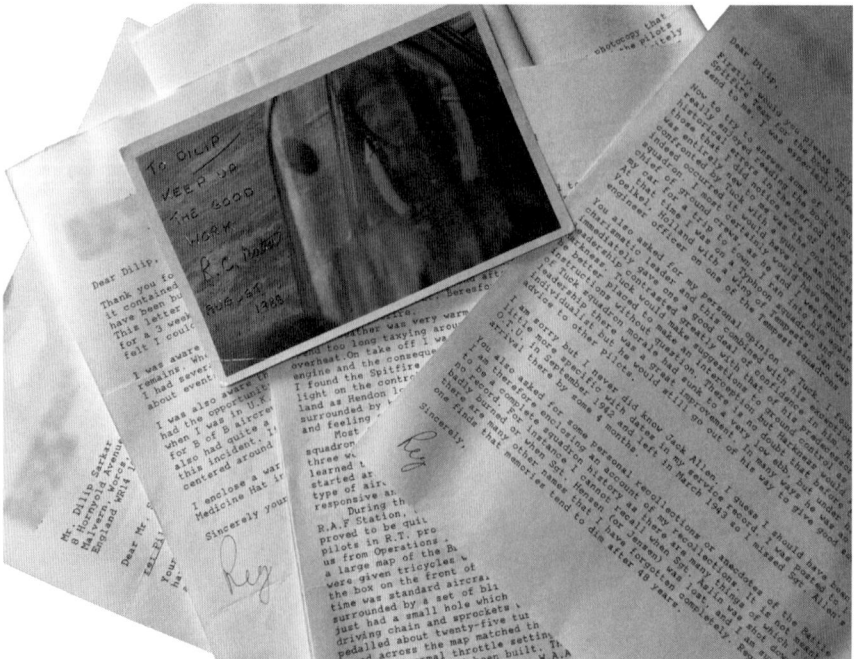

'Firstly, I should like to give a little background information on the Squadron, as such information is not always easy to glean from official records.

'During August and September, we had lost a considerable number of pilots and Flying Officer Blatchford and several Polish pilots arrived to take the place of those lost due to enemy action. As far as I can remember these replacements arrived in October. Thus, it would seem that Pilot Officer Surma had not been with the Squadron for very long when the incident on 29 October 1940 took place.

'At the time, we were stationed at North Weald and subjected to nightly bombings which surprisingly did comparatively little damage. During the afternoon of the 29th, a message came over the public address system to the effect that enemy aircraft were approaching from the north-east but there was no need to take cover. Almost immediately afterwards the Tannoy again burst into life with the following: "All personnel take cover! 247 and 249 Squadrons scramble immediately!" This latter command was most unusual and during my whole time with 257 it was the only time that I heard a scramble ordered in this way. The usual procedure was to use the dispersal telephone.

'On hearing this command all the fitters in charge of aircraft started engines and all pilots dashed for their planes. Before most of us had even begun to taxi out to take-off point, the attack by Me 109s had begun. Then everybody started to take off in all sorts of directions in order to get off the ground as quickly as possible. I distinctly remember seeing Sergeant Girdwood crash but then became too concerned with my own take-off and keeping my eyes peeled for attacking 109s. Once in the air it was a case of every man for himself as the 109s were all around and over us. Then all aircraft headed in the general direction that the retreating 109s had taken. It was impossible to join up any sort of a formation as we were strung out over many miles of airspace. Although I may have been detailed to fly as No 2 to Pilot Officer Surma, I never did see him the whole time I was airborne, and it was not until considerably later that I learned what had happened to him.

'The only recollections I have of Pilot Officer Surma are of a quiet, dedicated pilot, who, like almost all Poles, was most anxious to get on with the war and liberate his homeland. You must remember that the time we spent together would be limited to the time we were both at dispersal. In this setting the barriers between officer and NCO pilots tended to become blurred, but once out of this environment we messed separately and would see very little of each other. Usually, only those pilots on immediate readiness would be at dispersal. The others who would be on standby

169

would be in other parts of the 'drome until called to readiness over the Tannoy. Shortly after our replacement pilots arrived I was granted ten days leave in early November 1940 (the first I had had since June) and left the Squadron in mid-December. This too would tend to shorten the period of our acquaintanceship.

'I very much regret that I do not have any photographs of myself or any of the other pilots of 257 taken during the period.... The reason for the great dearth of photos taken on 'dromes during this period is that in the interests of security the taking of personal photographs was forbidden and cameras were strictly taboo. Any photos that did come out of this period were all official ones [author's note: not strictly true, as the snapshots in this book confirm; some surreptitiously circumnavigated the prohibition on personal photography at great risk of disciplinary proceedings!].

Reg continued with his recollections of the Polish pilot Karol Pniak:-

'He was a big man and had, I think, been a cavalry officer and thus had a very commanding manner. For this reason, he is the one Polish pilot that I can recall quite clearly. The usual range at which we opened fire on enemy aircraft was 100 yards, but this would not do for Karol: he would hold fire until within twenty yards in order to ensure that he obtained hits! On Armistice Day 1940, 257 Squadron intercepted the only Italian Air Force attempt to stage a bombing raid on England. During this interception, Karol, upon going in to twenty yards of the last surviving bomber, was surprised to see the rear gunner hold his hands above his head in the turret. He held his fire and escorted the Breda 20 in to a forced landing at Woodbridge in Suffolk. The Squadron insignia from this aircraft graced the walls of our dispersal up until the time I left.'

Well, this was obviously great stuff, and a response was soon winging its way to Medicine Hat with more questions. Reg replied on 21 May 1988:-

'I was born in Dover, Kent, and educated in the UK and Malta. I joined the RAFVR in March 1939 as a sergeant and commenced *ab initio* flying training at Air Service Training, Hamble, on week-ends and evenings. I completed this elementary training in June, then moved on to advanced training, and continued this when I was later moved to Portsmouth. I was called up on the outbreak of war and posted to 5 Service Flying Training School (SFTS), Chester, to complete advanced training. I graduated as a fully trained service pilot in April 1940.

'Upon graduation I was posted to 601 Squadron, Tangmere, but only remained with then for a few weeks before being posted to 257 Squadron which was then forming at Hendon. I stayed with 257 from May 1940 until Christmas 1940, when I was posted as an instructor to 9 SFTS, Hullavington, Wilts. In February 1941, I was posted to an overseas draft and a few weeks later arrived at 34 SFTS, Medicine Hat. In June 1941, I was commissioned and remained in Canada until January 1944.

'During this time I also served on 133 (Fighter) Squadron RCAF, which was forming at Lethbridge, Alberta, and as an instructor at No 1 OTU, RCAF, Bagotville, Quebec. I finished my time in Canada as an instructor with the Royal Navy Fleet Air Arm at Kingston, Ontario. By this time, I had been promoted to Flight Lieutenant.

'Upon return to the UK, I was granted leave and then went to 61 OTU, Rednal, Salop, for a refresher course on Spitfires and to try my hand at firing 20 mm cannon. From there I was posted to 175 Squadron, flying Typhoons, in May 1944.

'Unfortunately, at this time I came down with a bad attack of sinusitis which prevented me from participating in the D-Day invasion. When I was fit again I was posted to 245 Squadron, also with Typhoons, and joined them in Antwerp, Belgium, and it was from there that we participated in the attempt to secure the bridge at Arnhem. In January 1945, I took command of "B" Flight,

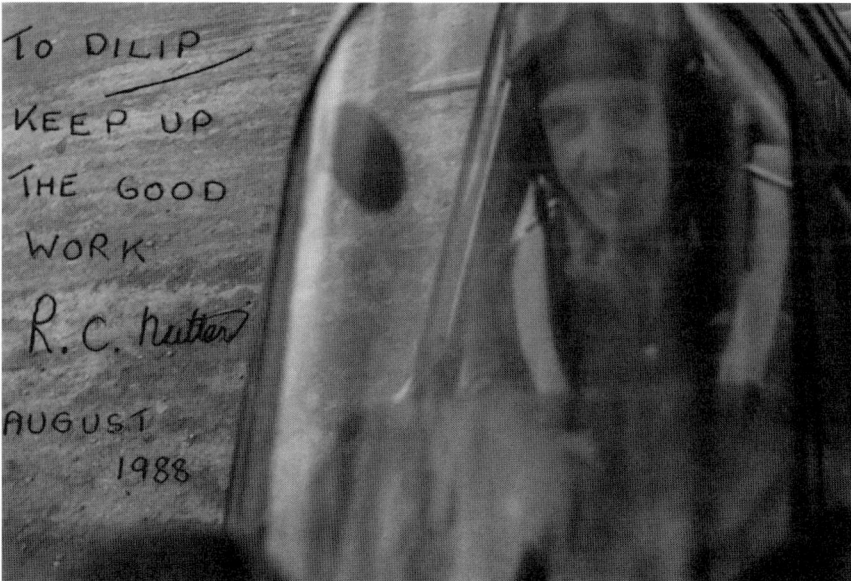

Reg Nutter instructing in Canada after the Battle of Britain.

175 Squadron, again on Typhoons, and stayed with this squadron until leading it back to the UK in September 1945, to be disbanded.

'During my service with 175, I was seconded to the Army for a time. I was attached to the 7th Armoured Division, the "Desert Rats", and my job was to ride in a tank with the forward troops. I crossed the Rhine and stayed with them until we reached the southern outskirts of Hamburg. I could contact Group HQ by radio and arrange for rocket-firing Typhoons to be sent to my area. Once the aircraft arrived in my vicinity I could brief them on the target and direct them into the attack. In a similar manner, I could obtain reconnaissance aircraft which could report directly to me on the condition of bridges, roads and the presence of enemy artillery. While serving with 175 Squadron I was awarded the DFC.

'I completed my military career on the HQ staff of No 83 Group at Schleswig, Germany, as Accidents Investigation Officer, and was demobilised in April 1946. In June that year I emigrated to Canada and have resided here ever since.'

Squadron Leader Bob Stanford Tuck DSO DFC commanding 257 Squadron in early 1941 – who Reg Nutter rated highly.

Back in those days, researching the Few's biographical details was far from easy. Unlike today, when, although far from infallible, encyclopaedic volumes and online sites abound, in those days such material was virtually unobtainable. For that reason a letter like Reg's was of enormous value and interest. As an expression of appreciation, I posted Reg a copy of Larry Forrester's 1956 *Fly For Your Life* account of Bob Stanford Tuck's war, including his time commanding 257 Squadron. On 2 July 1988, Reg replied:-

'I really enjoyed reading the book and found few historical errors in the period I served under Bob Tuck… One incident which was entirely new to me was the one concerning the two sergeant pilots confronted by Tuck with a gun. I am certain that if such an incident had indeed occurred, it would have been common knowledge throughout the Squadron. I most certainly would have heard about it from Jan Tyrer, the chief of ground crews, as he and I were good friends; he often borrowed my car for a trip to town. I ran into him again in the winter of 1944-45. At that time, I was on a Typhoon squadron and our Wing shared the 'drome at Volkel, Holland, with a wing of Tempests. Jan was then a flight lieutenant and Engineer Officer on one of the Tempest squadrons.'

As discussed in the previous chapter, the now late Larry Forrester, a Scot, was a writer more used to producing thrillers than historical works (and later lived in America, working in the film industry on such diverse movies as *Tora! Tora! Tora!* and *Star Trek: The Next Generation*), so a degree of embellishment is unsurprising. Reg continued:-

'You also asked for my personal opinion of Tuck. I found him to be a very charismatic leader and this, combined with his exceptional combat record, immediately gave one a good deal of confidence in him. His style of leadership contrasted greatly with that of his predecessor, Squadron Leader Harkness. Tuck would make suggestions to Ground Control as to how we could be better placed to make an interception, but Harkness would follow all instructions without question. There is no doubt that before the arrival of Tuck, Squadron morale had sunk to a very low ebb, but under his leadership there was a great improvement. In many ways he was an individualist but would still go out of his way to give sound advice to other pilots.

'You also asked for some personal recollections or anecdotes of the Battle. I am therefore enclosing an account of my recollections.

It is not meant to be a complete Squadron history as there are many things of which I have no record. For instance, I cannot recall when Sergeant Aslin was shot down and badly burned [author's note: 23 September 1940], or when Sergeant Henson was lost [17 November 1940], and I am sure that there are many other names that I have forgotten completely. Regretfully, one finds that memories tend to dim after forty-eight years.'

Reg had written the accompanying account in June 1988:-

257 (Burma) Squadron: May-December 1940

'Sergeant Don Hulbert and myself were posted to 257 Squadron at Hendon, from 601 Squadron at Tangmere. We arrived at Hendon about 23 May 1940, just as French resistance to the Germans was beginning to collapse. 601 Squadron had spent a lot of time in France prior to our departure.

'After going through the usual reporting-in procedure we met our new CO, Squadron Leader Bayne. I was assigned to "A" Flight, commanded by Flight Lieutenant H.R.A. Beresford. Our Spitfire aircraft were arriving in

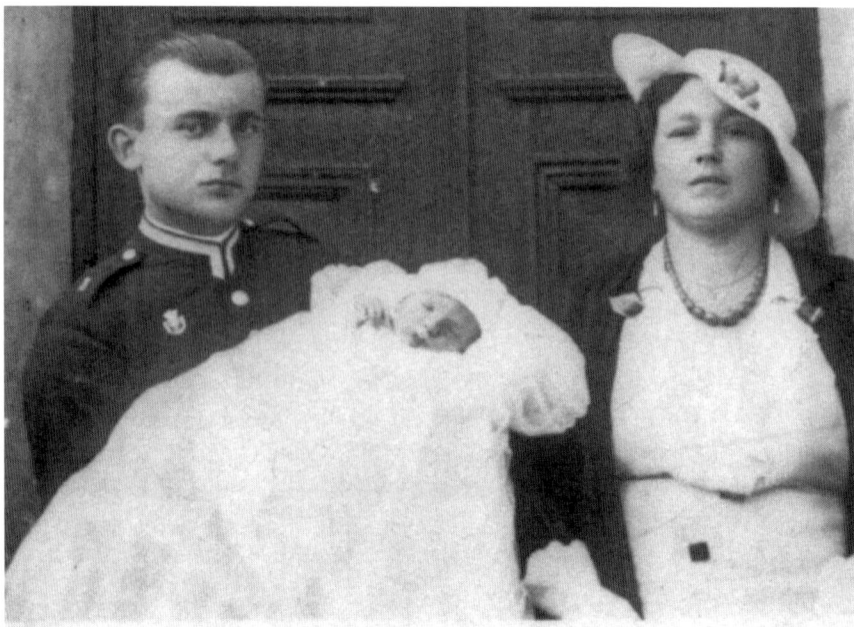

Franek Surma pictured in Polish Air Force uniform before the war at a family christening.

twos and threes, and after a short ten-minute check flight in a Miles Master with Flight Lieutenant Beresford, I was authorized to make my first flight in a Spitfire.

'The weather was very warm and I was warned by the groundcrew not to spend too long taxiing around or the aircraft would overheat. On take-off I was very impressed by the power of the Merlin engine and the Spitfire's rapid climb. In the air I found it a beautiful aircraft to handle because it was so light on the controls. I was somewhat disconcerted when it became time to land, as Hendon looked like a small green postage stamp, completely surrounded by houses. However, I managed to make a very creditable landing and, feeling quite proud of myself, took off and made another one.

'Most of the pilots joining the Squadron had neither been on a fighter squadron before, nor had they flown Spitfires. So we all spent the next three weeks or so working up on Spitfires. In the first week of June, we learned that we would be re-equipped with Hawker Hurricanes and shortly afterwards this type of aircraft began arriving at Hendon. On 14 June 1940, I made my first trip in a Hurricane and found it much heavier at the controls, far less responsive and somewhat slower than the Spitfire.

'During the working-up period, Don Hulbert and myself were sent to RAF Uxbridge for a course on radio procedures. This proved to be quite interesting as it had a two-fold purpose – to train pilots in R/T procedures and to train the controllers who would later control us from Operations Rooms. Marked out on the playing fields was a large map of the British Isles and a part of Western Europe. We pilots were given tricycles, which had formerly been used to sell ice cream! In the box at the front was a TR9 radio, which, at the time, was standard aircraft equipment. We wore headphones and were surrounded by a set of blinker-like boards, which restricted our vision. The driving chain and sprockets were arranged in such a way that when we pedalled 25 times the wheel moved round just once! Thus our speed across the maps matched the speed of fighter aircraft across the ground at normal throttle settings. Down in the stadium a complete Operations Room had been built. This was fully manned by trainee Controllers, WAAF Plotters etc. On top of the stadium was a spotter who passed our position, and the position of the person designated as the 'enemy', down to the Operations Room. The 'Controllers' could then vector us by radio to make interceptions. We both learned a lot from the course but found it somewhat difficult to sit down on our final return to the Squadron. Pedalling around in the hot sun in a serge uniform made one quite sore in a certain part of one's anatomy!

'By the end of June, Squadron Leader Bayne had us all whipped into pretty good shape. We had done a good deal of formation flying, air-to-ground and air-to-air firing. Around the beginning of July, the Squadron moved to Northolt where we practised "scrambling" from proper dispersal points. This airfield was also big enough for us to practise dusk and night landings.

'From my logbook it appears that the Squadron was declared fully operational on about 20 July 1940. At about this time a change of command occurred with Squadron Leader Harkness replacing Squadron Leader Bayne. We spent a good deal of the rest of the month operating out of Hawkinge, near Folkestone, with a return to Northolt each evening.

'Early in August three of our pilots, Pilot Officer the Hon. David Coke, Pilot Officer Carl Capon and myself, were chosen to perform VIP escort duties. My log shows a flight to Christchurch escorting an American VIP, and on 7 and 8 August 1940 we escorted the Prime Minister, Winston Churchill, who was a passenger in a De Havilland Flamingo piloted by Flight Lieutenant Blennerhassett. The route was Hendon to Northcoates, Manby, Coltishall to Hendon. This trip remains vivid in my memory as the PM persuaded his pilot to do some very low flying, for his personal amusement, across the Wash!

'During the first half of August, the Squadron also operated on a daily basis out of North Weald to provide escort to convoys proceeding up or down the East Coast. We also operated out of Tangmere on a daily basis to provide similar cover to shipping in the English Channel. On 8 August, whilst on a convoy patrol, the Squadron tried to intercept some bombers which were attacking a convoy, but we were "jumped" by enemy fighters. In this first major engagement we lost three pilots: Flight Lieutenant Hall, Flying Officer D'Arcy Irvine and Sergeant Smith. This loss, coupled with the recent change in command, dropped Squadron morale very sharply.

'On 15 August 1940, we moved to Debden. This airfield had only just been completed and was very modern. From here the Squadron operated out of Martlesham Heath on a daily basis. Again, we did a lot of convoy escort but did do some interceptions of larger raids in the London area. Sometime towards the end of the month, Debden was heavily bombed and the Squadron moved to Martlesham temporarily because Debden was out of action. It is funny how things stick in one's memory but I remember that the Sergeants' Mess at Debden had a grand piano. The only one I ever saw in an NCO's Mess, but the last time I saw it, just after the bombing, it was trying to hold up the concrete roof! During this period Sergeant Girdwood was shot down and slightly wounded, and Pilot Officers Chomley and Maffett were killed.

'September was a very busy month with the Squadron flying many sorties and getting involved in plenty of fighting. During this period the Germans were putting up really large fleets of bombers with heavy fighter escorts and the Squadron suffered further casualties, including Flight Lieutenant Beresford, Flying Officer Mitchell and Pilot Officer Bonseigneur, who were all killed. Flight Lieutenant Beresford was replaced as commander of "A" Flight by Flight Lieutenant Peter Brothers, who came to us from 32 Squadron. It was during this month that we had another change of command, with Squadron Leader R.R. Stanford Tuck taking over from Squadron Leader Harkness.

'On 2 September 1940, while the Squadron was patrolling off North Foreland, I managed to get some good bursts at a 109 which had swung

Above left: Another Peter Brothers snapshot, this time of 257 Squadron's Flight Lieutenant H.P. 'Cowboy' Blatchford DFC – later killed in action leading the Coltishall Wing.

Above right: Again Peter Brothers' album shares with us this photo of Flying Officer The Hon. David Coke, son of the Earl of Leicester and an Old Etonian, holding up his injured hand, referred to in Reg Nutters' letter. Coke would be killed in action the following year.

in front of me while attempting to attack the Squadron from the rear. He immediately dived, streaming coolant, but I lost sight of him in the thick haze.

'On 3 September 1940, whilst intercepting a force of bombers attacking North Weald, I stupidly allowed myself to watch the fall of bombs across the aerodrome, instead of watching my tail. I was promptly pounced upon by an Me 110. Although the aircraft was quite badly shot up and leaked petrol all over me, and I had received shrapnel wounds to my right side, I did manage to make it back to Martlesham Heath.

'On 7 October 1940 we moved to North Weald. The daylight raids by large fleets of bombers had ceased by this time and the night raids on London, and other major cities, had begun. During daylight the Germans began employing Me 109s and 110s as fighter-bombers. These were nuisance raids intended to keep the British defences at a constant state of alert and to demoralise the civilian population by the constant sounding of air raid alerts. These sorties flew at very high altitudes and were mixed with fighters carrying no bombs. Trying to intercept these nuisance raids was very tiring work because of the very high altitudes at which we had to fly with no form of pressurised cabin or flying suit. Sergeant Bobby Fraser was lost intercepting one of these raids over the south coast.

'On 12 October 1940, we were caught on the ground at North Weald by a low-level raid by 109s and 110s. During the ensuing attempt to scramble and intercept, Sergeant Jock Girdwood had the misfortune to take off right over a bursting bomb and was instantly killed.

'At the end of October, now that replacement pilots were beginning to arrive, I must have been granted a well-deserved leave, for my log book indicates that I did not fly between 29 October and 12 November 1940. During my absence the Squadron had moved to Martlesham Heath. On 11 November, led by Flight Lieutenant Blatchford, it intercepted the one and only attempted raid by bombers escorted by CR42 (biplane!) fighters. A Polish pilot, Pilot Officer Karol Pniak, forced one of the bombers to surrender. This was indicated to him by the upper rear gunner who stood up in his turret with his hands above his head. He attempted to guide the aircraft to Martlesham but the Italian pilot decided to make a crash-landing near Woodbridge, Suffolk. After this the weather deteriorated rapidly and in consequence there was little major enemy air activity and a good deal of our time was once again spent on convoy patrols.

'On 17 December 1940, the Squadron moved to Coltishall, Norfolk. The next day I left the Squadron to take up my new posting as an instructor in Training Command. I had completed 112 operational flights with the Squadron. I said goodbye to the only two remaining pilots who had been with it since its formation some seven months earlier, Pilot Officer The Hon. David Coke and Pilot Officer Carl Capon.

'Unfortunately, time dims one's memory and it becomes very difficult to put events into a definite time-frame. I have a whole kaleidoscope of memories which I cannot put into perspective. I can remember how glad we were when the old TR9 radio, which required hand tuning, was finally replaced by a push-button VHF set and we were actually able to communicate with one another. I am sure that many early casualties were caused by the inability of pilots to communicate with one another quickly and clearly. To illustrate a case in point I can clearly remember being at the rear of the Squadron with Pilot Officer Carl Capon when we were jumped by 109s over the south coast. I attempted to warn him of one on his tail but on talking to him later, after he had baled out and had returned to the Squadron, I found that my transmissions had not reached his ears. I can also remember David Coke returning from a battle over Portsmouth as mad as a hornet because some German gunner had nicked him in the little finger of his throttle hand, and Don Hulbert with a bullet in his leg from the rear gunner of a Ju 88. I can remember chasing a lone Do 17 reconnaissance aircraft in and out of clouds while listening to American jazz music which was coming over the Squadron frequency and rendering all other communications impossible.'

After the war, Reg joined other family members in the teaching profession, having attended university as a mature student. His letters, in front of me now, remain inspirational, and had the Atlantic not separated us I am sure that Reg would have enthusiastically supported our work in person.

Reg died in Calgary on 9 December 2014, aged 93. Fortunately, not all his memories of a life lived to the full were lost with his passing.

Chapter Nineteen

Squadron Leader Boleslaw 'Gandi' Drobinski VM KW DFC

Spitfire Pilot

'I wish to congratulate you and your Team,' wrote Squadron Leader Drobinski on 14 September 1987, 'who worked so hard and very successfully in order to accomplish the task in erecting the memorial to one of our Poles. By paying a great tribute to Flying Officer Franek Surma, you also paid a great tribute to all Polish airmen who lost their lives fighting for freedom in the Second World War.' Again, it was our project to research the history of Spitfire R6644 and remember Flying Officer Surma that first brought 'Gandi' and I together – although upon reflection, when we started

the project in 1986, neither Andy Long, then aged 17, nor myself at 24, fully understood the enormity of what we were doing and why this meant so much to the Poles.

On the night of 31 August 1939, Nazi Germany invaded Poland in an undeclared act of war. Simultaneously, German troops crossed the frontier along its entire length, attacking guards and forward defensive positions. At dawn, the *Luftwaffe* bombed aerodromes and major strategic assets throughout Poland. In spite of all the diplomatic unrest that summer, the German attack achieved complete surprise.

31 August 1939 was, however, the first day of mobilisation in Poland, reservists reporting to their units and operational squadrons dispersing to various airfields. Few, though, believed that war would actually break out, the reservists expecting little but an inconveniently long stay with the colours ahead of them. The Poles trusted that Britain and France would honour their pledge to support Poland in the event of Nazi aggression, and mistakenly believed that would be sufficient to deter Herr Hitler. Many expected the Soviets to side with the western Allies, unaware of the secret non-aggression pact signed by the foreign ministers of Germany and Russia on 23 August. On that day, Poland's fate was sealed. Although at 1100 hrs on Sunday 3 September 1939, Britain and France declared war on Nazi Germany after Hitler ignored their ultimatum to withdraw from Poland, in reality the western powers were not geographically positioned to provide military support. Poland was on her own.

Sixty-three German divisions attacked Poland, facing fifty-six Polish. The German attack was spearheaded by fifteen mechanised *Panzer* divisions, whereas the Poles only fielded two motorised formations. The enemy's superiority of arms was considered 8:1. Moreover, the German *Wehrmacht* was a modern force, equipped and armed to current standards, whereas Poland went to war with the equipment of 1925. Importantly, Germany's diplomatic successes of 1938 and 1939 had secured strategic advantages in that Poland's northern frontier and most of the southern was controlled by Germany, and the attack was made simultaneously from north, south, east and west. Offensives on both flanks and steady pressure in the centre provided for envelopment. Nonetheless, by the campaign's ninth day, German losses were such that it was clear that the Poles' determined fighting spirit had been overlooked – a factor emphasised by the propaganda machine preparing German public opinion for news of heavy casualties. This fighting spirit would define the Polish contribution to the Allied cause throughout the Second World War.

In 1939, Poland, even more than Britain and France, was ill-prepared for a war in which air power played a crucial role. The immense capital investment required to create and maintain a modern air force was simply beyond the means of this newly independent country. The technical inferiority of its air force made Poland vulnerable – but the bravery of her aircrews was beyond doubt.

The first German aircraft to be destroyed during the Second World War were two Do 17s shot down over Olkusz by Lieutenant W. Gnys, in total the Polish fighter pilots destroying 126 enemy aircraft during the campaign. The Polish fighter squadrons, including the Fighter Brigade and Army Co-operation units, lost fifty pilots and 114 aircraft, while the bomber force suffered ninety per cent casualties in aircrew and aircraft. By 14 September, losses were such that the Polish Air Force was unable to continue operations. Some squadrons lost their last aircraft on that day, others, threatened with being overrun, destroyed their remaining machines. On 17 September, fittingly in a violent thunderstorm, the few remaining Polish aircraft crossed the Rumanian border, ending the air fighting over Poland. On the same day, in another undeclared act of war, Russia invaded eastern Poland. Polish Air Force flying schools and experimental and maintenance units evacuated their personnel to Rumania and Hungary.

On 1 October, German troops entered Warsaw. Six says later, Polish resistance finally ceased – although the Polish Home Army would continue fighting a partisan war until the Germans were finally defeated five years later. From a Polish viewpoint the short, tragic, campaign was a consequence of unpreparedness, the outcome, against ruthless and efficient aggression, inevitable. Nonetheless, Poland's defiant spirit, refusing to surrender without a fight, no matter what the odds, set a benchmark of courage that would resonate throughout the Second World War. It is important to understand the Polish character, fundamental to which is a powerful sense of duty and love of country. For five hundred years, Poland fought two or three defensive wars every generation. Poles know full well, therefore, that material possessions, even the family home, can be lost – instantly. If that happens, anything that the enemy can use must be destroyed. Polish soil, however, cannot be destroyed, and neither can national solidarity, an iron will to endure whatever the odds. Consequently, the Polish nation has survived even when forced into exile. It is this long history of suffering and its profound effect on the Polish psyche that more than anything explains why, when Poland had fallen, the Polish Armed Forces trekked west to continue the fight. It explains why, when the call was made for the Polish

Pilot Officer 'Gandi' Drobinski serving with 65 Squadron at Turnhouse in September 1940.

Air Force to reassemble in France and later Britain, only those who were prisoners or those ordered to remain in Poland did not respond. For others, not continuing the fight and ultimately liberating Poland was unthinkable.

Organising the evacuation of the Polish Air Force was a huge task. First, crossing into such neighbouring states as Rumania, Hungary, Latvia and Lithuania, the Poles were interned. In Rumania, where the majority of air force personnel were interned, officers and 'other ranks' were immediately segregated. Unsurprisingly, Romania was unprepared for this influx of personnel, and things were chaotic. When the news was received that General Sikorski had re-formed the Polish government in France and was assembling the Polish armed forces there, this chaos worked to the Poles' advantage: many staged individual escapes, most travelling by boat via Constanza, Beirut, Malta and Marseilles. Amongst the Polish Air Force officer-pilots interned in Romania, at Slatina, was one Boleslaw Henryk Drobinski, who had been commissioned on the very day his homeland was invaded:-

'I was suffering from toothache so obtained a pass to leave the camp and visit the dentist. On producing my pass for inspection at the main gate, the Romanian guard said, "Where are the others? This pass is for Boleslaw, Henryk *and* Drobinski." Immediately, I ran back into the camp, collected two friends, and off we went. We caught the train to Bucharest and reported to the Polish Embassy. The next day we took a train to Paris, from there to Cherbourg, sailing to Southampton. I arrived in England in January 1940 and joined the RAF.'

On 25 October 1939, British, Polish and French delegates had met at the French Air Ministry to decide the best way forward. The Poles argued that their air force should be re-formed in Britain, given their familiarity with British aero-engines but ignorance of French equipment. The French countered that the Poles should be equally divided between Britain and France, believing that Polish squadrons could be quickly formed and would be welcome reinforcements on both sides of the Channel. Finally it was decided that 300 Polish aircrew and 2,000 ground staff would be stationed in Britain, the rest in France. This now meant that a large-scale evacuation had to be organised from the internment camps. Eventually the Poles reached

Pilot Officer Drobinski (second left) with, from left, Plt Off David Glaser; Sgt Oldnall (a replacement pilot); Sgt C.R. Hewlett; and Sergeant P. Mitchell, Tangmere, December 1940.

France and were passed from camp to camp until Lyon was made the central collecting area. From March 1940, Polish pilots began joining French squadrons. However, following the unprecedented success of Hitler's attack on the west, starting on 10 May 1940, once more the gallant and courageous Poles found themselves flying obsolete aircraft which were no match for the Me 109, and on the losing side.

Disappointed with the speed of the Allied collapse in France and Belgium, the Poles now had to reach England. Polish records indicate that towards the end of the Battle of France, the French fighting spirit had largely evaporated, it being necessary to use or threaten force against the French to facilitate evacuation. Ships were requisitioned, on occasion at gunpoint, and sailed to Gibraltar. Some Polish pilots were able to fly across the Channel in French machines, some crossed over in boats. No possible means of transport was overlooked by the Poles, whose only aim was to remain free and fight back.

Throughout the summer and autumn of 1940, refugee Polish airmen continued arriving in England, there joining earlier arrivals like Drobinski – nicknamed 'Gandi' by his new RAF chums owing to the thin physique he shared with the famous Indian leader! The Poles were frustrated, considering that their experience should immediately be put to operational use. Unfortunately this was far from easy, mainly because of the language barrier, in addition to the training the Poles would need to fly British aircraft types. The many foreign nationals, which included free Czechs, French, Belgians, Dutch, Norwegians and Danes, also needed to learn RAF procedures, which would take time.

Contrary to popular myth, there was no actual shortage of pilots. What was in short supply was combat experience. Few of the foreign nationals had actually experienced combat, and certainly not in modern, fast, monoplanes like the Spitfire and Hurricane. In July 1940, two all-Polish fighter squadrons, 302 and 303, were formed, with Polish officers shadowing British commanding officers and flight commanders, but many more such squadrons would be required before all of the foreign nationals were actively back in the fight. By August 1940, however, some of the early arrivals were sufficiently trained and conversant in English to be posted to RAF fighter squadrons. Slowly but surely, the Poles were getting back in the game.

Gandi was commissioned into the RAFVR on 27 January 1940 – an early arrival – inducted into the RAF at Eastchurch, and then, from 1 June 1940, kicked his heels at the big Polish collecting camp at Blackpool.

On 22 July he was posted to Old Sarum for evaluation, a week later reporting to 7 OTU at Hawarden for conversion to Spitfires. Successfully completing the course, on 22 August 1940 Pilot Officer Drobinski reported to 65 Squadron at Hornchurch – right in the thick of it. There he replaced Flying Officer Franek Gruszka – reported missing two days previously – and joined Pilot Officer Wladyslaw Szulkowski, a 30-year-old pilot who had served with 65 Squadron since 5 August 1940. On the day Gandi arrived at Hornchurch, Szulkowski struck a blow for Poland when he made his first combat claim, an Me 109 destroyed. On that day, 65 Squadron operated from the forward airfield at Manston, intercepting a large formation of bombers and fighters off Dover. From that sortie, Sergeant Michael Keymer failed to return; having chased the Germans back to France, he was shot down over the French coast and baled out. Breaking both legs upon landing, Keymer was allegedly shot by a German officer on the spot. This was a fighter squadron at war.

Amongst 65's personalities at Hornchurch was one Pilot Officer Brendan 'Paddy' Finucane, destined to become a leading ace and remembered by Gandi (in an undated letter from 1987): 'I had three practice dogfights with Paddy. He was a quiet man, not much for drinking as a rule and not much time spent by him in the bar. He was a very good pilot and very determined. It is a travesty of justice that he was forced to ditch his Spitfire in the Channel after his Spitfire's radiator was hit by a machine-gun from the ground.' Paddy was never seen again.

Upon arrival at Hornchurch, Gandi was checked out in the dual Miles Master by Pilot Officer Couzens, then the following day flew a Spitfire for an hour practising 'circuits and landings'. On 24 August 1940, Pilot Officer Drobinski spent an hour and twenty minutes flying a 'sector recco', familiarising himself with the local area – but returned to find Hornchurch being bombed! Gandi went after the raiders but noticed that his fuel gauge had dropped to zero. Forced to abandon plans to attack the bombers, the Pole glided into land 'like a slalom skier'. No record of this flight exists in the 65 Squadron ORB, it having been a non-operational flight – but the sortie is clearly recorded in Gandi's personal flying logbook. On 27 August it was decided to rest 65 Squadron, which was moved north to Turnhouse, 'to train new pilots and to give rest to those pilots who were so heavily engaged in the south' (ORB). According to the ORB, Pilot Officer Drobinski's first recorded operational flight with 65 Squadron was another 'sector recco' in company with Pilot Officer David Glaser on 1 September 1940 – thus qualifying for the coveted Battle of Britain Bar to the 1939-45 Star – but a similar flight made the previous day is also recorded in his logbook, indicating that official records are sometimes incomplete and

SQUADRON LEADER BOLESLAW 'GANDI' DROBINSKI

Squadron Leader Drobinski (seated, fourth from left), with Flight Lieutenant Kazek Budzik on his right, commanding 303 Squadron and flying P-51 Mustangs in 1945.

confirming that often a variety of sources are required to determine an accurate account. From then onwards, flights from Turnhouse (and Drem) were training flights, including the dogfight practice mentioned with Paddy Finucane. On 29 November 1940, 65 Squadron returned to 11 Group, based at Tangmere, although owing to the winter weather, operations were comparatively limited. On 26 February 1941, 65 was relieved by 616 Squadron, flying north for rest once more at Kirton-in-Lindsey. A few days later, on 2 March 1941, Gandi was posted to 303 (Polish) Squadron at Northolt. It was now, back with his fellow countryman, that Gandi's real war began.

A month after Gandi's arrival, No 1 Polish Fighter Wing was formed at Northolt, initially comprising the Spitfire-equipped 303 Squadron, together with the Hurricanes of 302 (Polish) and British 601 Squadron. Things, however, were changing (as is explained in more detail in subsequent chapters). Fighter Command had just been reorganised, with all sector stations hosting a three-squadron wing, led by a new appointment, the Wing Commander (Flying). Moreover, Spitfires were replacing the Hurricane in frontline squadrons in preparation for the so-called 'Non-stop Offensive', in which Fighter Command would be taking the war to the *Luftwaffe* in north-west France. On 15 May 1941, elements of 303 Squadron flew a sweep around St Inglevert – Pilot Officer Drobinski and Sergeant

Squadron Leader Drobinski (second right) and his senior pilots, including Flight Lieutenant Budzik (extreme left).

Belc comprising White Section, shooting up a taxying Ju 52 and some airfield installations before turning for home, attacking three ships, one of which Gandi set on fire, and strafing an E-Boat. On 18 June, 303 Squadron flew down to Merston, a Tangmere satellite, participating in a bomber escort sortie. Gandi claimed his first aerial victories: two Me 109s destroyed. Three days later, the RAF mounted its greatest effort to date: a 'Circus' in which no less than seventeen 11 Group fighter squadrons were involved, escorting a handful of 2 Group Blenheims to attack the German airfield at St Omer. The Polish Wing, led by the Canadian Wing Commander Johnny Kent, took off from Merston at 1143 hrs. Near St Omer, Kent saw a *Rotte* of Me 109s climbing below him, turned into the attack and destroyed one of them. Sergeant Belsa was attacked and his Spitfire damaged. Back at Merston, Pilot Officer Drobinski reported:-

'I saw two Me 109s in line astern going in to attack two Spitfires below me. I turned sharply to starboard and attacked one of these E/A and gave it a very short burst from 3-600 yards to try and frighten him off the Spitfires. I then closed in from above and astern, gave him another short burst at 400 yards. Smoke and flame appeared immediately and E/A went straight down. This is confirmed by Sergeant Palak. I then turned and saw three or four Me 109s above and behind. I was then at 15,000 feet. AA fire prevented me from making any attack, so I turned west, climbing and joined with two Spitfires of my Squadron. I then noticed two Me 109s flying low towards France. I dived and repeated my attacks, going up below one of them, and firing a short burst of cannon and machine-gun from fifty yards. Black smoke and flames immediately appeared and the E/A went straight down. The other pilots of the Squadron saw this E/A crash into the sea.'

The crash site of Flying Officer Franek Surma's Spitfire R6644, at Madresfield, Worcestershire.

Both Me 109s were claimed as destroyed.

The first, however, was not, in fact – but it was flown by one of Germany's two leading aces: *Oberstleutnant* Adolf Galland, Kommodore of JG26. Galland and his wingman, *Feldwebel* Bruno Hegenauer, were the first defending fighters to intercept the 'Beehive', diving through the escorting Spitfires and attacking the bombers. Just eight minutes after scrambling, at 1232 hrs, Galland sent a Blenheim hurtling earthwards in flames. Galland then damaged another Blenheim but was then attacked by Pilot Officer Drobinski. The German ace dived away, escaping into cloud, making a forced landing, streaming white coolant and with a seized-up engine, at nearby Calais-Marck. The 109 destroyed by Wing Commander Kent was that of Bruno Hegenauer, who baled out.

That 'season' of 1941, throughout which the day fighting over France was relentless, Gandi claimed seven enemy aircraft destroyed and one probably destroyed. For this feat of arms he was awarded both the Cross of Valour (KW) and the *Virtuti Militari* (VM, 5th Class), followed by the DFC. After destroying another Me 109 on 13 March 1942, Gandi was rested and posted as an instructor, then returned for another tour with 303 Squadron. Having subsequently served as a flight commander with 317 Squadron and on the Polish Defence Minister's staff, on 26 September 1944 he took command of 303 Squadron – at Coltishall – where one of his flight commanders was Flight Lieutenant Kazek Budzik: 'Gandi was a great commander, very fair, great pilot, great leader. I enjoyed serving with him.'

After the war, Squadron Leader Drobinski left the RAF in 1946 and applied for a British passport: 'They told me that when I landed in 1940 it

Above left and right: Flying Officer Surma after baling out of Spitfire R6644 on 11 May 1941, and at Bosworth Farm, Madresfield, awaiting transport back to Baginton.

was as an illegal immigrant, so the five years I had spent in England didn't count! I was so disgusted that I went to live in America, but returned in 1960, helping my father-in-law on his farm, who was unwell by that time.'

On 12 September 1987, our former Malvern Spitfire Team excavated the crash site of Flying Officer Surma's Spitfire R6644, at an event open to the public and aimed at promoting the annual RAF Benevolent Fund's 'Wing's Appeal'. Surma had crashed near the village of Madresfield, just outside Malvern, having baled out due to an engine fire on 11 May 1941. Although he survived, the Polish ace was reported missing six months later, on 8 November 1941 – so we felt that the 26-year-old pilot deserved to be remembered somehow. It was decided to build a memorial cairn at the junction of Jennet Tree and Hawthorne Lanes, where Franek peered over the hedge at the wreckage of his aircraft. The Mayor of Malvern hosted a civic reception on-site, and our honoured guests were Polish Battle of Britain pilots Squadron Leaders Gandi Drobinski and Ludwik Martel, along with Polish Air Force Association Secretary Tadek Krysztik. As we walked smartly from the crash site to the memorial, which Gandi and Ludwik unveiled, Gandi turned to me and said, 'You know, in 1945, because of the situation with Stalin, we Poles were told not to turn up at the big victory parade in London. *This* is our victory parade, and we have waited a long time for it.'

On 24 November 1987, Gandi arranged for Air Vice-Marshal Alec Maisner to host a luncheon at the Polish Air Force Association's London HQ for members of our team, which Gandi, Ludwik, and other wartime Polish pilots attended. There then followed a moving ceremony in which I was presented an Association badge and made an 'Honorary Pole' in recognition of the team's work, which I was honoured to accept on behalf of everyone involved with the project. Then, on 4 June 1988, Gandi attended the opening of our exhibition, 'Spitfire!', at Tudor House Museum, Worcester, again attended by a host of former pilots and Dr Gordon Mitchell, son of Spitfire designer 'RJ' and our President. The previous evening, Gandi arrived at my Malvern cottage – unknowing that within awaited a surprise: Flight Lieutenant Kazek Budzik, one of his two flight commanders on 303 Squadron and whom Gandi had not seen since 1945! It was an emotional reunion and a privilege to have witnessed it.

12 September 1987: Former 66 Squadron Battle of Britain Engine Fitter Bob Morris, showing two of the Polish Few, Squadron Leaders Gandi Drobinski and Ludwik Martel, some of the items recovered by the Malvern Spitfire Team that day from the crash site of Spitfire R6644.

Gandi would talk and write freely about how the Poles were treated after the war, the bravery of his fellow countrymen, especially the casualties, and lavish praise upon those involved in research and remembrance, but he would never talk about his own wartime experiences. On Boxing Day 1991, the Soviet Union was dissolved, the 'Iron Curtain' finally crashing down and opening up the former Soviet Bloc to the western world. On 13 August 1992 Gandy wrote to me:-

'Only a couple of days ago I received airline tickets to fly to my homeland. It is the first reunion in Poland since the end of the war. Naturally, as you I am sure will understand, I am very excited to see my country for the first time since 1939. The reunion takes place from 3 to 7 September 1992.'

On 23 September 1992, Gandi, a true gentleman, added, 'As you know I have been in Poland taking part in the Polish Air Force reunion, for the first time in fifty-three years taking place in the country of my birth. There were over 820 persons taking part in the reunion, which, as you mentioned in your letter, it was indeed a very moving experience.'

Nearly four years later, I received a call from Gandi, thanking me for our years of friendship and for what our team had done to further the cause of remembering the part played by Polish aircrew – adding almost as an afterthought that he wanted me to know this because he was dying.

On 26 July 1995, Squadron Leader Gandi Drobinski VM KW DFC passed away peacefully in his sleep.

Left: Squadron Leaders Drobinski and Martel unveiled the Team's memorial to Flying Officer Surma, beside Jennet Tree Lane, Madresfield, which was the first such commemoration for an individual Polish fighter pilot in the UK.

Below: Squadron Leaders Ludwik Martel (left) and Gandi Drobinski on that very special day back in 1987.

Chapter Twenty

Squadron Leader Bob Beardsley DFC
Spitfire Pilot

On 16 June 1997, Bob Beardsley, a long-standing friend and correspondent, wrote to me: 'I cannot believe that we ever looked so like schoolboys! All the air and groundcrew (in the photograph) were in "A" Flight and all are now deceased (at least the pilots are!) and it was very strange to see us all twenty years old! I was lucky to survive three tours of Spits plus one on Meteors subsequently, but this history is far back and memories grow very inaccurate! So much for all the aces now new researchers have cut the scores down to size!'

It must have been strange indeed for these men, in their dotage, with time on their hands, to reflect upon the most exhilarating of days flying fighters in their youth. Indeed, as Flight Lieutenant Ron Rayner DFC,

Sergeant Bob Beardsley of 41 Squadron (extreme right) with his great friend Sergeant Terry Healey (to Bob's right), with the South African Johannes Jacobus le Roux (second left), and an unknown pilot at Hornchurch in late 1940/early 1941. Le Roux would later be the man to remove Germany's commanding *Feldmarschall* from the Normandy battlefield when he strafed Erwin Rommel's staff car, wounding the 'Desert Fox'. Neither Healey or Le Roux survived the war.

a contemporary of Bob's in 41 Squadron during 1941, said to me in 1993, 'There isn't a day gone by I haven't thought about it, about what we had to do, but I think of it increasingly the older I am getting.' Bob is right about the fallibility of the human memory of course. Over time, memories fade, details become blurred, and the retelling can become exaggerated or shaped by later events. Nonetheless, certain events are so indelibly impregnated on one's mind that they are impossible to forget. Bob also wrote down for me the most vivid of those from 1940/41, which we will explore here.

A Londoner, Robert Arthur Beardsley was born in Charlton on 19 January 1920. Educated at Roan School, Bob joined the RAFVR in 1938, learning to fly at Gravesend, and was mobilised on 1 September 1939. After service flying training, Sergeant Beardsley was, unusually, posted directly to 610 Squadron at Biggin Hill, on 27 July 1940, three days later reporting to 7 OTU at Hawarden for conversion to and operational training on Spitfires. On 12 August, that process complete, Bob returned to 610 Squadron at 'Biggin on the Bump'.

Three days after Sergeant Beardsley's arrival at Biggin Hill, the *Luftwaffe* launched its *Adlerangriff* – Attack of the Eagles – at which point the Battle of Britain proper began. Over the next three weeks the assault's emphasis shifted firmly to battering 11 Group's all-important Sector Stations – including Biggin Hill. On 25 August 1940, German fighters prowled up and down the Channel, hoping to provoke a reaction from Fighter Command, but the RAF sensibly ignored these sweeps. At 1600 hrs, a huge raid of over 300 enemy aircraft approached Weymouth, a great air battle rapidly. Then *Luftflotte* 2 again targeted Hawkinge, Major Adolf Galland leading the whole of JG26 on a *freie hunt*. Over Dover, the Me 109s were intercepted by Spitfires from Kenley's 616 Squadron, and Biggin's 610; Bob Beardsley was amongst the latter, and wrote to me about that day:-

'We received a scramble to patrol Dover–Folkestone and on approaching the coastal area saw a number of Me 109s crossing inbound at 90° to our course. I had a wild burst at a 109 crossing me at 90° full deflection and was immediately hit by fire from another on my tail, which affected my aileron control. Not being able to sustain effective action I returned to Biggin Hill,

Sergeant Terry Healey taking a professional interest in the 'plumbers' working on his Spitfire's guns at Hornchurch.

where I was congratulated on my first "kill", which my No 1 confirmed, in flames – and I didn't see it happen!' – although no JG26 loss cross-references to this claim. The record shows that the Spitfires unfortunately came off second-best in this confrontation. 610 Squadron's Pilot Officer Gardiner baled out wounded over Dover, but 616 Squadron's Sergeants Westmoreland and Wareing were both missing, the latter eventually confirmed as a prisoner of war. Bob continued:-

'On 29 August, I claimed a Do 215 (probable) and an Me 109 escort as damaged. On 30 August I attacked a He 111 as it was heading for home. I was short of ammunition after a scrap with a couple of escort fighters, but as one engine was smoking badly I followed up and put the other engine out. I followed it down until it landed off Hythe and a couple of aircrew got out onto the wing root. Three Hurricanes who had arrived later claimed a third each!

'On 31 August, after a defensive patrol over Westerham area, Biggin was bombed and we landed at Croydon – where we were also bombed!

Above left: Sergeant Healey has been joined by Sergeant John Gilders; killed in a flying accident in February 1941, his remains would not be recovered for burial until 1994.

Above right: More 41 Squadron pilots at a muddy Hornchurch during the winter of 1940/41. At left is Sergeant Robert Angus, who would become another victim of Major Werner Mölders. Centre is Flying Officer Tony Lovell DFC, and at right Pilot Officer Roy Ford.

Sergeant Terry Healey being 'photo-bombed' at Hornchurch, circa 1940!

There was a Duty Pilot's hut surrounded by sand bags near the perimeter track and we made a dash for it with Squadron Leader Peter Townsend of 85 Squadron. In retrospect it was rather hilarious as too many pilots tried to get under the Duty Pilot's bed!

'We were ordered back to Biggin and landed to find it had been badly bombed again and was covered in craters. I had to extend my run to hop over the bomb holes and it carried me over the perimeter track. I was out of air for the brakes and rolled gently into a pile of barbed wire, outside an army tent, whereupon the Spit toppled slow motion onto its nose. As I stood up in the cockpit to evacuate a trio of squaddies clutching mugs of tea came out of the tent to find their exit blocked by a propeller and a huge Merlin! They looked quite pale!

'I was told to grab some clothes and report back to the Flight as we had been relieved. Only seven Spitfires left for Acklington. I was one of the lucky pilots.

'After a week's leave (in London!) I was posted on my return to Acklington, to 41 Squadron at Hornchurch, about five miles from home. I was flying again on 18 September 1940 and claimed two Me 109s damaged over Tonbridge area. At this time we were using Southend (Rochford) as our forward base and it was for me no action, although I flew two or three sorties daily, until the last week when it brewed up again.

'On 30 September 1940 we were ordered to patrol Portsmouth–Beachy Head. Before we reached Portsmouth, we saw bombers and fighters returning home separately, and I attacked a Do 17. Both engines were smoking badly and there was no return fire or evasive action. I followed him down over the Channel to 5,000 feet where I spotted a Me 109 solo, going home below me. I tucked in behind and fired my remaining ammunition – when he reached about 1,000 feet he rolled onto his back and dived towards the sea. However, at this stage I was closer to France than England and on turning north again was horrified to spot six Me 109s behind me as I turned for the coast on the horizon! I managed to evade by popping in and out of small clouds at 2,000 feet but one persistent fellow chased me back to within sight of Hythe and hit me with cannon shells, one of which broke the throttle linkage, but luckily the engine continued at full power (where it had been for some time!). I had no radio or hydraulics and the engine was now smoking and clanking. I, however, was praying as hard as I ever had. At 1,000 feet I was hit again and the engine packed up. I could see Hawkinge on the cliffs and reckoned I could just about make it when a lone Hurricane of a Polish squadron flew towards me and scared the 109 pilot off. I blew down my undercarriage (no flaps) and stretched my glide and, my prayers being answered, made a good landing inside the fence! The Station Fire Engine followed. I stood on the wing root and jumped off, the Spit continuing, pursued by the Fire Engine! (Incidentally, the Head Fireman was a very disliked Corporal from the flying training school at Lossiemouth and now an LAC! We had cut turves and placed them on top of the chimney in his quarters on our last night of our course there and smoked him out!). As I walked to the Control Tower a He 111 flew slowly over the airfield at 1,000 feet on the way home. The Bofors gunners were firing frantically some ½ mile behind, knowing nothing about deflection shooting, and I was hopping up and down, swearing heartily as he disappeared towards France!'

Bob's next combat was fought on 25 October 1940 (by coincidence seventy-nine years ago to the day as I write this):-

'This day, the CO, Squadron Leader Don Finlay, had lent me his new Spit Mk II, donated by the Observer Corps, as my aircraft was unserviceable, with the admonition that I was not to "bend it"! We were patrolling Maidstone and attacked our usual target, the escorting fighters. I hit my target, which caught fire, and was immediately hit myself with a cannon shell through the engine. I made for Hawkinge and landed safely without causing any damage. I was greeted by the Station Commander (again!) who said "I hope you are not going to make a habit of this, Sergeant!" I returned to Hornchurch by

198

train and underground via London – parachute on my lap! I was greeted by my CO who demanded to know what I had done with his aircraft! He was not amused – well, it was a *new* Spitfire and a *Mk II*! The CO of Hawkinge apparently recommended that I was put up for a DFM but our own CO was not at that time recommending for an award anyone who had not achieved five kills. The aircraft was apparently repaired and fought again.'

As previously explained, with the change in high commanders after the Battle of Britain, Fighter Command pursued an offensive policy, 'reaching out' to the Germans in north-west France. Certain of these new operations were codenamed 'Circus', complex affairs requiring much planning and coordination, and involving many aircraft. On 10 January 1941, Circus No 1 was despatched against ammunition supplies hidden in the Forêt de Guînes. Six Blenheims of 114 Squadron were closely escorted by Spitfires, 41, 64 and 611 Squadrons contributing top cover. Bob Beardsley flew on that historic sortie:-

'I was flying with another experienced sergeant pilot as "Arse-end Charlie". We were in the coastal area, heading outbound, when I saw six Me 109s in my rear-view mirror. Before I could give a warning, I received the "full dose" from their leader. This attack damaged my aileron control and my radio would not transmit. However, by chance the E/As did not follow me down as I dived frantically to catch up with the Squadron. My other "rear-guard" had not seen anything happen to me, and as I was unable to contact the Squadron I tagged on behind, at the same time discovering that I had neither guns nor flaps. Obviously, the pneumatic system had been damaged. I let the Squadron land at Hornchurch and flew a large circuit; with no ailerons it must have been clear that I was in trouble! Thank heavens that the engine was undamaged. I blew down the undercarriage, using the emergency bottle and landed safely on

Sergeants Bob Beardsley and Terry Healey, Hornchurch 1940.

199

flat tyres! I was met by the fire engine and driven back to dispersal to be greeted by the Flight Commander with "Where the hell have you been, and where is your aircraft?", most definitely not the "How are you, old chap?" that I thought the situation merited! When he finally realised the situation and condition of the aircraft (Cat 3, written-off) he was somewhat mollified! I was rather hacked off as it was *my* aircraft!'

On 23 February 1941, 41 Squadron was rested at Catterick:-

'From 1 March 1941, 41 Squadron remained at Catterick (their home station), while we "oldies" trained new pilots and the senior pilots were posted to other units. I was posted to a night-fighter squadron at Ayr, but this was cancelled as someone with experience was needed to shepherd the young, new, pilots (I was just twenty-one!). We also took part in a number of convoy patrols and scrambles, plus night-flying, a very unpopular practice on Spitfires. I was commissioned in June and stayed with the Squadron, moving to Merston, a Tangmere satellite, on 27 July.'

As explained in previous chapters, by this time Fighter Command had been reorganised, the Spitfire replacing the Hurricane as the frontline day-fighter,

Sergeant Bob Beardsley at Catterick in 1941 – all of his Spitfires were named 'Eileen' after his wife.

The Olympian Squadron Leader Don Finlay DFC, CO of 41 Squadron, snapped by Bob at Catterick.

Bob Beardsley: Spitfire pilot.

and every sector station hosting a wing of three squadrons. The Tangmere Wing, of which 41 Squadron was now part, had been in action since the spring of 1941, led by the legless Wing Commander Douglas Bader:-

'On 7 August 1941, we took part in our first sweep since January, of the Lille area and lost Graham Draper who was taken as a PoW until 1945. On this sortie I was leading a rear cover section of four. We were the low squadron of the Wing led by Douglas Bader, and as I looked into my left rear I saw an Me 109 closing on my port sub-section, so close that the cannon orifice in the propeller boss was *very* apparent! I called "Break port!" and we all went hard at it! The attacking aircraft had *not* fired and I called the Wing Leader that we had been attacked by *Messerschmitts*. To my amazement, Dougie replied "Only Hurricanes, old boy!" I failed to see the joke and next moment the Wing was engaged – and I saw no more "Hurricanes"! He did say "Sorry, old boy!" when the Wing was attacked! Two days later we swept the same area and our Squadron was not engaged but "DB" was attacked and baled out. During the month of August, I flew a dozen sweeps, including close escort to Blenheims, one of which dropped DB's replacement leg, and our Squadron lost four pilots. During September, I flew almost every day but only three sweeps are listed in my log book. Perhaps the powers that be realised that sweeps achieved very little and counted the casualties. On 10 October 1941, I was Gazetted for the DFC, much to my surprise, and posted on rest as an instructor at 58 OTU, Grangemouth, having spent fifteen months on 41 Squadron.'

Also at Catterick, from left, Sergeants Bob Beardsley, 'Mitch' Mitchell and Frank 'ITMA' Usmar.

Bob was unusual in that he had a bulging album of snapshots from those wartime days – including two of his wife, Eileen, and himself at Buckingham Palace for Bob's DFC investiture. In one of those pictures Eileen is holding her husband's gallantry award, bursting with pride – and quite right too!

Flying Officer Bob and Eileen Beardsley at Buckingham Palace for Bob's DFC investiture on 10 March 1942.

Proud as punch: Eileen with Bob's DFC outside the Palace.

Eileen and Bob Beardsley pictured at their 60th wedding anniversary party in July 2000.

After a period instructing, Bob returned to operations, with 93 Squadron, probably destroying a FW 190 over North Africa on 25 November 1942. After another rest instructing, he joined 222 Squadron, a part of the 2nd Tactical Air Force's 135 Wing, with which he flew on D-Day and the 'Long Trek' from Normandy, engaged in highly dangerous low-level strafing and dive-bombing operations in support of the army. Flight Lieutenant Beardsley DFC left the RAF in 1945, re-joining four years later and converting to jets. After eventually retiring from the service in 1970, Bob became a school teacher. Over the years we corresponded extensively about this and that, with Eileen also contributing to the exercise about life in general. It was a sad day when Eileen wrote that Bob 'has virtually no memory now'. Bob left us on 17 October 2003.

Whatever academia may think of oral and first-hand accounts, to me Bob's writings are a priceless treasure trove of information about those exciting days when, 20 years old, he flew Spitfires in action during Britain's most desperate hour.

Chapter Twenty-One

Flight Lieutenant Harry Welford AE
Hurricane Pilot

In front of me I have a veritable mountain of letters from Harry Welford, a prolific correspondent, the first of which, dated 29 May 1988, read (in part):-

'Last week I stayed with my ex-flight commander (Francis Blackadder) and his wife, who is my second cousin, and amongst other things we talked of the Battle. He showed me your letters, which I found very interesting, and in fact I was in the same Flight (of 607 Squadron) as "Chatty" Bowen and Frankie Surma, having been transferred over to "B" Flight just before we flew to Tangmere to relieve 43 Squadron. Strangely enough, there was a story about the two which I jotted down.

'We had a very intrepid and garrulous fighter pilot in Flight Lieutenant Jim Bazin's Flight called "Chatty", who seemed to have continued success in combat. One of our Polish pilots called Frankie envied Chatty's successes and wished he could borrow his luck. Chatty was known to carry a toy stuffed elephant as his mascot and Frankie pleaded and cajoled Chatty into lending it to him for a sortie in which Chatty wasn't flying. After much argument and some pushing from other members of the Flight, it was agreed provided the mascot was returned to Chatty's machine for his sortie.

'Anyhow, Frankie came back jubilant as he had a "probable" to his name and as promised he returned the mascot to the Flight Rigger, who stored it in the cockpit as he had been told. Next trip Chatty was on, he missed the mascot and cursed Frankie, who said he'd returned it. Later, Chatty was shot down and it was surmised that his change of luck was through lending the elephant. The twist to the story was that the mascot was in the aircraft all the time but had dropped down, jamming the controls and was found in that position when the aircraft was salvaged.'

Again, this is yet another example of a previously unrecorded story, existing only in Harry's memory.

"Chatty" was Flight Lieutenant Charles Earle Bowen, a pre-war Short Service Commission officer who had fought with 607 'County of Durham' Squadron of the AAF during the Battle of France, opening his account as a fighter pilot. Further successes followed. On 26 September 1940, KG55's He 111s, escorted by Me 110s of ZG76, executed a devastating attack on the Supermarine factory at Woolston, Southampton. According to the 607 Squadron diary, the Squadron's Hurricanes were in action between 1550 and 1630 hrs that day, over the sea six to twelve miles south of the Needles. Bowen was scrambled at 1505 hrs, and was shot down and baled out over the Isle of Wight at 1620 hrs. Pilot Officer Franek "Frankie" Surma, however, was scrambled at 1600 hrs

Pilot Officer Harry Welford, an auxiliary airman of 607 'County of Durham' Squadron.

and destroyed an Me 109 off the Needles at 1610 hrs. The pair could not have met on the ground as Harry described, if the records are correct. The exact facts of the tale may well have become blurred over time, but there would undoubtedly be some truth in it. Unfortunately Flight Lieutenant Bowen was reported missing on 1 October 1940, Pilot Officer Surma on 8 November 1941, so neither survived to provide confirmation.

Harry continued:-

'We all liked Frankie, who went from strength to strength, teaching us all "Nostrovia" at pubs in the evening. We understood Chatty was recommended for a DFC but owing to his death never received it as it is not awarded posthumously.'

On 12 June 1988, Harry wrote again:-

'The time Franek Surma and I were in "B" Flight together seems extremely short, only six days, but the loss of lives occurred so rapidly that the experiences of a lifetime could be crammed into a few days.
   'There were, I think, three Poles transferred to us at the same time as we lost five pilots on our very first sortie at Tangmere, two of them were my best friends. One in particular, Stuart Parnall, had operated in Norway and only just got out by the skin of his teeth by a sea evacuation. It seemed very sad that he should be shot down so soon. His brother was killed a week or so before.
   'Your details (regarding timings) do seem to fit in with my story (about the mascot) to some extent. Franek was the sort of person who immediately became popular and when we had a beer in the evening he would teach us how to say "Nostrovia" (good health, I think, in Polish). Anyhow, he impressed me so that the story, which could have been second-hand from someone writing to me in Ashford Hospital, was so true to character of Franek and Chatty that it became "fact". Certainly, before I was shot down Franek had tried to borrow Chatty's mascot then. He used to call Chatty his "lovelee boy" – which infuriated Chatty beyond reason!

On 25 June 1988, Harry added:-

'It is now forty-eight years since the Battle of Britain and not only are our recollections somewhat dimmed but there is a tendency to dramatize, perhaps even fantasise, and it is a shock to be told what the records say.

'You confirm the fact that there were three Polish pilots in the Squadron, and I recollect a short, stocky, rather serious man, who would have been Jan Orzechowski. If I remember, he smoked incessantly with a cigarette holder which was unusual to the British, but then the Polish officers tried to strike a pose, one would imagine, to keep their end up with us easy-going, casual, Britishers. They were certainly good, but quite mad and fearless pilots. Franek was more relaxed and met us half way, probably because he spoke more English.

'After the Squadron was rested, in October 1940, and was split up, one of our Sergeant Pilots, Burnell-Phillips, became a flight commander and used to fly in close formation in aerobatics with two Poles, and one day they all collided and were killed. I wondered whether Franek had been one of them, now I know otherwise.'

Over time, I persuaded Harry to record his memories of the Battle of Britain period, which he completed and sent me with a covering letter on 16 November 1994. Extracts are reproduced below:-

The First Flight

During 1939, my cousin Robert got permission to take me up to the Auxiliary Air Force base at Usworth and give me a 'flip', parlance for 'flying experience'. It was a fine day and ideal to get the feeling of 'no longer being earthbound', as my cousin put it. However, I knew that what goes up must come down again, so I was nervous. I was strapped in the front cockpit of an Avro dual control trainer with Robert in the rear. This seemed odd to me as I had expected the passenger to sit behind. Anyway, we taxied out and Robert spoke to me through the intercom, swung into wind and took off. After a circuit of the airfield we did a trip over the local countryside pointing out such landmarks as Penshaw Monument, the River Wear, and, of course, Sunderland and Newcastle further north. All of these sights will remain in my memory as pointers to the aerodrome itself. My cousin asked how I liked it and my response was enthusiastic, whereupon he suggested performing the odd aerobatic. Before I could respond he dived steeply and performed a loop followed by a slow roll. My stomach was not feeling so good and I was quietly sick over the side. Robert must have seen my distress because he went down to land, by which time I was all right again. We joked about it but one of the senior officers must have spotted the mess in the cockpit and gave poor Robert a ticking off for doing aerobatics during an air experience exercise. He then made Robert clean up the cockpit.

607 Squadron (Auxiliary Air Force)

607 Squadron AAF was formed on 17 March 1930 as a day-bomber unit, but it was not until September 1932 that personnel were able to move into the site at Usworth for training. In December, the first Wapitis were received and operated until September 1936, when Demons replaced them, the Squadron's role being changed to fighters. Soon after the Munich Crisis the Demons were replaced by Gladiators, which were currently used for operational training when I started my elementary training on Avro Tutors. The Squadron went over to the Continent for the Battle of France with Gladiators but were then equipped with Hurricanes, and returned after Dunkirk to re-form at Usworth with Hurricanes.

It was on 4 December 1938, my 22nd birthday, that I was very pleased to be accepted for training with 607 Squadron. I had already had one or two instructional flights.

In the early part of 1939, I was at the works during the day, getting in as much time as possible to complete my apprenticeship. During the evenings it was a case of working up the college subjects. At the weekends I was spending more time at the aerodrome having lectures and being given dual in flying and Link Trainer work.

607 Squadron had the services of a regular RAF adjutant and assistant adjutant, who not only did the routine duties of adjutant but also had the responsibility of instructing trainee officers and NCOs, who would become AAF flying personnel. There were, of course, regular airmen and other personnel on the staff, in charge of whom was the Station Commander, 'Tubby" Mermagen. He was a great character, completely unflappable, and quite awe-inspiring to the likes of lesser-mortals like me. In the evening or on a dining in night, he was always impeccably dressed and would drink all night without batting an eyelid until he passed out and was carried to his room by his faithful batman! Even 'In Vino Veritas' he looked dignified without a hair of his head ruffled, and what was more, next day he was bright as a button.

Summer Camp

The Squadron's annual summer camp in 1939 was actually a prelude to war. None of us would be out of uniform for the next six years. Many would not survive for one year, let alone six. The summer camp concerned was at Abbotsinch, near Glasgow, which was the home base of 602 Squadron, another Auxiliary unit which was holding summer camp elsewhere.

607 Squadron summer camp, 1939, Abbotsinch. All pictured are pilots, from right to left: Stuart Parnell, J.B.W. Humpherson, Francis Blackadder, Harry Radcliffe, Harry Welford, unidentified, Lancelot Smith (CO), Jim Bazin, George White, Peter Dixon, Monty Thompson and Tony Forster.

We pilots flew our machines up there while the ground crews were transported by road in advance of our arrival, erecting tents and marquees for servicing and messing facilities. The Gladiators took off in squadron formation and were a sight to be proud of, while we trainees followed in our Avro Tutors, in open order, led by the instructors. I was very proud to be flying solo on the longest cross-country I had done, although I was following the leading instructors and just wished that some of my fancied girlfriends could see me now!

In May 1939, I was commissioned into AAF as a Pilot Officer, and called to full-time service on 24 August 1939. In October, I completed my Service Flying Training and then went to 6 OTU at Sutton Bridge to learn how to fly Hurricanes. There we became familiar with all aspects of our Hurricanes and concentrated on aerobatics and more unconventional versions of them to avoid enemy attacks. We also did a lot of formation and simulated attacks and fighter tactics. A favourite exercise was to go up in pairs with an experienced pilot and then he would tell you over the R/T to follow him in all the manoeuvres he carried out. He aimed to lose you, and generally did, then got on your tail and the situation was reversed. Afterwards you discussed the different tactics of defence and attack, and the instructor would then advise you according to his experience.

The Harvard and Hurricane

Having previously only flown biplanes with fixed-pitch airscrews and no flaps, I required instruction on these additional facilities. I was therefore given dual instruction in a Harvard aircraft, which had most of the Hurricane's refinements, but not all, and nowhere near the power of its 1,280-HP Rolls-Royce Merlin engine. It was in the air when I started worrying how, in the name of heaven, I was going to get this thing called a Hurricane down again. I did a few manoeuvres and a couple of circuits, got my wheels and flaps down, my God how the speed dropped and how the attitude changed! I was coming down too steeply, I opened the throttle and she assumed a more gentle, engine-assisted, approach. I touched down and throttled back but then realised that I had not got much more aerodrome to pull up in. Hell, I was on the ground and intended to stay there. It being a grass airfield, I did not roll too far but far enough even with judicious braking to be just short of chopping the far hedge with my propeller. Nobody worried very much because I was sent off formation flying for the very next trip the same day.

607 Squadron pilots at Usworth immediately before participating in the Battle of France. From left to right: Harry Radcliffe, Robert Pumphrey, Jim Bazin, J.B.W. Humpherson, unidentified, Dudley Craig, Joe Kayll, Alan Glover and Tony 'Nit' Whitty.

Practising dog-fights at OTU

At Sutton Bridge we were converted to operational aircraft and became familiar with them in all aspects of flying, concentrating on aerobatics and more unconventional versions of them to avoid enemy fighter attacks. We also did a lot of formation and simulated attacks and fighter tactics. A favourite exercise was to go up in pairs with an experienced pilot and then he would tell you over the R/T to follow him in all the manoeuvres he carried out to avoid you. He generally could lose you, then he got on your tail and you tried to shake him off. Afterwards you discussed the different aspects of attack and defence, and the instructor would advise you according to his experience.

Six hours on Hurricanes and ready for combat

After six hours on Hurricanes, some of us were detailed to stand by to be flown over to France to replace some of the losses which our Squadrons were suffering out there, including 607. A Rapide and a Bombay were already on the aerodrome to take us when another signal came through cancelling the flight. This was 6 June 1940, when the capitulation of the French was about to take place. Anyhow, we resumed our training until 15 June.

A new posting and a chance to meet old friends

I was posted to 607 Squadron, which had returned to Usworth, our Home Station. I was very happy to be posted to 607, and better still to be with them re-forming at our Home Station where we could renew our contacts and relationships with our old friends and family. The sad thing was the gaps in the ranks of those lost out in France and coming across from Dunkirk. Of the twenty or so pilots that I knew, six were killed later; my cousin was shot down over France and captured; another, Peter Dixon, was shot down near Dunkirk and managed to get to one of the 'Little Ships' on the troop evacuation run when it received a direct hit and everyone was lost. Later, information is that he was shot down and descended by parachute into the sea. He was picked up and taken to a Dunkirk hospital where he died of his injuries.

Francis Blackadder and 'A' Flight

I had the choice of which Flight I should go to and naturally chose 'A', as the Flight Commander was Francis Blackadder, as he was the friendliest, acting like a 'Dutch Uncle' in my earlier days in the Squadron.

'A' Flight of 607 Squadron pictured at Tangmere in September 1940; from left: Sgt Anderson and F/Sgt Atkin (armourers); Sgts R.A. Spyer and W.G. Cunnington, Fort (Engine Fitter), and A.C. Ventham (Rigger), Flt Lt W.F. Blackadder (Flight Commander), Fg Off M.M. Irving, Plt Off Watson (Intelligence Officer), and Plt Off M.R. Ingle-Finch.

As we were both rugby players he got me in the AAF team. Anyhow, that was my choice, but it was a disappointment that my best friend, Stuart Parnall, went into 'B' Flight – because it would mean not only that our Squadron activities would be divided but also our time off. Stuart had flown Gladiators in Norway and was pretty pleased to be back in one piece. He was one of the world's natural gentlemen. He'd had a public-school education and I think gone to university, was several years older than me but despite his extensive experience never treated us in any way other than equals. One could not have chosen a better companion or friend, either in the service or out. Back at Usworth there were two other newcomers to 607 Squadron, namely Bob Lauder and Scotty Lenahan. We all became good friends, though sadly not for long.

The first big encounter with the enemy
One Thursday we were to have a big encounter with the enemy, our first. And one considered on a par with the sort of attacks experienced by 11 and

12 Groups in the south. It was 15 August 1940 and at 1230 hrs we were going off duty for twenty-four hours when the whole Squadron was called to Readiness. We heard from the Group Operations Room that there was a big 'flap' on, that is a warning of imminent enemy action along the NE coast. We waited out at dispersal points, at "Flights", for half an hour, then scrambled in squadron formation.

I was in a feverish state of excitement and quickly took off and climbed up to our operational height of 20,000 feet ready to patrol the coast. We kept receiving messages over the R/T of forty or fifty plus "Bogeys" approaching Newcastle from the north. Although we patrolled for over half an hour, we never saw a thing. Just as I was expecting the order to "Pancake", I heard the senior flight commander shout "Tally Ho!", and "Tally Ho" it was! There on our port side at 9,000 feet must have been 120 bombers, all with swastikas and German crosses as large as life, having the gross impertinence to cruise down Northumberland and Durham's NE coast. These were the people who were going to bomb Newcastle and Sunderland and our loved ones, friends and relations who lived there.

I chased a Heinkel and filled that poor devil with lead

I'd never seen anything like it. They were in two groups, one of about 70 and the other about 40, like two swarms of bees. There was no time to wait and we took up position and delivered No 3 attacks in sections. As only three machines at a time, in formation, attacked a line of 20 bombers, I just couldn't see how their gunners could miss us. We executed our attack, however, and despite the fact that I thought it was me being hit all over the place, it was their machines that started dropping out of the sky. In my excitement, during the next attack I only narrowly missed one of our own machines while doing a "split arse" breakaway – there couldn't have been more than two feet between us! Eventually, spotting most of the enemy aircraft dropping down with only their undercarriages damaged, I chased a *Heinkel* and filled that poor devil with lead until first one, then the other engine stopped. I then enjoyed the sadistic satisfaction of watching the bomber crash into the sea. With the one I reckoned to have damaged during our first attack, these were my first bloods, and so I was naturally as elated as anything. The Squadron suffered no losses, but claimed six He 111s and two Do 17s destroyed, five He 111s and one Do 17 probably destroyed, and four He 111s and one Do 17 damaged, although we now know that in fact there were no Do 17s amongst the German formation.

Resuming author's commentary:-

The attack on northern England by 15 August 1940 became known as the '*Junkers* Party' by the RAF, 'Black Thursday' by the *Luftwaffe*. While certainly the size of this raid was comparable to those being made on southern England, there was one significant difference: owing to the distance involved, the escorting enemy fighters were Me 110s – usually no match for a Spitfire or Hurricane; there were no Me 109s involved. 607 Squadron, like many other units, would soon take a turn in 11 Group and find how traumatic the increased tempo of operations was – entirely because of the Me 109.

Harry continues:-

'I shall always remember 8 September 1940, because this was the day after the evening that Betty Elise and I became engaged, but our move to Tangmere, in 11 Group, was confirmed that day. We were to relieve 43 Squadron, whose CO, "Tubby" Badger, had been shot down earlier in September, and since which time the Squadron had been led by Flight Lieutenant Tom Morgan. Now, barely half the original complement of pilots was capable of operational duties.

'Of course it was a tragedy so far as Betty was concerned but, though I felt the same, there was a war to be fought and we were trained fighter pilots. This was the beginning of the end, and as we all climbed into our Hurricanes having bid our 'adieus' that fine September day, I wondered how many of us would see Usworth or Newcastle again. Strange as it may seem,

Pilot Officer George Drake's Hurricane P2728: Missing in Action for 32 years.

Pilot Officer George Drake: the first missing Battle of Britain pilot to be recovered post-war.

dirty, smoky, old Newcastle was to us seventh heaven when compared with the rolling green fields of southern England.

'We arrived, however, at a completely blitzed aerodrome where we were greeted by the remnants of 43 Squadron, some on crutches, others with an arm in a sling, and yet another who had had his face torn apart by an exploding cannon shell, with a head swathed in bandages. Though they had suffered so many casualties it was quite amazing to see them walking about. Needless to say they were very pleased to see us, having just been up on the third sortie that day, and were still waiting for news of the latest casualties.

'We only had time to refuel when we were called out on an operational trip that evening. There was no interception, however, and no casualties. The next morning, to my great disappointment, I was not called upon to fly and later the Squadron went off. In the event I was the more fortunate, as of twelve Hurricanes *six* were shot down. Three officers were killed and three sergeants wounded. Amongst the casualties were Stuart Parnall, my best friend, Scotty and the young South African George Drake. They were all lovely people, just like Alex Obelenski and "Ching" Mackenzie, with whom I would have flown to hell, if necessary, in glorious comradeship.'

Again, resuming author's commentary:-

With little experience, 607 Squadron had arrived at one of the 'hottest' sector stations at an extremely busy time. Without time to adjust to the new operational conditions, it was inevitable that the lethal 109s would harshly treat the 'County of Durham' Hurricanes. Yet again, this RAF squadron, new to the fray, went on patrol flying the useless vic formation, and paid the price. As ever, the 109s had the advantage of height, sun, and used the excellent *schwarm* tactical formation. This divided each *Staffel* into three sections of four aircraft in line abreast, the aircraft well spread out so there was no fear of collision, enabling the pilots to search the sky for the enemy. In the event of combat, the *Schwarm* would split into two fighting pairs of leader and wingman, the *Rotte*, so the fundamental principles were both flexibility and mutual support.

Harry goes on:-

'Somehow we could not believe it. No one talked about it and we all hoped for news to filter through from some remote pub or perhaps a hospital. No news came, so we hardened ourselves to the worst: "Killed in Action". We bit back our tears and our sorrow. It was "You heard about Stuart and Scotty? Rotten luck, wasn't it?" Someone would add, "And young George, bloody good blokes all of them." After that epitaph, the matter would be dismissed with the ordering of another round of drinks to avoid any trace of further sentiment.'

The remains of Pilot Officer George Drake, killed on that fateful interception on 9 September 1940, were not found until recovered by aviation archaeology enthusiasts in 1972. Harry wrote to me about George on 11 July 1995:-

'Yes, I knew George Drake, but only for a very short time. He came as a replacement to 607 at Usworth during the reformation after the losses in France... I think he was in "B" Flight, but my concern was more with my contemporaries Stuart Parnall and Scotty Lenahan. George Drake always seemed to me very young, with a boyish open face, but beneath the surface was latent belligerence. He had a constant inquiring mind and seemed much interested in how the other half, we Brits, lived. No bad thing as he would expect to be amongst us for some time. I don't remember any particular incident but a feeling was that he was too young to be thrown into battle. I think he was barely out of his teens, but then so were others; perhaps less so, though, on auxiliary squadrons. I was in "A" Flight first, then transferred to "B" Flight as I wanted to be with my friends, Stuart and Scotty. When we moved to Tangmere, I was not selected to fly on the operation on 9 September 1940, when we lost six out of twelve: Stuart, Scotty and George killed, and three sergeant pilots who survived. Experience counted for little. It still hurts to talk about it.'

Losses did, in fact, often especially affect auxiliary personnel, given that these units, in which nepotism was rife, were all locally raised, old school and family friends, business associates and family members consequently serving together. Casualties, understandably therefore, had a most depressing effect on these units.

By 17 September 1940, 23-year-old Pilot Officer Harry Welford was a veteran. On that day 'B' Flight scrambled at 1505 hrs on the squadron's fourth sortie of the day, Harry flying Blue 2. On this occasion,

Above and below: Pilot Officer Franek Surma (left) and Flight Lieutenant Charles Bowen playing 'pax' at Tangmere, September 1940. Both would be reported 'Missing in Action' in due course. Note that Bowen is wearing a highly prized German fighter pilot's *schwimmweste*, a superior life preserver to the RAF's 'Mae West'.

six Hurricanes patrolled the Biggin Hill/Gravesend line at 17,000 feet. Between 1500 and 1600 hrs, a multi-wave enemy fighter sweep crossed the south coast, each wave comprising two *Gruppen* of Me 109s (some sixty fighters). Suddenly 'B' Flight was bounced from above and behind, as Harry remembered in notes accompanying a letter dated 6 February 1992:-

'When attacked we were warned to break formation. I broke and took evasive action, as a result of which I lost the Squadron. As we had instructions to re-form rather than fly alone, I saw a large group of fighters ahead, which I then intended to join up with until I realised that they were Me 109s! I fired a quick burst at them, but an unseen 109 fired at me and hit my air intake with a cannon shell. I did a quick flick roll that dropped me below cloud. No 109s about but a lone Hurricane that guarded my tail as I force-landed. The engine had seized and looking down I saw a field in which I thought I could land. As I approached, glycol and smoke streamed from the engine. When I opened the hood, these fumes were sucked through the cockpit and impaired my vision. The field was actually smaller than I thought, but there was a wattle fence that acted like a carrier's arrester hook. The plane then skidded across the second field but was brought to an abrupt halt by a tree at the far end, cracking my head on the reflector sight. Blood poured down my face, and thinking that the plane might catch fire I undid my straps and jumped out, only to fall flat on my face because my leg, which had been wounded by shrapnel, collapsed on me. Two farm workers rushed over and picked me up, putting me on a section of wattle fence. They told me that there was a German plane in the next field with the pilot in it, very dead. I regret now that I declined their offer to show me, but at the time I felt pretty dicky.

'In hospital I gave my report to our flight commander, Flight Lieutenant Jim Bazin, who acknowledged that I had shot down the 109 in the field next to where my Hurricane crashed. Now, however, I am not so sure as we have not been able to identity a potential candidate from the German crashes that day. Anyway, I was thereafter in hospital for a while with "Tubby" Badger, 43 Squadron's former CO, who was very brave, always laughing. Sadly, he ultimately succumbed to his wounds, which was a great shame, as he was a fine man.'

Research into this combat suggests that Harry was shot down by *Hauptmann* Eduard Neumann, *Gruppenkommandeur* of I/JG 27. 'Edu's' logbook, a copy of which he kindly sent me on 6 December 1991, confirms that he shot down two

Hurricanes during this action, the other probably being 607 Squadron's Sergeant Landesdell, who was killed. Neumann was very experienced, having fought in the Spanish Civil War, and later became *Kommodore* of JG 27, which went to North Africa in 1941. There, one of Neumann's pilots became one of the most incredibly successful fighter pilots of all time: Hans-Joachim Marseille, the 'Star of Africa'. Ultimately, Neumann's personal victory tally was thirteen, and he later became leader of the German fighter forces in Italy. As Harry said, 'A distinguished chap, then. Doesn't make me feel so bad about being shot down!'

On 15 December 1988, Harry wrote:-

'I reckon my score in the Battle was three or four, all bombers, though when I was shot down I had fired a burst at some 109s and it was said, by the farm workers who picked me from my crash, that a 109 had come down in the next field with the pilot very dead. Not confirmed.'

Harry really finished his own story in the letter of 25 June 1988:-

'As a result of my "accident" (shot down!) I lost my operational flying category and went into Training Command as an instructor. I got married

To Dilip *"Nachromia! Harry Welford*

Flight Lieutenant Harry Welford (extreme right) while flying Spitfire Mk IXs in 1944 with 220 Squadron.

Harry Welford (right) pictured with 607 Squadron stalwarts Wing Commander Francis Blackadder OBE and Wing Commander Joe Kyall OBE DSO DFC, at Durham Cathedral on 14 November 1993.

and did three years until I was Acting Squadron Leader Instructor, by which time I volunteered for operations again. I lost my rank confirmation and after retraining got posted as flight lieutenant to 220 Squadron on Spitfires and Tempests, in Belgium, Holland and Germany, until the end of the war in Europe. I was posted to India, but as my demobilisation category was due it was sadly cancelled, though by then, after six years of war, we were heartily sick of it. I did try to get a Permanent Commission but was turned down.'

Harry became an engineer, settling in Sidmouth, Devon, from where he often travelled to attend my various events; he died at home on 6 October 1996, having been looking forward to attending the launch of *Bader's Tangmere Spitfires* at Worcester Guildhall the following week. Sadly, it was not to be.

Chapter Twenty-Two

Flight Lieutenant William Walker AE
Spitfire Pilot

Early on, I developed an interest in 616 'South Yorkshire' Squadron of the AAF, again owing to my research into the history of Spitfire R6644. The squadron's ORB, however, is poor, providing scant detail of flights, making it impossible to identify individual aircraft. The only way forward, therefore, was to compile a list of pilots known to have served with the units between the dates this Spitfire was on charge, and trace survivors, requesting a check of their logbooks – should, indeed, that all-important document also survive. Amongst these men was one William Louis Buchanan Walker, who responded to my inquiry on 24 March 1988:-

'I have checked my log book but can find no record of having flown R6644. I notice that I flew several very adjacent numbers, R6633, R6696 and

R6693, but "your" plane is absent. This may be because the plane was in "B" Flight whilst I was in "A", but this is only a guess.'

Nonetheless, this fired up further voluminous correspondence over many years and another enduring friendship. On 20 April 1988, William wrote, 'Thank you for the photograph of Donald Smith's grave, which I shall add to my album. He was such a nice chap and a very good pilot. It is sad that the best pilots seemed to get killed while the hams like myself survived. They were exhilarating days but one lost so many good friends, who were all so young.

'You are quite right, the picture of me sitting in a Spitfire was taken at Brize Norton when I was training on Harvards – and at that time I hardly dared to think that I might actually fly one! The machine had come out of the Maintenance Unit on the aerodrome and was on the forecourt awaiting delivery to a squadron.'

On 2 January 1995:-

'I am sending you herewith my account of those early days of the war… which will enlighten you as to how we lived, hoped and worked.'

Greatly assisted by William's discovery of an old wartime diary, extracts from that account are reproduced below:-

'I joined the RAFVR at Kidlington on 2 September 1938, whilst working at Oxford (for Hall's Brewery). The age limit for enlistment was twenty-five. I was actually over twenty-five but fortunately had sent in my application a few days before my birthday and was accepted largely, I suspect, because of an acute shortage of volunteers. I was pupil No 26 and do not think we ever exceeded thirty pupils whilst I was there. I remember my Instructor saying that it was a very lucky number, being twice thirteen – as a survivor, I think his prediction was about right! I was enrolled as an AC2 but because no airman below the rank of sergeant was allowed to fly an aircraft I was promoted to sergeant the following day.

'With so few pilots to train, the instructors had very little to do during the week so I used to travel to the aerodrome during my lunch hour and have a lesson before returning to work. It was during one of these visits that I made my first solo, on 28 September 1938, in a Magister, the day the Royal Navy was mobilised. The following day Mr Neville Chamberlain, our Prime Minister, returned from Munich after his meeting with Daladier, Hitler and Mussolini. After landing at Croydon he waved his piece of paper signed by himself and Hitler, agreeing never to go to war. Had my patriotic response been premature? No matter, I wished to fly and the RAF were teaching me for free and I was enjoying all the delights of a private flying club and the company of several other enthusiasts.

'In October 1938, my company moved me to Romford and I was posted to the flying school at Stapleford Abbotts, where I continued my training on Tiger Moths, which was a sheer delight. Sadly, this tranquil and pleasant existence was to end rather abruptly with the invasion of Poland, and at the outbreak of war on 1 September 1939 I was called up. I duly reported to the RAFVR HQ in Store Street, just off the Tottenham Court Road, and was immediately sent home to await further orders. On 13 November, I received a telegram with orders to report to the Railway Transport Officer at Liverpool Street Station, 1100 hrs, 15 November, fully kitted, carrying kitbag for posting, signed No 1 London Town Centre. I duly reported and learned that my destination was Cambridge. On arrival we were met by an officer and a couple of sergeants and we marched to Pembroke College where I and many others were to be billeted. After my first RAF meal at 1500 hrs, which consisted of sausage and chips and a sort of custard pudding, we were allocated rooms.

'My room, which had been stripped of all furniture, carpets and curtains, was on the top floor of a block forming the quadrangle of the College. I shared the room with "Wimpy" Wodehouse who was later to join 616 Squadron with me but was sadly killed when he crashed during night-flying training in a Spitfire. We were issued with a thirty-inch iron bedstead, four RAF issue blankets and a paillasse which was a bit short of straw – but I had observed an old sofa in the passage with a rather dirty cushion which I used to supplement the straw, and this at least avoided lying directly on springs.

'The winter of 1939 was particularly severe and snow lay several inches thick. There was no heating in the block and keeping warm was a problem. Washing involved a walk across the quadrangle

Pilot Officer William Walker of the RAFVR in 1940.

in the blackout. My diary reminds me that on my first sortie into Cambridge I purchased a torch and a can for collecting shaving water. These modest purchases went some way to improve a way of life!

'Some airmen had been at Cambridge for several weeks and we learnt that the food at Pembroke was considered better than at some other colleges, that life was quite pleasant and the average stay was five to eight weeks. Tea at 1800 hrs consisted of soup, eggs and chips, and an apple. There were still a few undergraduates at the College and they arrived for their dinner as we were leaving the dining hall. After tea, Sergeant "Potts" Wood, who later killed himself, and Sergeant Wallis, when they crashed in a Harvard at Brize Norton while "beating up" the home of a girlfriend, and I went into town for a few beers. To leave the College you booked out at the Porter's Lodge, now called the "Fire Picket". You were given a number which you had to repeat upon returning, to be booked in. We returned soon after 2100 hrs to what promised to be a very cold night. I put my greatcoat, pullover and all my clothes over the blankets in an endeavour to keep warm. So ended my first day on active service.'

For the new recruits, life continued in a round of ground lectures on various subjects connected with service life, drill and route marches. On 8 January, William received 'Great news: I heard this evening that I have been posted to Brize Norton together with "Rubbergoods" Thorogood, Wodehouse, Potts and a couple of others. We are due to go on the 31st. This is grand as Brize Norton is close to Oxford, which I know well. As most airmen have been posted to the north of England or Scotland I count myself very lucky... After two weeks of great expectancy and living in dread that our posting would be cancelled, we set off on a cold morning, 17 February 1940, with several inches of snow, for Brize Norton. The train journey was notable for its length. We left Cambridge at 0930 hrs and eventually arrived at Oxford, where we had a meal at mid-day, and finally reached the aerodrome at 1700 hrs. We were put in quarters which did not come up to our expectations at all. Before we left, we heard that we would get bedrooms with central heating, hot and cold water and good messing. We were sadly disillusioned. We sleep in a wooden hut which is heated with one combustion stove in the centre. There are four of us in the hut, "Rubbergoods" Thorogood, Doug Ward, McClure, and I. After about two days, however, we have settled in and our hut is quite comfortable and homely. The messing arrangements are appalling as the Sergeants' Mess is hopelessly overcrowded. The reason being that Brize Norton was an officers' flying school and very few

The result of Pilot Officer Walker's first night solo!

sergeants were trained there. Consequently, the Officers' Mess is enormous and the Sergeants' Mess very small. However, with a sense of humour we are muddling through.

'I am put on Harvards which pleases me a lot as nearly everybody wanted to go on single-engined aircraft. The course (No 45) was virtually split in half between Harvards for fighter training and Oxfords for bomber training. The weather is appalling with much snow and the aerodrome has been unserviceable for several days. We have still done no flying to date (Thursday 22 February 1940) but we are still hoping! Great excitement today. I actually sat in a Harvard and started it. Not a very difficult manoeuvre but after so many months at Cambridge any sort of contact with a plane is a thrill. There are a great many planes around as this is also a maintenance unit, and I have seen Blenheims, Lysanders and Wellingtons. The course is scheduled to last ten weeks but this may vary according to the state of the war. After five days I feel like I have been here for weeks and Cambridge seems very far behind. I think I will like it here although the work promises to keep us busy.

'23 February 1940 I had my first flight of forty-five minutes in a Harvard, with Pilot Officer Marsh as instructor. This embraced taxying, take-off, effect of controls, straight and level flying, stalling, climbing, gliding and landings. Flying Harvards, which was one of the noisiest planes and must be most irksome to local residents, was sheer delight and a real uplift from Magisters and Tiger Moths. We had several rugby matches which relieved the tension and, of course, I made full use of the squash court which adjoined the Officers' Mess. The lectures were interesting and extremely well presented. My greatest problem was the Morse Code: although I achieved a pass mark I never really mastered it.

'I had my first ever night flight of forty-five minutes on 30 March 1940 with Flight Sergeant Holman as instructor, and after a further forty-five-minute flight with Flight Lieutenant Sykes on 1 April, I was despatched on my first solo night flight. I took off into complete darkness after leaving the flare path. There were no ground lights due to the wartime blackout and there was no moon. I must have become completely disorientated and in a matter of minutes I crashed into a field. The plane was utterly smashed but by some miracle of fate my starboard wing had hit the ground with such force (around 200 mph) that the entire engine had broken away from its mounting and had spun off to finish some distance away. This had not only saved my life but had prevented the aircraft from catching fire. I climbed out of what remained of the cockpit and walked with my parachute across several fields back to the aerodrome and into the locker room where several pilots were hanging about as all night flying had been abandoned. They were completely surprised when I walked in as they were certain that I had "bought it" as several ambulances and vehicles had been despatched to find the wreckage and bring back my remains, if any. Somebody produced a flask of whisky and suggested that I must need it, but I said "Better not, in case somebody smells my breath." I scarcely had a scratch and no bones were broken. I then returned to the Mess and went to bed.

'The following morning, I was given a medical check-up which revealed nothing untoward and was told to report to the Chief Flying Officer, Squadron Leader Jarman, in his office. It was with some apprehension that I approached his office in the Control Tower having just smashed up one of his £10,000 Harvard aircraft. I noticed several instructors with him as I entered. He greeted me with a smile and said "Let me rub your back – you have a charmed life." He then asked if I wanted to go on extended leave but I said I wanted to continue the course. He said I could do this so long as I appreciated that the crash was due to my error and there were no funny little men playing about with the controls, and added that he could replace planes but pilots were in short supply. I was then given many hours in the Link Trainer and another 3.50 hours dual night-flying before being allowed to go solo at night again. This occurred on 9 May, when I made two landings with the plane unbroken! In retrospect it was probably rather crazy to send me solo after only ninety minutes night flying but as many other pilots had about the same night tuition and flew without mishap, I must have been slow to adapt to this alien environment. My spectacular crash was to benefit one enterprising airman in the Photographic Section who photographed the crash and sold postcards for sixpence a card, making quite a sum.

'My course continued without any further major mishap. My log book reveals that I failed a Navigation Test on 25 March 1940 but passed it two days later. On 17 April, I passed the Group Commander's Flying Test and an Instrument Flying Test. On 25 April I was awarded my "wings" and commissioned as a pilot officer. I was posted to 616 Squadron at Leconfield, arriving on 18 June 1940. Wimpy Wodehouse and I were commissioned together and shared a room at Leconfield. His death was very tragic. During August we were both flying Spitfires at night when he suddenly dived straight into the ground and was killed. Another friend from Cambridge and Brize Norton, Sergeant Walsh, who also joined 616 Squadron at the same time as me, was practising "dog-fighting" during August when he suddenly spun-in from a steep turn at 5,000 feet. He failed to recover from the spin, hit the ground and was killed.

'I did have two further night crashes, in Spitfires, at Leconfield which the Squadron records charitably referred to as "heavy landings". It is also of interest that when I was at Turnhouse, flying Lysanders, I was given a night vision test which I failed!

'Looking back to the time when so many of us on Course No 45 had such high hopes and felt invulnerable it is terribly sad that some would not survive a year, would never see the enemy and all their hard work and training should prove fruitless. Whilst they were just casualties of war in the records they are a reminder to me of many happy days of friendship that are well worth recalling and should be remembered.'

On 25 January 1995, William wrote more about his experiences at Leconfield:-

'Soon after arrival, I was told to report to the Squadron Commander, Squadron Leader Marcus Robinson, who asked me what aircraft I had flown. I told him that I had flown Magisters, Tiger Moths and Harvards, whereupon he said that he could not allow me to fly a Spitfire until I had flown some other operational plane. The only plane available was the Fairey Battle bomber which was abandoned at the airfield but was kept serviceable. Flying Officer "Teddy" St Aubyn was detailed to instruct me thereon and we walked over to the plane which was dispersed on the far side of the aerodrome. As we approached I saw

Spitfire Mk I Spitfires of 616 Squadron at Leconfield in early 1940.

that the plane seemed very large, much bigger than a Spitfire, and far larger than any plane I had previously flown. Teddy showed me the instruments as he sat in the cockpit and then told me to climb into the rear seat which was some distance back and where the navigator/bomb aimer would normally sit. From this position it was, of course, not possible to see what the pilot was doing. He made a couple of landings then climbed out and told me to take over. I climbed in and taxied the elderly aircraft across the field, noticing that the large wings seemed to flap slightly as we covered the uneven field. Having reached the far edge of the field, I turned into wind and opened the throttle. The plane very gradually gathered speed and eventually reached about 90 mph and I became airborne. I climbed to about 1,000 feet and flew around feeling most elated having succeeded in getting the plane into the air. The plane handled well and it was really exciting to feel it responding to the controls. To see the large wings dipping and rising as I banked was a wonderful new experience and a cherished memory. I made two landings, whereupon I was ordered to instruct Sergeant Walsh. I showed him the instruments and he climbed into the rear seat. I did two more take-offs and landings before sending him solo!

'The following day, 23 June 1940, I flew a Spitfire Mk I on my first solo. During the following week I flew a total of eighteen hours on Spitfires doing various exercises such as cloud flying, camera gun practice,

The Three Musketeers: Fg Offs Jack Bell and Teddy St Aubyn with Plt Off William Walker immediately before taking off for Kenley on 19 August 1940. Only William would survive the war.

formation flying, sector reconnaissance etc. On 1 July, I was detailed to do a practice "battle climb" with an operational pilot and another pilot also under training. It was a glorious summer day with splendid visibility and we climbed to 20,000 feet. It was sheer joy to be flying such a lovely aircraft in such beautiful conditions with the English landscape spread out far below.

'Suddenly, a message came over our radio to inform us that a "bandit" was in the area and we were given a course to steer in order to make contact. This was the first possible encounter with the enemy since the Squadron had arrived at Leconfield and our leader was in no mind to inform Ground Control that he was flying with two non-operational pilots. We all opened our throttles and set off on the course given. I was flying a Mk I Spitfire which was rather slower than the others and I was soon left behind. After a few minutes I saw them well ahead, attacking a Do 17. I had never fired the guns, apart from camera-gun practice, and had no idea what to expect, but I turned the firing button on the joystick to "Fire". When I eventually reached the enemy plane the other two pilots had vanished. I closed in with the Dornier well in my gunsight and pressed the button hard. I could see tracer bullets hitting the plane which suddenly caught fire and spiralled down, crashing into the North Sea. It was a moment of considerable elation and excitement. I then returned to base and taxied to our dispersal. I jumped out and went to our Flight Office where the Intelligence Officer was awaiting my report. I recounted the events I have just described and had almost finished when the Flight Sergeant came in and said "Excuse me Sir, but did you know that your guns were not loaded?" This announcement was a very sad anti-climax to a remarkable morning. My plane had been used for camera-gun practice and had not been re-armed – nor was there new film fitted to the camera-gun. I then realised that the tracer bullets which I had seen were not from my guns but from the Dornier firing at me. The other two pilots had obviously hit the plane before I arrived but the fire did not start until after my arrival. The story of my "kill" remained the subject of much hilarity at my expense for quite a while. Nevertheless, it was still a thrill to hear on the radio that our aircraft had shot down a raider in the North Sea that morning. As an aside, I had been made operational after nineteen hours on Spitfires!!'

Flying from Leconfield, 616 Squadron was involved in the 'Junkers Party', the action fought off the north-east coast on 15 August 1940. On that occasion the Germans had not expected to find Spitfires and Hurricanes so far north, wrongly believing that all available single-engine fighters must have already been committed to battle in the south. From the aerodromes in Norway, from whence these raiders came, England lay beyond the range of the Me 109, so consequently escort was provided by Me 110s. The latter proved inadequate to the task, however, and the Germans took a beating, so much so in fact that the *Luftwaffe* never again tried to attack the north in daylight. 616 Squadron engaged fifty bombers and a gaggle of 110s at 15,000 feet, ten miles off Flamborough Head. Subsequently, eight bombers were claimed as destroyed, four probably destroyed and two damaged, all for no loss. The absence of Me 109s, however, gave the inexperienced defenders a false impression of air fighting – soon to change, drastically.

On 19 August 1940, 616 Squadron flew south to Kenley Sector Station, in 11 Group. Only the previous day Kenley had been hit hard, and so the Station bore little resemblance to the formal and orderly environment left behind by 616 at Leconfield. On 23 November 1994, William remembered:-

'The early days of war were interesting in so far as we were so unprepared for what was to come. It is my lasting regret that I did not have more operational training – trying to pick it up with the Squadron straight from flying school was a pretty haphazard affair.

'The Mess at Kenley was a rather sombre building and far removed from the modern, light and cheerful Mess at Leconfield. Kenley bore many scars as witness to damage and loss of life caused by enemy action.

An atmosphere of purpose prevailed and we found ourselves having to respond to a life of far greater activity than at Leconfield where only a few minor raids had disrupted our existence.'

Three days later, the squadron experienced its first clash with the enemy whilst operating from Kenley: Green Section was bounced over Dover by a *Staffel* of JG 51's Me 109s. Within seconds Pilot Officer Hugh 'Cocky' Dundas was taking to his parachute, his Spitfire in flames, and a cannon shell damaged Pilot Officer Lionel 'Buck' Casson's fighter. Sergeant Wareing, however, claimed a 109 destroyed in the resulting skirmish.

On 25 August 1940, 616 Squadron was vectored to intercept a raid comprising twenty Do 17s escorted by a *Gruppe* of Me 109s. Before reaching the bombers, the Spitfires were bounced and broken up by the 109s. Sergeant Westmoreland was killed and Sergeant Wareing was 'Missing' (later reported as a prisoner). In response, the auxiliaries claimed two enemy aircraft destroyed and a probable.

William Walker:-

'We were very unsure of ourselves at this time. Everything happened so quick, and of course our formations of vics and lines astern were all wrong. There was so little information available to us. Very little was passed on by those squadrons that were relieved as they just couldn't wait to get the hell out of the place! Fighting in the south, where the 109s always seemed to have the advantage of height and sun, was very different indeed to chasing after unescorted bombers up north.'

That having been said, 616 Squadron's initiation was not as brutal as experienced by some unfortunate squadrons. Studying the casualty lists, every now and again a squadron suddenly appears and suffers a far greater number of losses than the average. Inevitably, if one delves a little deeper, this invariably occurred when the squadron in question met Me 109s in strength for the first time. The period of adjustment to the infinitely fiercer tempo of combat can, therefore, only be described as traumatic.

26 August 1940 was a traumatic day for William, who sent me an account of those events on 23 November 1994:-

'It was still dark when the Orderly awoke me with a cup of tea at 0330 hrs that morning, just two days after my twenty-seventh birthday, which had

Sgt Marmaduke Ridley, pictured at Leconfield with Fg Off Jack Bell. On 26 August 1940, Ridley was shot down and killed over Dover by *Hauptmann* 'Joschko' Fözoe, *Staffelkapitän* of 4/JG51.

passed unnoticed amid the current level of activity and excitement. I drank my tea slowly and gradually awakened to another day. It seemed such a short while since we had been "stood down" the previous evening at about 2100 hrs, and after which a few beers refreshed our spirits before bed. However, I dressed and went down to breakfast, always a quiescent occasion at the unearthly hour of 0400! The sound of aero engines could be heard in the distance, indicating that the groundcrews were already busy. One was so accustomed to the drone of engines that it passed almost unnoticed amid the clatter of cups and plates.

'Following breakfast, I joined other pilots outside the Mess. We all climbed aboard a lorry and were driven to dispersal, to remain at "Readiness", where a hut and a few tents constituted the Squadron's base. A few days earlier the Duke of Kent had actually paid us a visit at our modest location to wish us well.

'That day I was allocated Spitfire R6633, and was to fly in Yellow Section led by Flying Officer Teddy St Aubyn, a former Guards officer. The plane stood within fifty yards of our hut and so I walked over and placed my parachute in the cockpit with the straps spread apart and ready for wearing immediately I jumped in. Two of the groundcrew stood by the plane with the starter battery plugged in. I walked back to the hut as the sun rose and added a little warmth to a chilly start. Pilots sat about either reading or exchanging the usual banter that had become routine. We had spent many months in this way, which was now a way of life. At 8 a.m. our second breakfast arrived at dispersal, and was just as fulfilling as our breakfast of four hours earlier: coffee, eggs, bacon, sausages and toast to replenish our undiminished appetites.

'The telephone suddenly rang in the dispersal hut, and a shout went up of "Yellow Section Scramble! Patrol Dungeness/Dover Angels 20!" This sent me running for my Spitfire. I leapt on to the wing and was in the cockpit, parachute strapped on, within seconds. I pressed the starter and the engine fired immediately. The groundcrew removed the plug from the cowling and pulled the remote starter battery clear. I waved the chocks away and taxied the aircraft, following my Section Leader and Sergeant Ridley to the end of the runway for take-off. Within minutes, Yellow Section was airborne. We headed east, climbing quickly and passing through cloud, reached our patrol course in some fifteen to twenty minutes. We flew in a wide formation that day, in fact, and had been airborne for about an hour without sighting an enemy aircraft when suddenly several Me 109s appeared.'

High above and unseen by Yellow Section, however, was the entire JG 51 (about 100 Me 109s), led in person by the *Kommodore*, Major Werner Mölders (the exalted "Father of Modern Air Fighting") on a *geschwader-* strength *freie hunt*. Dropping behind and below the Spitfires, Mölders selected William Walker's Spitfire and attacked from the blind spot:-

'When the 109s hit us, I banked sharply to port, towards a 109, but suddenly my machine was raked with bullets. The one that attacked me did so from below and behind, I never even saw it. The flying controls ceased to respond and a sudden pain in my leg indicated that I had been hit. Baling out seemed to be a sensible option. My two comrades, St Aubyn and Ridley, had both vanished.

'I pulled back the hood and tried to stand up but realised that I had not disconnected the radio lead, which was still plugged in, and had to remove my helmet before I was free to jump. The aircraft was still banking to port, so jumping out was easy, I was still at 20,000 feet and pulled the ripcord immediately. A sudden jerk indicated that all was well and that I was on

Above left: *Hauptmann* Fözoe recounts a successful combat over England.

Above right: *Der Oberkannone*: Major Werner '*Vati*' Mölders, the so-called 'Father of Modern Air Fighting' and Kommodore of JG51 – who shot down Pilot Officer William Walker on 26 August 1940.

my way down. I looked around but could not see a single aircraft. Below there was 10/10ths cloud. I had no idea where I was. It seemed to take ages to reach the clouds and passing through I realised that I was still over the Channel. Thinking that I would soon land in the sea prompted the thought that I had better remove my heavy flying boots. I did this and let them fall. I watched them spiral down for what seemed like ages and then realised that I was much higher than I thought. I inflated my Mae West and eventually landed in the sea. I easily discarded my parachute and could see the wreck of a ship sticking out of the water a few hundred yards away and swam to it. I reached it and climbed on, sitting there for about half an hour until a fishing boat came alongside and I clambered aboard. I was now extremely cold from my immersion and wet clothes.

'The fishermen gave me a cup of tea, well laced with whisky, as we headed for land. When about two miles offshore, an RAF launch came alongside and I was transferred to it. By this time the tea concoction had worked quite disastrously on my cold stomach. Fortunately there was a loo aboard to which I retired with some relief. I was still enthroned when we reached Ramsgate harbour. An aircraftman kept knocking on the door and enquiring whether I was all right. It was some time before I was able to emerge! I was carried up the steps to a waiting ambulance, by which time quite a crowd had gathered and gave me a cheer as I was put in the ambulance. A kind old lady handed me a packet of cigarettes, so I decided that being shot down was perhaps not such a bad thing after all!'

Yellow Section's Sergeant Marmaduke Ridley had not been so lucky, however: he was dead, having been shot down by *Hauptmann* 'Joschko' Fözoe, *Staffelkapitän* of 4/JG 51. Yellow One, Flying Officer St Aubyn, had been shot down by *Oberleutnant* 'Pips' Priller, *Staffelkapitän* of 6/JG 51. The Spitfire caught fire but the wounded pilot managed to crash-land at Eastchurch. 616 Squadron also suffered other losses, including the death of Pilot Officer Moberley and another pilot wounded.

On 26 August 1940, 616 Squadron had lost seven of the twelve Spitfires flown on operations that day; two pilots were dead and four more wounded. Pilot Officer William Walker was one of the lucky ones. The squadron's Orderly Clerk, clearly a master of the understatement, recorded that it had been 'a very unfortunate engagement'. William summarises the day's events as 'traumatic'. More accurately for the squadron as a whole, they could be described as 'catastrophic'. Since having arrived at Kenley a week previously, seven Spitfires lost, four pilots wounded and four killed.

The following day, whilst in transit between Ramsgate Hospital and RAF Hospital Halton, William Walker stopped off at Kenley to collect his belongings:-

'While there I asked my driver to take me to dispersal so that I could say farewell to any remaining pilots. It proved a sad occasion, however, as the squadron had suffered severe losses and very few pilots actually remained operational.

'It was almost 2200 hrs when we arrived at Halton RAF Hospital, where I was put to bed. Unfortunately, by this late hour, the kitchens had been closed for some hours but a wonderful night nurse produced an equally wonderful and indeed appropriate meal: scrambled eggs!

'After breakfast the following morning, doctors appeared and attended to the officers in my large ward of some 20 beds. Nobody came to see me, however, and apart from getting rather painful, I was beginning to worry about gangrene. The previous 48 hours had been somewhat traumatic to say the least, so my concern was not entirely unjustified!

'At noon the head doctor, a group captain, did his rounds. As he passed my bed he asked what I was in for. I told him that I had a bullet in my leg.

He said "Oh yes, and who is looking after you?" When I told him that I had yet to see a doctor despite having arrived the previous night I thought that he was going to have a convulsion! He literally exploded and his wrath remains a vivid memory. Never were so many doctors torn off a bigger strip. It was action stations from then on, and within just 10 minutes I was in the operating theatre.

'When I regained consciousness, the surgeon was by my bedside. He said "I think you may like to have this", and handed me an armour-piercing bullet. He

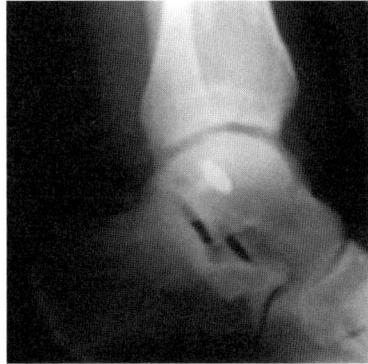

The 7.92mm machine-gun round firmly lodged in William Walker's ankle.

then told me that as he was prising open the bone in my leg to extract the bullet it shot out and hit the ceiling of the operating theatre! I still possess it today as a cherished souvenir.

'Fortunately, my sense of humour never quite left me, and when a doctor later asked how my accident happened I assured him that I was not the victim of an accident, but of a determined attempt on my life by a German fighter pilot!'

On 3 September 1940, 616 Squadron, comprising just eight of its original members who arrived at Kenley on 19 August, was relieved by 64 Squadron. In those fifteen days, 616 had lost a total of eleven Spitfires destroyed and three damaged. Five pilots had been killed, six wounded and one captured. In response, the squadron claimed the destruction of ten enemy aircraft destroyed, three probably destroyed, and six damaged. Of this 'bag', seven destroyed, two probables and three damaged were claimed by one man: Flight Lieutenant Denys Gillam AFC. For this feat he was awarded the DFC.

William Walker, his leg in plaster, was sent to complete his treatment at the Palace Hotel, Torquay, which had been converted into an RAF Hospital. Another patient there at the time was Flight Lieutenant James Brindley Nicholson, as William remembered:-

'A telegram arrived for him. Nick's response was simply "Well, what d'you make of that?" He was genuinely puzzled, and not a little embarrassed, that of hundreds of brave deeds performed by RAF fighter

August company: while convalescing at Torquay's Palace Hotel, Pilot Officer Walker (on drums) and other wounded aircrew formed a band – on vocals is Flight Lieutenant James Brindley Nicolson, Fighter Command's only VC of the Second World War.

pilots that summer, his had been singled out for this very great honour. His was the only Fighter Command VC because due to the speed of fighter combat it is difficult to find witnesses, supporting evidence being a prerequisite. At first 'Nick' got into trouble for being improperly dressed because he refused to stitch the maroon ribbon onto his tunic. In the end I think he adopted the attitude that he was accepting the medal on behalf of us all. He was a good sport, in fact, and we enjoyed playing together in a four-piece band that we formed with other wounded pilots down at Torquay.

'On 1 May 1941, I was considered fit enough to return to operations, so I re-joined 616 Squadron, which was then a part of Wing Commander Douglas Bader's Wing at Tangmere and was much changed. When I reported to the Wing Leader he tore me off a strip for being so careless as to have been shot down, which I thought was a bit off, to say the least. Suffice to say that I did not take to him, and he not to me, so three weeks later I was posted to

FLIGHT LIEUTENANT WILLIAM WALKER AE

The opening of the Malvern Spitfire Team's 'Spitfire!' exhibition in Worcester in 1988. Back row, from left: the author; Flt Lt William Walker*; Wg Cdr Roger Boulding*; Sqn Ldr Gandi Drobinski*; Fg Off Ken Wilkinson*; Flt Lt John Down*; Flt Lt Tony Pickering*; Front row, from left: Fg Off Bob George (Spitfires and Meteors); Mrs Helen Budzik; Flt Lt Kazek Budzik; Sqn Ldr Bob Pugh (Wellingtons); Flt Lt Hugh Chalmers (Spitfires); Fg Off John Lumsden (Mosquitos and Brigands post-war).

an Aircraft Delivery Flight at Hendon. Later that summer, of course, it was announced that Douglas Bader himself had been shot down and captured by the Germans!'

On 20 May 1941, William was posted away from 616 Squadron and the Tangmere Wing, beginning a long period variously associated with both the Aircraft Delivery Flight and 116 Squadron, the Anti-Aircraft Calibration Flight. After the cessation of hostilities, Flight Lieutenant William Walker was 'demobbed' on 1 September 1945, 'Duty Carried Out'.

In civilian life, William returned to the brewing business, eventually retiring as Chairman of Ind Coope. In retirement, from 1988 onwards, he became a great friend, travelling miles to attend signing and other events, and was a passionate supporter of the Battle of Britain Memorial Trust, which published William's book of poetry. Like another of the Few, my old friend Wing Commander Christopher 'Bunny' Currant, William used verse to document and help rationalise his memories and feelings. Today, at the National Battle of Britain Memorial, high on the chalk cliffs

William Walker with the author in 2000, displaying Major Mölders' bullet removed from his ankle sixty years before.

overlooking Folkestone and distant French coast, the names of the Few are proudly recorded on the Sir Christopher Foxley-Norris Wall. William Walker is personally remembered there, and his superb poem 'Our Wall' is prominently engraved:-

Here inscribed the names of friends we knew
Young men with whom we often flew.
Scrambled to many angels high,
They knew that they or friends might die.
Many were very scarcely trained
And many badly burnt or maimed.
Behind each name a story lies
Of bravery in summer skies;
Though many brave unwritten tales
Were simply told in vapour trails.
Outnumbered every day they flew,
Remembered here as just "The Few".

William left us on 21 October 2012, aged 99, and remains missed by many.

Chapter Twenty-Three

Air Marshal Sir Denis Crowley-Milling KCB DSO DFC*
Hurricane Pilot

Living in Malvern during the 1980s, it was not long before I came into contact with Air Marshal Sir Denis Crowley-Milling, an 'Old Boy' of Malvern College and at that time President of the Old Malvernians. 'DCM' had immeasurable respect and admiration for his friend and inspiration, Group Captain Sir Douglas Bader, about whom he would not tolerate a bad word. It is easy to understand why.

Born in Flintshire on 22 March 1919, after Malvern College DCM (also known as 'Crow'), became a Rolls-Royce apprentice, joining the RAFVR and commencing elementary flying training in 1937. Mobilised on

1 September 1939, after the usual induction, service and operational flying training, Pilot Officer Crowley-Milling was posted to 615 Squadron, flying Hurricanes, in France on 14 May 1940 – four days after Hitler's shocking attack on the west. After the Fall of France, the 21-year-old fighter pilot was posted to 242 Squadron, a Canadian squadron, at Biggin Hill on 6 June DCM returned to France with 242, covering the evacuation of British troops from the Atlantic coast, the squadron settling afterwards at Coltishall in 12 Group. Disillusioned and disorganised, lacking strong leadership, morale and operational efficiency was low. As we have previously heard from Air Commodore Mermagen, 'DB' was promoted to Acting Squadron Leader and sent to sort out the 'Bolshie' Canadians. This the legless dynamo did in short order, morale rocketing to a whole new dimension. By 10 July 1940 – the Battle of Britain's start-date – 242 Squadron was back on 'Top Line' and operational once more. All this achieved by a leader and fighter pilot without legs.

As DCM told me in 1988:-

'Douglas was the most incredible man and leader anyone could ever meet or serve under. He led by example and inspired everyone under his command. He was, of course, a legend in the RAF anyway, and much older than most of us, a mature, married, man of the world. We would have followed him anywhere – and frequently did.'

During the Battle of Britain, again as we have already heard, a tactical argument arose, powerful political support being achieved for the 'Big Wing' concept, an idea pushed forward by Squadron Leader Bader and backed by his Group Commander, Air Vice-Marshal Leigh-Mallory, as the Air Marshal explained in a letter dated 19 July 1996:-

'The "Big Wing' interest is in the tactical argument under the circumstances that developed at one stage in the Battle of Britain, i.e. end of August and early September 1940. I do not believe it is a subject for a whole book, it is a chapter in the Battle and was tried out on but few occasions. If the timing and positioning were right and the enemy did what you expected, it could result in hitting the German formations earlier and with more fighters, i.e. higher attrition. The very first Duxford Wing (three squadrons) was not used until 7 September 1940. The vital factor in the Battle was of course *Reichsmarschall* Göring's change in tactics, making the whole weight of attack on London, thus allowing our radar and frontline airfields to recover.'

Old Malvernian Denis Crowley-Milling (second left), then a Rolls-Royce apprentice, while undertaking elementary flying training with the RAFVR at Derby in 1937. In the white flying suit is Alan Feary – later killed in action flying Spitfires with 609 Squadron during the Battle of Britain.

On 7 September 1940 – on which day the codename CROMWELL was broadcast (invasion imminent) – Squadron Leader Bader led the 'Duxford Wing' into action over London for the first time, comprising the Hurricanes of 242 and 310 Squadrons, covered by the Spitfires of 19. On that fateful day, 'Black Saturday', the Germans began the relentless round-the-clock bombing of London. Bounced while climbing over, Bader later described what followed as 'windy work'. The 242 Squadron Intelligence Report described what befell Pilot Officer Crowley-Milling in the ensuing combat:-

'Red 3 (Pilot Officer Crowley-Milling) flying in vic formation sighted AA fire to the east. He climbed to meet E/A and engaged a flight of twenty bombers. He fired a two second burst at left-hand rear bomber, then observed Me 110 just behind last bomber. He fired four second burst at Me 110, setting port engine on fire and starboard engine smoking. Red 3 was then attacked by Me 109, receiving cannon shell in radiator, one in left aileron and one behind pilot's seat.'

Pilot Officer Denis Crowley-Milling – note the brass 'VR' insignia.

DCM span away from the fight, making a successful forced landing on the former airfield at Stow Maries. The armoured glass windscreen of his Hurricane (P3715, LE-H) was shattered. LAC David Evans of 242 Squadron's ground crew wrote telling me that 'He was lucky: there was a spent 7.9mm bullet jammed in the space between the front and rear screen.' The 110 that DCM accounted for was also attacked by Red 4, Sub-Lieutenant R.E. Gardner, and crashed at Little Burstead. It was DCM's first combat claim, this being followed by others under Squadron Leader Bader's leadership, resulting in the award of a DFC on 11 April 1941. By that time, DB was Wing Leader at Tangmere, where Flight Lieutenant Crowley-Milling joined him on 13 June, to take over a flight of 610 Squadron at Westhampnett. It was this period that the Air Marshal and I mainly communicated about. As DCM wrote on 16 March 1995:-

'I think the main point for all of us (about 1941) was that we were now on the offensive, taking the battle over to the Germans, following the Battle of Britain.'

21 June 1995:-

'I will give thought to 9 August 1941. The greatest impression was the uncanny silence on the R/T. Douglas always kept up a running commentary. Had the worst happened?'

A few days later a postcard arrived from Sir Denis, accompanying the following notes:-

'This, of course, is all written from memory, as the thoughts come to mind relaxing here on Madeira Island. I cannot be sure of the exact dates and some of the names escape me. I am covering the period from around November 1940 to August 1941, when Douglas Bader was shot down.

There was no collision with a 109. General Galland confirmed this laughingly to DB and named one of his pilots who performed the deed! I believe this was at the time when we were all gathered together to take part in "This is Your Life" with DB the victim. I followed, shot down a week or so after him, I think, on 21 August 1941.

'Very soon after Leigh-Mallory took over 11 Group from Keith Park in late 1940, he had DB promoted to Wing Commander, to command the Tangmere Wing. 242 Squadron was at Martlesham Heath, near Felixstowe, at the time. We were all very disappointed to see him go – he had really put the Squadron through its paces and built up a splendid fighting unit from a bunch of mainly Canadians – and a Bolshie lot they were, to start with. Squadron Leader "Treacle" Tracey took over but was killed in a collision with another Hurricane in a matter of weeks, I seem to recall. Then Squadron Leader Whitney-Straight, the pre-war millionaire racing driver (an American by nationality).

A snapshot speaking volumes regarding the frustrations and mood of certain 12 Group pilots during the Battle of Britain – especially Squadron Leader Douglas Bader (third from right) and his pilots of 242 Squadron, pictured here. From left: Plt Off Willie McKnight DFC; Fg Off Eric Ball DFC; Bader; Plt Off N.N. Campbell and Plt Off Crowley-Milling.

Pilot Officer Crowley-Milling, in black pre-war flying suit, at Coltishall in 1940.

'DB found 610 Squadron at Westhampnett (Goodwood) in poor shape and low morale. He sacked the Squadron Commander and both Flight Commanders and brought in Flight Lieutenant Ken Holden, Flight Lieutenant Tony Leigh-Knight and myself, ex-242 Squadron now stationed at North Weald. He had already taken Stan Turner to command 145 Squadron. From then on, one never looked back, "sweeps" over Northern France daily, very often twice a day, escorting a few Stirling bombers to make sure that the German fighters reacted. I felt rather sorry for the Stirlings operating, as what must have been a dramatic change, in daylight and attracting all the "flak"! As usual, DB kept up a running commentary from the time we approached the French coast to the time we left on return. Also coming over the ether as we saw the French coast approaching was the voice of Squadron Leader Stan Turner – "OK chaps, put your corks in!" – in other words, now is the time to be looking out for German fighters and don't be scared! The Germans listening on the ground to our radio chatter thought this must be an order to switch on some special equipment! After the war, I learnt from one of my pilots who had been shot down and a PoW that during his interrogation the Germans asked him what does this "Put your corks in" mean? We both had a good laugh!

'There were, of course, numerous encounters with Me 109s, mainly from Galland's St Omer wing – all are documented… Though it is recorded that the losses in fighters covering both sides were not in our favour, for us it was taking the fight to the Germans in their own airspace for the first time, in a big way, since the Battle of Britain. We were inspired by it all and our morale was very high. I was somewhat dismayed to learn that ACM "Bing" Cross in his wartime book claimed that the pilots in DB's Wing were near to mutiny at one stage. To me, things were quite the reverse, and as you may have heard from JEJ (Johnnie Johnson), he wrote to Bing, supported by "Cocky" Dundas and I, to this effect. Squadron Leader Billy Burton, Commanding Officer of 616 Squadron, certainly was fed up,

246

as he was never given the chance to lead his own Squadron, DB always led it and he always wanted Cocky and JEJ with him. I can well understand both sides – DB wanted pilots he was thoroughly familiar with in combat, and they with him, while Billy Burton, a Squadron Leader, never had the status of one. You could say he tried "desperately" to persuade DB to lead each of the three squadrons in turn, i.e. with different pilots round him on each operation, but Burton failed for obvious reasons and it must have got him down. You must know the pilots you lead and depend on, on the ground as in the air.

'The loss of DB in August left us all stunned. The uncanny part about it all was the terrible silence on the radio all the way home to Tangmere on that fateful day. The colourful language and running commentary had suddenly ceased, and left us all wondering what could have happened. Was he alive or dead? Had his radio failed? Naturally JEJ (and I am sure he was with him on that day) must have been more in the picture, but not much as I don't think anyone actually saw it happen. I know we were above thick cloud on the way home and asked the Tangmere Controller to give us a bearing to steer to base, and it was way out in accuracy and unbeknown to us we were flying up the North Sea and just scraped into Martlesham Heath with hardly any fuel left – so it was indeed a day to remember.

'I think it was the next day when a few of us were with Thelma Bader in their married quarter at Tangmere – I believe Cocky and possibly JEJ were

Pilot Officer Crowley-Milling's 242 Squadron Hurricane, P3715, at Coltishall – note the two-colour propeller spinner cap.

Pilot Officer Crowley-Milling outside his parents' home displaying the shattered windscreen of P3715, in which he was badly shot up on 7 September 1940.

there and I – when the phone rang and after speaking Thelma came back to join us, all very calmly, and said "Douglas is safe and a prisoner."

'We later, maybe a day or two, heard that the Germans were offering a safe passage to an RAF Lysander to land in France with a new artificial right leg, which of course DB had to leave behind before being able to bale out of his tail-less Spitfire. Somebody high up the chain of command, possibly Sholto Douglas, C-in-C Fighter Command, refused the offer, and decided the leg should be dropped by parachute during the next daylight bombing with the Tangmere Wing escorting. Paddy Woodhouse may already have taken over the Wing by this stage. You know the rest of the story. We clearly saw (or I certainly did) the leg released from the bomb bay of one of the Blenheims as the formation passed over St Omer and carried on to bomb the steel works at Lille, I recall. So ended our time with DB leading and encouraging us in the air – for some of us ex-242 Squadron it was fifteen exciting months from early June 1940 to August 1941. A never-to-be-forgotten experience that stood us in good stead to the day we were stood down for a rest from operational flying. For me, it was October 1943, less August to December 1941, when I came home via the French escape organisation, having been shot down around a week or so after DB as I recall, 21 August 1941.

'It was one of the worst days (or the worst day) for the Wing, as you well know. I think you mentioned in your last letter that the Wing lost very many aircraft that day. Naturally, I remember it only too well, and I did not meet Paddy Woodhouse again until 1943, when I was given command of a Typhoon fighter-bomber Wing, and by then he was a Group Captain. As in my mind I rather blamed him for not calling off the operation because at that time there was too much cloud cover for us to give adequate support to the bombers above. In the past, if cloud cover was reported or forecast over the target area that particular day's sweep was called off. The main object was to take the fight to German-occupied France and shoot down German fighters. Flying lower, as we did under broken cloud, to keep the bombers in sight was a distinct advantage and the

'DCM' was a confirmed 'Baderphile' and part of the Tangmere Wing's privileged 'inner sanctum', an elite within an elite. Here the legless Wing Leader practises his drive between sweeps at Westhampnett.

Me 109s picked off Spitfires through gaps in the clouds, and it all finished off with a running fight all the way to the French coast – but I never made it! Just one shell in the back of the engine, missing the fuselage fuel tank immediately behind it at an extreme angle of 70° from a 109 which dived past the nose of my Spitfire and out of sight below me (a good or maybe lucky shot). My Merlin engine kept going but gradually lost all the glycol cooling fluid, and with the engine temperature right off the gauge, it was clear that I was not going to make it home – an overheated engine could start a fire. So I shut it down, rolled my Spitfire onto its back and pulled through into a dive, hoping the 109s would leave me alone, which happily they did. One Me 109 followed me down but made no attempt to attack me and stayed out of firing range. No doubt he had seen the trail of boiling glycol from my aircraft. He watched me land wheels-up in a field, then promptly did a victory roll at low-level over the top of me as I climbed out of the cockpit, really rubbing it in that he had shot me down! The day of chivalry at that stage of the war appeared not to be dead.

'So ended my part of flying with the Tangmere Wing.'

Wing Commander Douglas Bader at Westhampnett in the 'season' of 1941. After Sir Douglas died in 1982, 'Crow' and friends founded the Douglas Bader Foundation charity, assisting the amputee disabled community as a living memorial to their friend and inspiration.

Flight Lieutenant Crowley-Milling's 610 Squadron Spitfire while serving as a Flight Commander in 1941. That 'season' he was shot down over France, successfully evading and making a 'Home Run' across the Pyrenees.

Aside from the foregoing account, which took some persuasion, the Air Marshal steadfastly refused to record his own experiences, whilst equally robustly encouraging me to concentrate on the 'supporting cast'. For that reason, Sir Denis's account is a significant one.

Sir Denis Crowley-Milling and Sir Douglas Bader remained firm friends in war and peace, until 'Dogsbody' died on 5 September 1982. On 27 October, a memorial service for Sir Douglas was held at the 'RAF Church' of St Clement Danes – after which a new charity was launched in the great man's name: The Douglas Bader Foundation. Appropriately, the first Trustees were Air Marshal Sir Denis Crowley-Milling, Air Vice-Marshal Johnnie Johnson and Group Captain Sir Hugh Dundas. The Foundation exists to uphold the name and story of Douglas Bader as a positive role model and inspiration to the amputee community, to which the charity continues to provide all manner of assistance.

Air Marshal Sir Denis Crowley-Milling died on 1 December 1996. Sir Denis would, I know, be delighted to know that the Douglas Bader Foundation, his great friend's lasting legacy, remains a thriving concern – long after all of the Tangmere Wing's 'inner sanctum' joined their swashbuckling Wing Leader in some better place.

Chapter Twenty-Four

Squadron Leader Jerzy 'Jurek' Poplawski VM KW

Hurricane Pilot

My interest in Spitfire R6644 and Flying Officer Franek Surma led me to locate another of the Polish Few, Squadron Leader Jerzy 'Jurek' Poplawski, who I found in Buenos Aires in 1987. Over the years, I would receive many air mail letters from Jurek, the first of which, dated 6 October 1987, in part read:-

'It is extremely interesting to read a story of one's own life written in so much detail by a young man of twenty-five who didn't even live through

the time of those events. It really makes me think that it was all worthwhile when your generation recalls in such a real way.'

Some confusion at first existed regarding Jurek's final retired rank and decorations, which he clarified on 28 March 1988:-

'I have no knowledge of being promoted to wing commander, nevertheless, if it did happen it would have been a very pleasant event. Now let's clarify the question regarding the DFC. I know for certain that my name was submitted on a few occasions for that decoration but on the other hand I also know that I did certain things I shouldn't have done, i.e. low flying over a prohibited area. It happened at one of the RAF stations in north-east England. Later on, the Station Commander became an important personality at Fighter Command HQ, and that was it. Anyway, today this is not important any more but I took (rather late!) note of it and in my conversations with my son and daughter I often make it clear to them that whatever happens you must always behave properly – it makes life easier.'

Born in Hodel, Poland (not 'Model' as incorrectly reported in certain sources), on 1 October 1919, Jurek achieved his early ambition and, according to his personal logbook, became a cadet at the 'Officers' Flying School, Deblin 1937', passing out with a commission in 1939. Initially he was posted to a light-bomber squadron, flying PZL 23 'Karaś', but before he could fly operational sorties after the German invasion on 1 September 1939, Jurek was evacuated to Romania. From there he and comrades travelled to France, arriving in Marseilles on 29 October 1939, then made their way to England, landing on 27 January 1940. On 25 January 1993, Jurek wrote:-

'I was first stationed at RAF Eastchurch when I arrived in England from France, and the first town I knew was Sheerness. In the future, every time I flew over Sheerness and Eastchurch I couldn't help thinking of those first days in England and the happiness I found after escaping from Poland following the German invasion.'

At Eastchurch, Jurek was commissioned as a pilot officer in the RAFVR, spending June and July 1940 at the Elementary Flying Training School, Carlisle. On 12 August, Pilot Officer Poplawski was sent to the Army School of Cooperation at Old Sarum for evaluation, where he was selected for fighters.

Consequently, on 12 August, Jurek reported to 5 OTU, Aston Down, for conversion to Hurricanes. On that day, he was checked out by Flying Officer Martindale in the Tiger Moth, in which type he spent the rest of that week flying various solo training flights.

On 20 August, Pilot Officer Maloney flew dual with Pilot Officer Poplawski in a Harvard, and after a number of 'Circuits and landings' in both that type and a Miles Master, Jurek first flew a Hurricane on 25 August. On 5 September, Jurek's operational training was considered complete, during which he had flown 18.15 hours on Hurricanes. His flight commander, Flight Lieutenant Prosser Hanks DFC assessed the young Pole's performance as 'Average'. It would not be to 11 Group, over which the Battle of Britain now raged, that Pilot Officer Poplawski would be posted, but to 111 Squadron at Drem, in Scotland. Having already been heavily

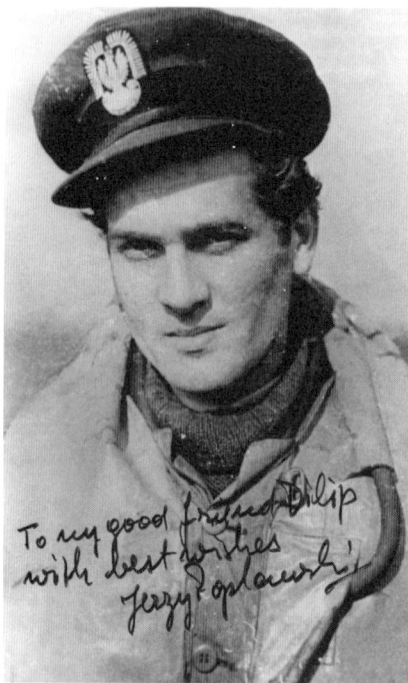

Above left: Pilot Officer Jurek Poplawski, pictured at Northolt serving with 308 Squadron in 1941.

Above right: Pilot Officer Poplawski (left) with an unidentified pilot after joining 308 Squadron at Baginton in March 1941. The unit would soon re-equip with Spitfires.

engaged in the Battle of Britain, flying from Croydon and Debden, 111 had been sent north to rebuild and refit, there to receive replacement pilots and provide them further training. On 13 September, Jurek made his first flight with 'Treble One', a formation practice sortie, after which days were spent on such training exercises as dogfighting, aerobatics and air firing. On 21 September, Pilot Officer Poplawski qualified for the Battle of Britain Bar to the 1939-45 Star when he scrambled with 111 Squadron to intercept an unidentified radar plot. The sortie was uneventful – but Jurek was now one of the Few. On 26 September having accumulated more experience on Hurricanes, Pilot Officer Poplawski was posted away from 111 Squadron to join 229, at Northolt, on the outskirts of north-west London, in 11 Group's frontline.

Jurek's letter of 28 March 1988 remembered those days:-

'I spent most of my Battle of Britain time with 229 Squadron, commanded by Squadron Leader Freddy Rosier, who later retired as a most distinguished and senior air marshal. I knew him and his wife very well. Although I did not shoot anything down during the Battle of Britain, I did fire at several enemy aircraft. I think that I was so excited that I trembled too much and as a result my aim was not good!'

Pilot Officer Poplawski's first operational flight with 229 Squadron's 'B' Flight was a patrol from Northolt on 2 October 1940. Thereafter, Jurek was a regular member of 229 Squadron's line-up, flying patrols daily. On 6 November, 229 Squadron took off at 1430 hrs to patrol the Croydon Line at 15,000 feet. The Hurricanes were vectored to Kenley and Horsham where they encountered 10/10ths cloud reaching from 2,000 to 24,000 feet. Blue Section became separated from the rest of the squadron in the bad visibility, Sergeant Frank Twitchett landing at Hatfield, where an undercarriage leg buckled on touch-down; Pilot Officer Poplawski, however, was missing. No news was received of his status for some time – then, with relief, it was learned that Jurek had force-landed at Streatley, west of Hitchin, having run out of fuel. And so, with the worsening winter weather, the patrols went on, every day, until on 15 November, 229 Squadron flew to Wittering in 12 Group, there to rest for a week. On 22 November, the Hurricanes flew to another new base, Speke, there to provide some protection to Liverpool and Manchester, and from where endless convoy patrols were flown over the Irish Sea. Jurek would make his last patrol with 229 Squadron on 7 March 1941, after which he bade Squadron Leader Rosier farewell and travelled to

Baginton, near Coventry, there to join 308 'City of Krakow' Squadron – a Polish fighter squadron:-

'When I was posted to 308 Squadron, I found some friends of my own age or thereabouts, but most of them were already experienced pilots in Poland, and that had to be respected. As I remember, at first I used to fly on the wing of my Flight Commander, but I don't recall his name now. This was really the start of my active war, in action against the enemy, because the Battle of Britain itself had been quiet for me.'

Amongst those new friends was Pilot Officer Franek Surma, as Jurek explained in that first letter:-

'Franek Surma was a good friend of mine, a bit shy when you talked to him. Perhaps we were all a bit quiet, trying not to think of tomorrow. It would be wrong to say that we had no fear. After all, we were human beings and as such we all knew what fear was. But we also had a code of how we conducted our lives, a sense of duty, that made us control our fear. And that fact was perhaps the most important in our lives. We both talked about it a lot.

'We had a mascot, a black "Scotty" dog which was particularly attached to Franek Surma, and vice-versa. Another friend of Scotty's was a pigeon, who used to follow wherever the dog went. When Scotty stopped and rested, the pigeon either stood next to her or just simply stood on her back. This little story is perhaps important background minutia because Franek liked Scotty very much and the dog responded to him more than anyone else.'

308 Squadron had been formed from Polish personnel at Speke on 12 September 1940. Five days later the new unit's first aircraft arrived, a Fairey Battle in which its handful of original pilots amused themselves flying 'circuits and bumps'. Then, on 27 September, 308 Squadron moved to Baginton airfield, the adjacent *Oak* public house soon being adopted as the squadron's unofficial HQ. Soon the squadron's Hurricanes arrived, but the unit would not participate in the Battle of Britain, which remained ongoing. Along with those airmen like Pilot Officers Gandi Drobinski, Franek Surma and Jurek Poplawski who were embedded in RAF fighter squadrons, two Polish fighter squadrons did fight in the Battle of Britain: 303 Squadron, based at Northolt, and 302 Squadron, which flew operations temporarily with the Duxford Wing. Today, long after the Iron Curtain's collapse, the Polish effort receives much acclaim and exposure, and rightly so, but let it not be

Above left: Pilot Officer Poplawski whilst serving with 308 Squadron and No 1 Polish Fighter Wing at Northolt during the 'season' of 1941.

Above right: Pilot Officer Tadek Stabrowski, who also went to the assistance of the Spitfire being attacked by a Me 109F over Dunkirk. Stabrowski was reported missing in 1943 – and only identified recently through DNA testing, having been buried as an unknown Polish airman in a French coastal cemetery.

forgotten that during the summer of 1940, Fighter Command was a multi-national force – and the Czechs of 310 Squadron, also based at Duxford, were heavily engaged. 308 Squadron's time, however, was yet to come…

On 24 November 1940, Wing Commander Oliver and Sergeant Mieczyslaw Parafinski recorded 308 Squadron's first victory when he destroyed a Ju 88 reconnaissance bomber which crashed near Cirencester. Parafinski had, in fact, been a member of the Polish Air Force's 122 'Krakow' Squadron, with which he had destroyed a He 111 fighting over his homeland in 1939 (sadly, on 26 February 1941, Parafinski crashed and was killed near Northampton owing to oxygen failure). Franek Surma was also amongst the combat experienced Polish pilots posted to 308 Squadron in March 1941, and he also found himself in action against a Ju 88 reconnaissance machine, along with Pilot Officer Bozek and Sergeant Kremski. On 26 March 1941, Surma's section intercepted the intruder 3,000 feet over their airfield, causing great excitement. Hit, the bomber dived away and was lost in the gloaming. A few days later, in readiness for the forthcoming Fighter

Command offensive, 308 Squadron exchanged its tired old Hurricanes for equally tired Spitfire Mk IAs. The aircraft involved came from 65 Squadron, which was upgrading to the newer Mk II in preparation for another frontline tour. The Poles were able to convert to Spitfires at Baginton, unmolested by the enemy, although pilots, including Jurek, flew many patrols investigating 'X-Raids' at a time when, owing to the night Blitz, German reconnaissance aircraft were most active. On 1 June 1941, however, things changed when 308 Squadron moved south, to Chilbolton, there also receiving Spitfire Mk IIs, and four days later joined No 1 Polish Fighter Wing at Northolt. The scene was now set for action.

On 2 April 1988, Jurek wrote:-

'From Northolt we flew patrols over convoys off Portland Bill, Swanage and Bournemouth, but we were mainly employed on operations over France, escorting small numbers of bombers and forcing the German fighters up to fight. These were impressive operations involving literally hundreds of Spitfires and the German fighters did not disappoint. This was, of course, a totally different situation to the Battle of Britain, and quite soon afterwards, really, it now was us having to cross the Channel twice and if brought down over France we were likely to be captured. We were in action pretty much daily, or so it seemed, losing pilots and scoring combat successes ourselves – Franek Surma was one who did well, I remember.'

Another who 'did well' was Jurek himself, although typically that was never mentioned in our correspondence. On 4 September 1941, Pilot Officer Poplawski scored his first kill while flying an escort sortie that evening to Fruges; attacked by twelve Me 109Fs, Jurek later reported that 'I turned to my left and made a head-on attack. I got within fifty yards and fired two bursts from both my cannon and machine-guns. I saw my bullets striking the cockpit area

Hauptmann Johannes Seifert – who shot down Flying Officer Surma but was himself killed in action later in the war.

when the enemy aircraft turned onto its starboard wing and went into a vertical dive, which became a spin. I followed it down to 10,000 feet and saw it crash into a wood. Having become separated from the Squadron, I returned to Northolt alone.'

On the evening of 16 September, 308 Squadron flew a fighter sweep over the Pas-de-Calais, engaging Me 109s from JG2 and 26. Pilot Officer Poplawski claimed a victory in unusual circumstances:-

'I saw one Me passing on my starboard side and decided to chase him. As I did so, I observed tracer bullets converging about thirty yards in front of me and, turning sharply to the right, saw one Me above, and I was attacked by another from the rear at the same time. I saw my Squadron in front of me but was unable to catch up with them. I lost height in a series of turns, keeping a careful watch on my attackers. I flew low across the Channel, pursued by the Me's, which kept me under fire. I continued taking evasive action and when about five miles out to sea, the Me on my starboard side was about to attack. I saw tracer bullets emerging from the Me on my port

General Sosnkowski with pilots of 315 Squadron at Ballyherbert, County Down, on 14 August 1943. Squadron Leader Poplawski is behind the General's raised hand.

side and turned towards the Me on my starboard side. I then made sharp turns to port, getting beneath an Me which was attempting to attack me from the port side.

'I then throttled back and as soon as the Me had overshot, I pulled up and got above and dived towards him. Realising that as soon as he straightened out he would be in immediate range of my guns, he continued to dive and failed to pull out in time. The aircraft skidded into the sea and I saw half the fuselage and tail submerge. Meanwhile the other Me had climbed and was circling over the first, but made no further attempt to attack me. No rounds fired!'

It is likely that the hapless German pilot was *Oberleutnant* Erwin Biedermann, a nine-victory ace, of 9/JG26, who was killed. A few days later, on 21 September 1941, Jurek sent another Me 109F into the sea just off the French coast, and on 27 September set another on fire, which was 'burning nicely as it crashed into a row of houses west of Amiens'. On that day, Jurek's Spitfire was shot up over France so badly by a 109 that he was unable to reach Northolt, instead crash-landing at Biggin Hill. According to the 308 Squadron diary, his Spitfire was 'riddled'. On 13 October, on 'Circus 110A', a raid to Arques, Pilot Officer Poplawski enjoyed the distinction of recording 308 Squadron's fiftieth kill, an Me 109 between Mardyk and St Omer:-

'I attacked one of a formation of seven Me 109s that were trying to manoeuvre to the rear of 308 Squadron and make an attack. The Me dived towards the ground and I followed him down until he was at about 300 feet. I gave him two bursts with cannon and machine-gun fire from three-quarters astern on the port side, closing from 100-150 yards. I saw my bullets striking the enemy aircraft and, at the same time, I saw a very big gun and its crew straight in front of me. I saw what I took to be the officer in charge with his right arm uplifted. I gave a quick squirt and saw men falling to the ground, the officer's uplifted arm flying into the air. The gun did not fire but I had overshot the Me. Pilot Officer Wandzilak, my No 2, saw it crash into the ground, emitting black smoke.'

The last operation of the 1941 'Non-Stop Offensive' was Circus 110, in which the Northolt Polish Wing was detailed to fly as Close Escort for twelve Blenheims attacking the railway repair facility at Lille. While the bombers cruised at 14,000 feet, 303 was to proceed at that altitude with 315 Squadron at 15,000 feet and 308 a thousand feet higher.

General Sosnkowski decorating Polish pilots; Squadron Leader Poplawski has just received the *Virtuti Militari*.

The Exeter Polish Wing's squadrons were to fly at 21, 23 and 26,000 feet, the Biggin Hill Wing providing top cover at 24, 25 and 28,000 feet. The 'Beehive's' withdrawal was to be supplied by 12 Group wings. Only problem was, it all went badly wrong from the outset. Firstly, only six Blenheims arrived over the rendezvous point at Manston. Then, as the Northolt Wing turned to take up their allotted positions, 308 Squadron was blinded by the bright sun and lost the remainder of the formation. Consequently Ground Control provided Squadron Leader Pisarek, the CO, a course to steer, and 308 Squadron set off for France. The main formation crossed the French coast east of Gravelines, hit the target then turned for home over Arras. Anti-aircraft fire was heavy throughout the operation, but although Me 109s harried the 'Beehive', all of the bombers were escorted safely home. Unfortunately, the RAF fighters fared somewhat less well.

Having been unable to locate the main party, 308 Squadron was ordered to patrol between Calais and Dunkirk, mainly inland, between 16,000 and 25,000 feet. Towards the end of their patrol, Pisarek's Spitfires were bounced by a large force of I/JG26 Me 109s over the French coast. Pilot Officer Poplawski reported:-

'I went to the assistance of a Spitfire that was being attacked by an Me 109F. I got on the Me 109's tail and from 200 yards above I gave a short burst from my cannons. I saw an explosion in the starboard wing and the Me turned onto its side with the starboard wing down. I fired another burst from both my machine-guns and cannons. Volumes of black smoke appeared from the Me, which started to dive down sideways. As four Me's were approaching to engage me, and were higher, I decided to join a formation of our aircraft in the distance.'

Pilot Officer Tadeusz Stabrowski:-

'I saw a Spitfire being attacked by an Me 109F and went to its assistance, engaging the enemy aircraft from above and astern. I gave it a burst of both cannon and machine-guns at 300 yards. The Me wobbled badly and I knew that I had hit it. I followed up my attack and fired three more bursts. The Me quivered and wavered more and more, thick black smoke pouring from the underside of the fuselage. It dived towards the sea near the French coast. Being short of ammunition and petrol, and a long way from base, I could not chase the Me and returned to England.'

It is likely that both Polish pilots attacked the same Me 109F.

For the RAF, Circus 110 was a disaster: at least seventeen Spitfires were lost, with fourteen pilots killed or captured, including a wing commander and three squadron leaders. Of those casualties, six pilots remained missing – amongst them Flying Officer Franek Surma.

In his letter of 6 October 1987, Jurek wrote:-

'The whole flight lasted an hour and fifty-five minutes. I believe that it was Franek Surma's Spitfire being attacked by at least one Me 109. The German attack that day was so sudden that it surprised me in its intensity. We tried to assist but, if I remember correctly, I had a warning from Squadron Leader Pisarek to "Break left!" quickly, which I did. Apparently, there were more Me 109s coming down to attack me so, being short of petrol,

I could not hang around. Therefore I did not see what happened to either Franek or the Me 109 that I had attacked. I also remember that there was another Me 109 in my way, between me and the one shooting at Franek Surma. That is really all I can remember of the whole action.'

When I researched German combat claims many years ago, it was apparent that Flying Officer Surma had been shot down over Dunkirk by *Hauptmann* Johannes Seifert, *Kommandeur* of I/JG26, an ace and holder of the Knight's Cross; he would be killed in action fighting the American daylight bomber offensive. Pilot Officer Stabrowski, I discovered, was himself reported missing in 1943 (but more recently was identified through DNA testing, having been buried as an 'unknown').

Jurek Poplawski made a new life in Argentina after the war, and is pictured here (right) with Prince Karol Radziwell in Buenos Aires, 1993. The pair became friends when together at Eastchurch, upon arrival in England in early 1940.

An analysis of Fighter Command losses on 8 November 1941 confirms a total of six Spitfire pilots reported missing in the Dunkirk area that day, including Flying Officer Surma. In 2018, while researching the burials of unknown airmen in cemeteries along the French coast, the Commonwealth War Graves Commission confirmed that the remains of one particular airman 'Known unto God' in the Dunkirk British War Cemetery had been recovered by the French from a Spitfire crash site near that port on the date in question: 8 November 1941. Unfortunately, exhaustive enquiries with the French authorities yielded no further information. Of the six missing Spitfire pilots, two were lost south of Le Touquet, so can be discounted. There is, therefore, a 1:4 chance that this unidentified airman at Dunkirk could be Franek Surma. Only a DNA test with living relatives could resolve this, but this is contrary to CWGC policy. In the case of Stabrowski, although another British War Cemetery on the French coast was involved, the grave was specifically that of an unknown Polish airman – giving the Polish authorities jurisdiction. This is a complex and emotive subject, and one I will be investigating in my forthcoming *Missing in Action: Finding the Fallen of the Second World War*. As things stand, whether or not the unknown Dunkirk airman is Franek Surma, we will never know.

For Jurek Poplawski, the war went on, that day in the winter of 1941 being just one in a long war, and, as he wrote: 'It all happened a long time ago.

Jurek Poplawski with his wife, Maria, in February 1993.

This was the most exciting time of my entire war, although later stages, such as the Dieppe Landings and D-Day period provide unforgettable memories.'

A month after Flying Officer Surma was lost, 308 Squadron was sent north to rest and refit at Woodvale. Jurek would remain with the 'Krakow' Squadron, also flying out of Exeter, Hutton Cranswick and Heston, until August 1942 – an unusually long time to fly and survive operational flying. After a spell instructing at 58 OTU, Grangemouth, Jurek was promoted to squadron leader and appointed to command 315 Squadron at Northolt on 16 April 1943. Four days later, he scored his final victory, an FW 190 destroyed over France. Remaining with 315 until February 1944, he then served as a staff officer with the Polish Air Force Inspectorate and at Fighter Command HQ. During his second tour, Jurek's logbook reflects a relentless round of operations, fighter sweeps, bomber escort missions and ground attack, all of which combined to etch a kaleidoscope of many memories. Decorated with the Polish *Virtuti Militari* Vth Class, and Cross of Valour with several bars, he left the RAF after the war, in 1947.

Jurek's son, Roman Poplawski, takes up the story:-

'In 1947, my father left the RAF behind and emigrated to Argentina, where he became Director of International Commerce for Cargill, a company in imports and exports, especially grain. He arrived in Argentina with virtually nothing except a few paper bank notes in his pocket and a bag. He couldn't even speak Spanish. But he did this to start a new life, and I guess that is why I am here, able to write to you today.'

Why, the reader may wonder, did Jurek not simply return to Poland after Germany was defeated in 1945? This was because Poland was now occupied by another dictator – Stalin – and absorbed into the communist Soviet Bloc, isolated from the democratic and capitalist west behind the so-called 'Iron Curtain'. Having had contact with and experience of the west, many Polish servicemen and women who did return home were persecuted, even imprisoned, by the Stalinist regime. Consequently, most had no choice but to make new lives elsewhere, exiled from their surviving families and homeland. For Jurek it all worked out, the same determination and courage he showed flying a Spitfire in combat seeing him through. Settling in Buenos Aires, Jurek happily married Maria Judith Molinari, the couple having a son, Roman, and a daughter, Maria, and grandchildren; he passed away in his adopted country on 21 June 2004, aged 84.

Jurek once told me: 'I am a lucky man. So many friends did not survive the war.'

Chapter Twenty-Five

Sergeant Ray Johnson
Spitfire Armourer

Long after the Battle of Britain, Air Chief Marshal Dowding wrote, 'I do not think that one should consider what happened in terms of individuals and personalities. It is more fitting to think of us as a team – men and women, aircrews and groundcrews, and operations and other staffs at all levels – in which everyone played an integral part. But for all the warmth of feeling for those with whom I was associated in fighting the battle, I think that we should remember, with very special esteem, those who did the actual fighting: the aircrews.'

When Churchill paid tribute to Fighter Command's airborne warriors, immortalising them as the 'Few' in his speech to the House of Commons on

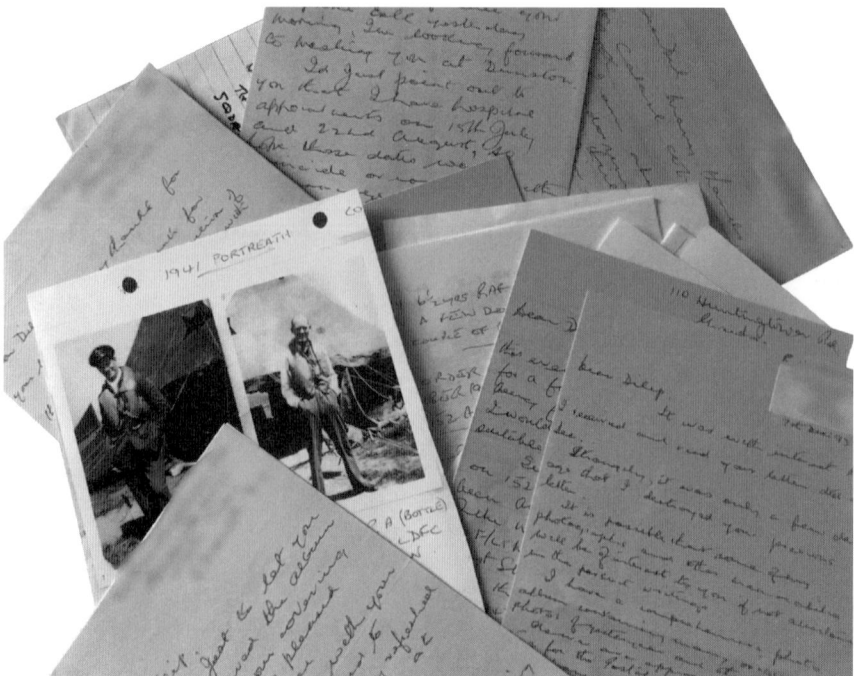

20 August 1940, Fighter Command's Sector Stations in southern England were being pulverised by the enemy – causing many casualties amongst the wider 'team'. For groundcrews – engine fitters, flight riggers and armourers – keeping the aircraft on 'Top Line' often meant working out in the open, the all-important fighters dispersed around airfields, frequently a long way from shelter. In this book's companion, *Battle of Britain 1940: The Finest Hour's Human Cost*, the wider sacrifice is both acknowledged and explored – and neither is it ignored here. While *Letters From The Few* essentially concerns aircrew, and Spitfire and Hurricane pilots at that, it is right that we also think about those young men and women on the ground, under fire, working tirelessly in difficult conditions. One such was Ray Johnson, who in 1940 was a 19-year-old Aircraftman 2nd Class (AC2) and an armourer on 152 'Hyderabad' Squadron.

Ray and I first met in 1993 when he answered my appeal in a service magazine for contact with groundcrew survivors who had served with 10 Group squadrons in the Battle of Britain. At the time, I was researching *Angriff Westland*, investigating the attacks aimed at Westland Aircraft. Full of boundless energy and enthusiasm, the pint-sized Ray, who lived in Grantham, fairly bombarded me with helpful correspondence, all kinds of details, addresses, and anecdotes. According to his service record, Ray was born on 4 September 1920, enlisting in the RAF on 12 July 1939. After training as an armourer at Padgate, Brize Norton and Pembrey, on 24 January 1940 AC2 Johnson reported to 152 Squadron at Prestwick where he found, in the words of 66 Squadron engine fitter Bob Morris, 'Every young man's dream: Spitfires!'

On 7 December 1993, Ray sent me a pile of cassette tapes on which he had recorded memories of his entire wartime service. Of summer 1940 and 152 Squadron he had this to say:-

'And then it happened. What is now known as the Battle of Britain started. Sometime around 21 July 1940, 152 Squadron moved south from Acklington to Warmwell in Dorset. An advance party, including myself, was flown down in a Handley Page Harrow, which was a high-wing monoplane, to Warmwell, which was a grass airfield inland of Weymouth and not far from the army camp at Bovington. In fact it was adjacent to the spot where Lawrence of Arabia was killed on his motorcycle. Warmwell was a pre-war practice camp, using the nearby Lulworth Cove bombing and gunnery ranges. About a week or so after our arrival, the Station Commander, a Group Captain, had the whole station parade; until then we had all operated from the concrete apron in front of the hangars, but the Groupie's address was to change all that. It went something like this: "One of these days in the not too distant future, the Hun is going to appear over those Purbeck Hills and knock three kinds of shit out of us. Therefore No 152 Squadron will disperse to the far side of the airfield in an effort to ensure that minimum damage will be occasioned. The hangar will only be used for major inspections and repairs." He was right about being hit. We were, several times, but luckily nowhere near as badly as some of the airfields in the London area.

'The Squadron's duties were in defence of the Portland naval base, Southampton docks, Yeovil aircraft factory etc, and throughout 152 Squadron managed to give a good account of itself, accounting for fifty or sixty confirmed victories. They were certainly hectic days, from dawn to dusk we were at dispersal. It seemed as though we were always at readiness, re-arming, re-fuelling, daily inspections of aircraft all seemed to follow each other without pause. It was certainly thrilling to see your aircraft return with its gun ports in the wing leading edges open and black streaks down the underside of the wings, indicating that it had been in action. Very often there was a victory roll before the undercarriage was lowered and the pilot brought it in to land. Sometimes, though, your aircraft did not return, and you were left wondering what had happened to it. Sometimes a Spit would land badly shot-up. One such incident occurred when Flight Lieutenant Boitel-Gill crashed his Spitfire

right into the corner of the airfield. The aircraft was absolutely riddled, we counted more than seventy holes, that is points of entry, and lost count. His undercarriage could not be lowered and neither could his flaps. Boitel-Gill was one of those unflappable types, he never rushed, always appeared casual. He was an inveterate cigarette smoker, using a long cigarette holder, that he always carried. This time, after alighting from the wreck, he calmly placed the cigarette in the holder and said "I thought I'd better put it in the corner, out of the way" – a really cool customer.

Ray Johnson while serving with 152 Squadron as an armourer in 1940.

'Another incident, Flying Officer Graham "Cocky" Cox landed with

268

his head and shoulders protruding above the cockpit, his seat supports having collapsed either due to enemy action or violent evasive manoeuvres. The seat was resting on the elevator and rudder controls. Flying Officer Christopher "Jumbo" Deansley was another who had a lucky escape, two in fact, twice crashing into the sea and being rescued each time. He later became a night-fighter pilot who survived the war.

'One day, Jerry started concentrating his attacks on airfields, and Warmwell did not escape. We saw a formation of about a dozen twin-engined aircraft approaching at 8,000-10,000 feet and drop their loads. It was all over in a matter of minutes. They were pretty accurate: the hangar and a number of aircraft were either destroyed or damaged, and then delayed action bombs kept exploding over the next few days. There was also a number of casualties amongst ground personnel. As practically all our waking hours were spent at the dispersal point, at the wooded end of the airfield, for years after in any panic the standard call was "Away to the woods!"

'On another occasion, towards the end of that long, hot, summer, half a dozen of us were having a snack in the canteen run by the WRVS, which was better food than the NAAFI, but a lone enemy aircraft bombed and strafed the camp at zero feet. It was a day of particularly poor visibility and I remember diving under one of the heavy hardwood tables, which were standard equipment in those days. A radiator in the heating system landed on top of it. Again, some were luckier than others.

'A sad loss during the Battle of Britain was that of 21-year-old Pilot Officer Douglas Shepley, who had only been married for six weeks and whose elder brother, a flight lieutenant, had already been lost over Dunkirk. His sister, a nurse, had been lost at sea when the SS *Lancastrian* was bombed and sunk. His family lived at Woodthorpe Hall, near Sheffield. His wife, "Biddy", and his parents raised a fund to buy a Spitfire, and a pub near the Hall is, to this day, still called the "Shepley Spitfire".

'From the beginning, the Squadron's mascot was a white bull terrier known as "Pooch". Now Pooch was not an easy animal to get on with, and if he only suspected that you were afraid of him that was sufficient to make your life a misery and a continual hazard. A very good mate of mine, the Squadron parachute packer, was one of these, and amongst his duties was a daily visit to the pilots' dispersal tent to carry out his inspection. I am sure that Pooch heard or sensed this coming from afar, and it was the duty of whoever was there to grab Pooch and picket him down [meaning, in this context, to tie the aircraft down for stability]. To do so was indeed difficult, for he had been known to move the NAAFI wagon, given a strong rope and enough encouragement! Pooch even until then had a somewhat colourful career having previously belonged to a Canadian officer pilot stationed at Digby. The pilot was with the RAF on some kind of scheme. When he returned to Canada, Pooch was given to Tommy Thomas who gave the dog to his wife as a present. For some time, understandably, she was scared stiff of the dog, but eventually they became very attached. When 152 Squadron re-formed in 1939, Tommy became Commander of "B" Flight and remained so until he was promoted to squadron leader and posted as a controller to Middle Wallop, Warmwell's Sector Station. His good lady had by this time relinquished ownership of Pooch, who was taken over by 152 and Flying Officer Cox in particular. Now Cocky Cox was equivalent in weight and strength to Pooch, but luckily his disposition was more docile! He and the dog became great friends. Wherever the Squadron went until sometime in 1942, Pooch was there and in every place the pilots sought female companionship for him, so much so that I am sure he had more than the rest of the Squadron put together!

'During the late summer and early autumn of 1940, the invasion of this country was more than a distinct possibility. Suffice it to say that the danger eventually receded and as the days shortened so did air activity and we were given a little time off. Bus trips into neighbouring Bournemouth and Weymouth were arranged, and evenings we would visit hostelries in the more immediate vicinity, such as at Woodsford, Puddletown, Broadmaine and Dorchester. Pilots had their own haunts, although occasionally our paths would cross, such as at the Gloucester Hotel in Weymouth, which was popular with all ranks.

'I managed a week's leave for the New Year of 1941. When I returned, I discovered my promotion to the exalted rank of Leading Aircraftman (LAC). The corresponding increase in pay was appreciated. In February 1941, the pilots very kindly threw a party for the groundcrews, and of course included themselves, at the Gloucester Hotel. It was a very heavy night indeed and a number of us had to have a whiff of oxygen for breakfast the following morning! Squadron Leader Boitel-Gill on such occasions would take up a Spitfire and treat us all to a session of aerobatics. One such "air test", as these flights were officially called, included another Spitfire flown by Flight Lieutenant W.D. David, who finished the war with a score of twenty enemy aircraft destroyed. After a mock dogfight the aircraft disappeared, flying very low towards dispersal at just 300 feet, wing-tip to wing-tip, each apparently trying to get lower than the other. When they landed, Dennis David's propeller blade had been damaged, which didn't do the engine any good.

SERGEANT RAY JOHNSON

Flight Lieutenant
Derek 'Bottle'
Boitle-Gill DFC.

'As frequently happened there were unfortunate occurrences. On 1 April 1941, of all days, we had a visitation by a nuisance raider. One of our pilots, Sergeant Fawcett, was killed by a single bullet while seated in the Sergeants' Mess. During the previous November, a young pilot joined us, Pilot Officer Allen. He made a good job of a crash-landing but was not so lucky a second time, when he went into some forest at Durweston, near Dorchester, after having been with us just a fortnight. Also, in November, Pilot Officer A.R. Watson crashed near Wareham for no apparent reason. The cynics on occasions such as this, and there were many at this time, said that it all went to prove that if your name was on it, it would find you – wherever you were. We had two Polish pilots, Sergeants Klein and Szlagowski, known as "Zig" and "Zag". Zig was shot down and crashed into the Channel, never to be seen again. Zag was inconsolable, but survived the war, dying peacefully in London long afterwards.'

Ray was immensely proud of his days with 152 Squadron, with which he remained throughout the Second World War. The Battle of Britain, however, was for survivors just a short period in a long war – emphasised by Ray's letter of 1 August 1995:-

'Throughout the last three years of the war, 152 Squadron, in chronological order, served with the 1st, 5th, 8th and 14th armies, coinciding with the period referred to by Churchill when he said "before Alamein no victories, after Alamein, no defeats", or words to that effect.

152 Squadron's groundcrew at Warmwell confirming the prevailing British spirit in 1940!

Ray Johnson pictured at Coningsby in 2002 with the Battle of Britain Memorial Flight's Spitfire PR Mk XIX, PS915 – painted in 152 Squadron's markings.

'To illustrate the point, the Squadron's activities during this period commenced with the Allied landings in North Arica, November 1942, at the time of the 8th Army's breakthrough at El Alamein, the subsequent advance to Tunis resulting in the expulsion of the enemy from Africa, the Sicilian invasion and landings on the Italian mainland at Salerno.

'Then, in November 1943, the move to India with involvement in the Japanese siege of Imphal, the eventual break-out followed by the drive through Burma, to the end of the war and dropping of leaflets on the Jap forces telling them that their leaders had agreed to the Allies' unconditional surrender terms.

'It is also worth noting that throughout the Second World War, the Squadron never took part in any victory parade or other celebration, as we were always on the move to some other place, and by the time I arrived back in the UK in January 1946, victory parades and celebrations were a thing of the past.

'I am both pleased and proud to have served virtually throughout these momentous war years with 152 Squadron and survived – unlike some of my comrades.'

Ray was demobilised in September 1936, after which he worked in engineering, living in Grantham. On retirement he devoted himself to his memories of 152 Squadron and was instrumental in seeking out other survivors from those wartime days. Hugely enthusiastic, Ray rarely missed a signing or lecture, distance irrelevant. He was later an inspiration to another comparatively young man, Rob Oliver, who set up and runs the 'Friends of 152 (Hyderabad) Squadron' (see: 152Hyderabad.co.uk).

Ray left us on 3 September 2016 – a day before his 96th birthday. He would be proud, I know, to be included in this book, and delighted that through the 'Friends', 152 Squadron is remembered and survives as a living community.

Chapter Twenty-Six

Group Captain John 'Cat's Eyes' Cunningham CBE DSO** DFC* AE

Blenheim & Beaufighter Pilot

Reams have been written about John Cunningham, which is hardly surprising: a wartime night-fighter ace and test pilot, his work on jet aircraft both launched and secured the post-war future of British aviation.

Born on 27 July 1917 at Addington, near Aylesbury in Buckinghamshire, son of the Dunlop Rubber Company's Company Secretary, John first experienced flight in an Avro 504 biplane aged just 9. This early inspiration was further fuelled by attending Whitgift School, close to Croydon airport. Many years later, John wrote to me from his Harpenden home on 15 December 1989:-

'I have always been obsessed with flight, always fascinated by birds and aeroplanes. Remember that Europe remained haunted by the Great War,

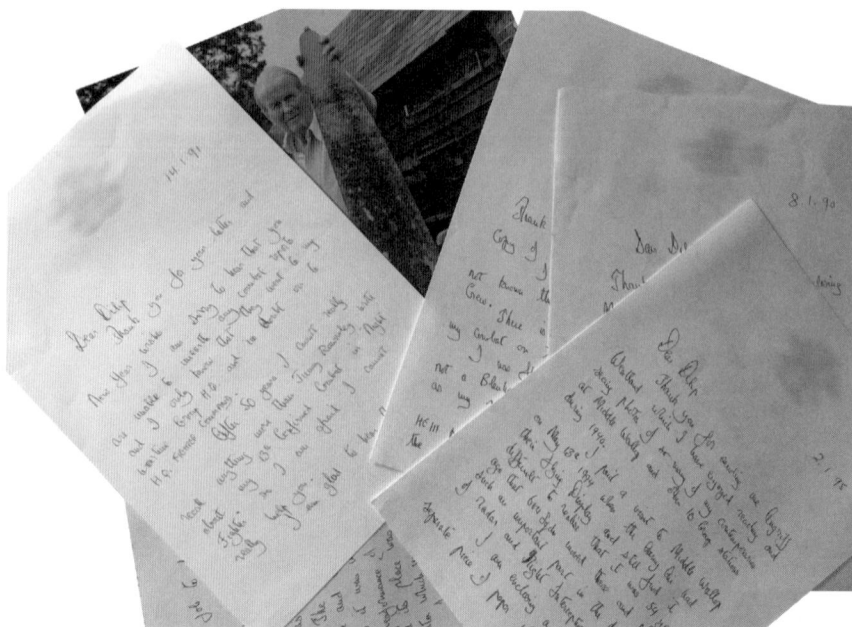

so my father was against me joining the air force. We compromised: I became a De Havilland apprentice, but then joined 604 'County of Middlesex' Squadron of the AAF in 1935, learning to fly during weekends at Hendon. After learning to fly, my career as a test pilot began when I was lucky enough to become a junior test pilot at De Havilland.'

On 24 August 1939, Flying Officer Cunningham was mobilised, joining 604 Squadron for the 'duration of the current emergency'. On 2 January 1995, John wrote:-

'604 Squadron was moved to Middle Wallop in July 1940, and was equipped with a fighter version of the Bristol Blenheim. Our intended role was as night-fighters.

'It was not until the arrival of the Bristol Beaufighter at the end of September 1940, which was equipped with an Airborne Interception (AI) radar set and four 20mm cannons, that we had any hope of intercepting the German bombers that droned over our Sector between the Isle of Wight and Lyme Bay on their way to the Midlands and further north.'

After the defeat of the German daylight bomber offensive, defending Britain at night presented a whole new set of problems for Fighter Command. As John has explained, dedicated, purpose-built night-fighting aircraft did not at first exist. Moreover, once an enemy aircraft had crossed the British coastline, owing to the limitations of the technology involved, it was initially safe from being tracked by radar, because the coastal Chain Home radar stations could only look outwards; once the intruder had passed inland, it was invisible to radar, meaning that the only means of interception was through visual contact assisted by searchlights. The *Luftwaffe*'s new aim was to bomb Britain into submission through directly attacking the civilian population and war economy. London remained the primary focus, as it had of daylight raids during September 1940, the intention being to batter the capital so extensively as to destroy civilian morale, making it impossible for the British government to continue the war. Nonetheless, while the RAF were faced with the difficulties of resolving nocturnal interception issues, the unanticipated switch to night attacks likewise presented the Germans with certain problems. Navigation and bomb-aiming were obviously more difficult at night, and beyond certain specialist units, there was a general lack of training in night-bombing. Moreover, the German bomber force's efficiency had been seriously reduced owing to the loss of so many experienced

Flight Lieutenant John Cunningham of 604 Squadron is presented to King George VI at Middle Wallop on 7 May 1941.

aircrews during the daylight battles. This deficiency in training, however, the Germans believed would be more than compensated for by their recently perfected radio guidance beams. First used in June 1940, by early October the *Knickebein* beam was compromised by British radio counter-measures, and the other options, the 'X' and 'Y' beam systems, were unsuitable for navigating large formations to their targets. Consequently, periods of bright moonlight were favoured for big attacks, when the target area could actually be seen. So, for both sides, the backroom war of electronic counter-measures, and deadly game of cat-and-mouse in the night sky, continued while bombs and parachute mines rained down on British cities during that terrible winter of 1940/41.

At Middle Wallop, inland of Southampton, 604 Squadron was perfectly located to prowl over the south coast and West Country, stalking enemy bombers travelling to and from their targets. On the night of 14 November 1940, 469 bombers dropped 420 tons of high explosive on Coventry, devasting much of the city and causing over 500 deaths. On November 19, Birmingham was attacked by 700 aircraft, and during December large-scale raids were made against Bristol, Plymouth, Liverpool, Southampton, Sheffield – and London. Indeed, on 29 December 1940, the 'X' beam was directed onto London, but KG100's pathfinders' marker flares were carried to a mile east and immediately north-west of St Paul's Cathedral. Seeing those fires burning, the main bomber force dropped their high explosive and incendiaries – burning the City of London.

On the night of the great raid on Birmingham, Flying Officer Cunningham was up on patrol from Middle Wallop in Beaufighter R2098, with Sergeant John Phillipson as his 'magician', operating the new AI radar. Picking up a contact, Phillipson guided his pilot to successfully intercept a Ju 88 of I/ KG54 over Brize Norton, which was destroyed. This was, in fact, the first victory recorded by an AI-equipped Beaufighter. John continued:-

'It was not until April 1941 that the Squadron really became effective and had considerable success in shooting down bombers at night.

'A night-fighter crew always consisted of a pilot and a radar operator, who worked as a team, and each man had to be highly proficient at his job to become a successful crew.'

Beaufighter R2101, the regular mount of Flight Lieutenant Cunningham and Sergeant 'Jimmy' Rawnsley, after they destroyed a He 111 on the night of 7 May 1941, in what became a 'Royal Command Performance', given the King's presence in the operations caravan. Afterwards the aircraft was taken up by another crew, who were forced to abandon their flight commander's favourite machine owing to damage sustained in combat with another raider.

By December 1940, inland radar coverage was resolved through the provision of mobile Ground Control Intercept (GCI) caravans. This, coupled with early warning of approach provided by Chain Home stations, and blind intercepts in the air made possible by AI, meant that the tide would turn. Middle Wallop Sector's GCI was located at Sopley, near Bournemouth, commanded by Squadron Leader John Brown, codename 'Starlight'. As John said: 'The improvements in radar coupled with the Beaufighter was really the thing that turned the tide. GCI tracked the bombers as they came in, vectoring us, then our own AI sets would pick them up, the operator taking over and guiding the Beaufighter to intercept.' By this time, John's regular 'magician' was Sergeant Cecil 'Jimmy' Rawnsley. Their first shared

The 'Royal Command Performance' He 111 belonged to 7/KG27 *Boelcke*, the crew of which are pictured here in happier times; from left: *Feldwebel* Heinz Schier; *Oberfeldwebel* Heinz Laschinski; *Felbwebel* Fritz Klemm; *Oberfeldwebel* Otto Willrich. (Via Allan White).

success came in January 1941 when John was awarded his first DFC; further kills followed in February and March; in April 1941, the Cunningham and Rawnsley pair destroyed seven more bombers, with others probably destroyed or damaged. This was an incredible result, especially when compared to the unproductive nights of only a few weeks before. To conceal the real reason for this change in fortunes, the press trumpeted that John's success owed much to his consumption of carrots, which improved night vision. This was also when the name 'Cat's Eyes' arose: 'It was all ridiculous,

From left, Laschinski, Klemm and Schier pose with their He 111, 1G+DR, the snap taken by the fourth crewman, Otto Willrich.

really, but helped the Ministry of Food promote the growing and eating of vegetables – which was important, of course, owing to rationing.'

On 7 May 1941, King George VI visited 604 Squadron at Middle Wallop, dining with the officers before inspecting the Beaufighter crews. Both John Cunningham and Jimmy Rawnsley were introduced, the King asking the latter whether he would 'get one for me tonight?' That night, the King moved on to the Sopley GCI, watching intently as Squadron Leader Brown identified an incoming hostile plot on his radar screen, passing details to Beaufighter 'R' for Robert, crewed by Cunningham and Rawnsley, prowling the night sky above. When Sergeant Rawnsley confirmed a 'fix' on the raider, Starlight's job was done. Realising that the plot was actually overhead, Squadron Leader Brown suggested that the King might step outside to watch the action. The unsynchronised throb of the enemy bomber's engines could be heard, then a far-off glow appeared momentarily in the night sky. John wrote:-

'The He 111 could be seen against a lightish sky, and, as usual, I positioned myself close in, below the target, then opened fire.'

The flight engineer, *Feldwebel* Fritz Klemm, was killed when the He 111 crashed at Weston Zoyland, Somerset.

The enemy aircraft was a machine of 7/KG27 *Boelcke*, and crashed at 2330 hrs at Anderson Farm, Weston Zoyland, Somerset, killing *Feldwebel*s Heinz Schier and Fritz Klemm; the more fortunate *Oberfeldwebel* Heinz Laschinski and *Feldwebel* Otto Willrich baled out and were captured. Inevitably, the combat became known as the 'Royal Command Performance'. Many more combat successes would follow for John Cunningham and Jimmy Rawnsley, who became the most famous night-fighter crew of the war.

After the big raid on London at the end of 1940, and further success of British counter-measures, the German bomber crews began losing confidence. By January 1941 there was so little confidence in the radio beams that large formations only penetrated inland during moonlight, and so the main focus of the attack shifted from London and inland cities to chief ports, including Plymouth, Bristol, Swansea, Cardiff, Hull and Southampton, to which the beams could be directed with the minimum of interference. By May 1941, preparations for Germany's attack on Russia were well underway, with flying and other units moving eastwards. To conceal this, a massive raid was made on London throughout the night of 10/11 May 1941. The heaviest of the whole Blitz, 550 aircraft participated, some making several shuttle-runs from their bases in France and Belgium – causing dreadful damage and loss of life. At the end of May, the vast majority of *Luftwaffe* units moved east, leaving only a small mixed force of bomber, reconnaissance and minelaying aircraft with single-engined fighters to continue a holding war against Britain. Arguably it was actually at that point that the Battle of Britain was truly over.

Without doubt, Germany had every opportunity to invade and defeat Britain in 1940, but had failed – largely owing to the lack of any continuous policy of attack. Certainly, large-scale destruction had been wrought upon British cities, including ports, and industry, but there had been

Above left: The observer (and aircraft captain) *Feldwebel* Heinz Schier was also killed.

Above right: The pilot, *Oberfeldwebel* Heinz Laschinski, baled out and survived, as did *Oberfeldwebel* Willrich.

no debilitating collapse in civilian morale, and by spring 1941, Fighter Command was stronger, by night and day, than it had been the previous year. The only option now lay in a blockade, combing air and sea attacks on British shipping to force surrender through deprivation of essential food and supplies. Alternatively, Britain's surrender could be forced after the defeat of Russia, which was anticipated to have been achieved by the autumn of 1941. Fortunately, these plans, like so many others, remained a pipe dream.

On 2 January 1995, John also wrote:-

'I continued to operate from Middle Wallop until the end of July 1942 – my last year as CO of 604 Squadron.

'The Beaufighter was a very fine war machine and the first successful night-fighter, but by 1943 it was not fast enough to deal with the higher performance of many of the later German aircraft and its place was taken by the Mosquito night-fighter, which was about 100 mph faster.

'Jimmy' Rawnsley and John Cunningham, night-fighters *par excellence*, pictured while operating the superb Mosquito later in the war.

'I was fortunate to be given command of 85 Squadron, flying Mosquito night-fighters from January 1943 to March 1944, operating from Hunsdon and West Malling in 11 Group.

'I paid a visit to Middle Wallop on 13 May 1994, when the Army Air Corps had their flying display. I still find it difficult to realise that it was fifty-four years ago that 604 Squadron moved there and played such an important part in the development of radar and night interception. They were exciting times.'

Those 'exciting times' I had the pleasure of discussing personally with the great 'Cat's Eyes' himself, when visiting him at home in 1990. It was daunting, as I recall, the prospect of meeting this awesome aviator. There was, however, no need for any apprehension: I found the great man so unassuming as to be almost shy, softly spoken and ever-helpful. What, of course, John would never mention is that he was awarded bars to both the DSO and DFC, and destroyed at least twenty enemy aircraft during the Second World War. In fact, he must surely be amongst the most distinguished British aviators of all time.

Group Captain John Cunningham, one of the Few, night-fighter ace and legendary test pilot, died, aged 84, on 21 July 2002.

Group Captain John Cunningham pictured at home by the author in 1989, with a He 111 propeller blade from his thirteenth nocturnal victory.

Epilogue

Hauptmann Hermann Kell
Heinkel 111 Pilot

In a book entitled *Letters From The Few*, the reader may ponder the legitimacy of including an enemy airman. History, however, including the human experience, must surely be inclusive to ensure a broader understanding of the past, so therefore this is arguably an *essential* component of this book.

Because of the language barrier, comparatively few accounts by German airmen who fought in the Battle of Britain have been published in English. The famous aces, at least those who survived, notably General Adolf Galland, have left behind their memoirs, but the reality is that such was the rate and extent of attrition, as the war went on, many of those who flew against England in 1940 were later killed. Moreover, there was no appetite in post-war Germany for tales of derring-do from former fighter pilots in

particular – whom civilians unfairly held responsible for having failed to prevent the devastation of German cities by the Allied strategic bombing campaign. Furthermore, and most importantly, post-war generations in Germany sought to distance themselves from Hitler's war, frequently seeking to avoid any association with the Nazi regime through admitting an ancestor who fought in the *Wehrmacht*. These are all reasons why more first-hand accounts 'from the other side' have appeared in English from those who were captured, made prisoner and settled in the former Allied lands. Many German aircrew prisoners were conveyed across the Atlantic to Canada and America, later returning to England whilst awaiting 'denazification' and repatriation. Some had nothing to go home for, their homes and families destroyed; others had formed romantic relationships in the countries in which they had been captive and so started new lives as immigrants. South America also beckoned as somewhere a German would not be discriminated against after 1945, a place of rich opportunity. Germany itself, of course, was divided between west and east, the latter under Stalinist control, behind the Iron Curtain, where there would be no chance whatsoever of promoting interest in any aspect of the Third Reich. It is also worth considering that most *Luftwaffe* units participating in the Battle of Britain later fought in Russia and were virtually annihilated on the *Ostfront* by 1945. It was not until 1956 that the last German prisoner was released from the *gulag* – and 356,700 German prisoners had died in Soviet captivity. All of these things, then, and more, explain why first-hand accounts in English by German aircrew from the Battle of Britain are comparatively rare – and eagerly sought.

The German narrative of summer of 1940 does not necessarily fit with our own. German historians argue that the Battle of Britain did not conclude until the end of May 1941, when Hitler's territorial focus shifted eastwards, immediately before the invasion of Russia. Indeed, some suggest that there never was a 'Battle of Britain' at all, because there was no serious intent, preparations or resources available to mount a seaborne invasion of southern England. The evidence, however, is contrary: Hitler, we know, did order the *Luftwaffe* to seize control of the air and preparations made for an invasion of England. Certainly, the opportunity was as unanticipated as it was unprecedented, owing to the lightning-quick advance to the Channel coast and Fall of France, but an opportunity it was nonetheless, which clearly Hitler tried to exploit.

One thing that is true is that the Battle of Britain was on a far smaller scale than the Allied strategic bombing campaign of Germany, which lasted years, by night and day, provoking certain *Luftwaffe* survivors to pour scorn on the very idea that a handful of brave RAF fighter pilots really did prevail against overwhelming odds. To those like JG2's Julius Meimberg, it was simply a case that an opportunity unexpectedly presented itself, that window then closing, owing to the changing seasons and the *Luftwaffe's* failure to destroy Fighter Command, the war's strategic focus consequently moving elsewhere – and that the air battles subsequently fought over north-west Europe in defence of Germany were of such a scale as to make the Battle of Britain's revered place in history disproportionate. In some ways that may be so, but the main point is that although neither side was decisively defeated by the Battle of Britain's end, Britain remained free – and Fighter Command had, therefore, achieved a victory. Conversely, upon conclusion of the Allied bombing offensive, German cities were in ruins, the country totally defeated. So the enormity of those air battles over Germany is irrelevant in this context for one simple reason: the *Luftwaffe* was soundly beaten by 1945, whereas by 31 October 1940, Fighter Command was not – and because Britain remained in the war, the liberation of Europe, with American help, four years later, was made possible. That, then, is why this victory – for that is what it was – remains of such fundamental importance to the war's ultimate outcome, and why it is justifiably so revered.

In this book, and its companion volume, *Battle of Britain 1940: The Finest Hour's Human Cost*, we have explored the composition of RAF Fighter Command, understanding that the comparatively small pre-war regular air force was supplemented by amateur auxiliary and reservist airmen. In that respect, the *Luftwaffe* was completely different, comprising as it did only professional airmen. Some of the *Alte Adler*, the 'Old Eagles', had been around before Hitler came to power in 1933, serving the Kaiser and subsequent Weimar regime, some from the 'officer class' so despised by Hitler. Others had first experienced flight as impressionable youngsters gliding in the *Hitler Jugend*, later joining Hitler's secretly rebuilt *Luftwaffe*, in which ability rather than social background was the key to advancement. What accounts have been published more often than not are from the younger breed of German airmen who joined the service after Hitler came to power in 1933. Outstanding amongst these is Ulrich Steinhilper's *Spitfire on My Tail* (produced in collaboration with British aviation historian Peter Osborne in 1989), an Me 109 pilot shot down by Spitfires and captured on 27 October 1940. Much rarer are accounts from those who served before Hitler became Chancellor of Germany. This is what makes the following account so special.

In 1994, I was approached at a book-signing by one Derek Boyling, a Briton who had emigrated to Canada and was temporarily in the UK on holiday.

HAUPTMANN HERMANN KELL

Above left: *Hauptmann* Hermann Kell

Above right: *Hauptmann* Kell at the controls of his 3/KG4 He 111.

Derek knew a former German wartime pilot who lived in Ontario, and inquired as to whether I would be interested in corresponding with him. Naturally I was, and soon, on 15 December 1994, the following lengthy and most welcome account arrived from my new correspondent – who was surprised and delighted in equal measure at the unexpected opportunity to record and share his experience:-

'I was born Hermann Otto Kell on 25 November 1914, the only child of my poor parents, August and Louise Kell, at Nabburg, a small town in Bavaria, Germany. I was brought up in a strict religious background. A death in the family stimulated an interest in medicine, and my dream was to spend a lifetime involved with medical research. I therefore learned Latin in my spare time as a fourth language.

'When I graduated from school in 1933, however, I realised that my parents were too poor to support me through university, so instead I applied to become one of the *Reichswehr's* 4,000 officers. Due to my humble origins I doubted that I would be accepted. I was. The only student from my college ever to have been commissioned. *Reichswehr* was the name given to the German armed force of 100,000 soldiers and 4,000 officers stipulated by the Treaty of Versailles in 1919. I was accepted under the aegis of *Reichspresident* von Hindenburg, before Hitler came to power. Members of the *Reichswehr* were actually prohibited from engaging in politics and were therefore the only Germans unable to vote at elections.

'After graduating in the top group from the German equivalent of West Point, I volunteered to become an officer in the *Luftwaffe*, although the air force did not officially exist at that time, a German air force having been forbidden by Versailles. My initial flying lessons, therefore, were not from a proper airfield but a country meadow near Celle. By 1936, aged twenty-one, I possessed all pilot's licences and was promoted to the rank of *Leutnant*. I became the *Flugleiter*, or airport manager, at Gotha/Thuer. Amongst other things, I was responsible for air traffic and safety.

'In 1937, I was selected by the German Air Ministry, at the age of twenty-two, to be one of only two Luftwaffe pilots flying officials to and from foreign countries on a weekly basis. The flights were often of eight to ten hours duration over the open sea, without weather information, auto-pilot or radio. We were flying the first all-metal aircraft, the Ju 52. On 1 January 1939, I was the only junior Luftwaffe officer promoted to *Oberleutnant*. The only other promotions that day were about eight *Obersts* and Generals.

Hauptmann Kell and observer.

288

HAUPTMANN HERMANN KELL

Hermann Kell again flying his He 111 – with a passenger with the appearance of the archetypal *Gestapo* man!

'I then served first as an *Oberleutnant*, then as *Hauptmann* and *Staffelkapitän*, with 3/KG4 *General Wever*. I flew the He 111 operationally in both Poland and Norway, and was awarded the Iron Cross II Class on the fifth day of the Second World War. A few days before the Blitzkrieg in the west commenced, I was ordered back to form a new training school on a deserted aerodrome, to prepare new KG4 crews for operations against the enemy. At the start of one of those training flights, an engine failed. I immediately took control from the student and landed the He 111 in a large forest over which we had been flying. The young navigator was killed, two were wounded, but four were unhurt. I was in a coma for two months, but after regaining consciousness I returned to my 3 *Staffel* on crutches in July 1940 – in time for the Battle of Britain.

'The next order I received cost me several nights' sleep: devise tactics for the laying of mines in the Irish Sea harbours, with the help of two engineers who supplied me the required technical data. The giant mines were to descend by parachute. They had to be dropped from a height of 100 metres above the water of the harbour approaches. Anti-aircraft fire could therefore prematurely end any mission. Fortunately, I had a brainwave: I flew at 100 metres at just the minimum speed and power to remain airborne. The acoustic-guided searchlights were therefore misled, and searched at greater

Battle damage to *Hauptmann* Kell's He 111 during the Polish campaign in 1939.

heights whilst I flew over their heads! A test flight over a harbour in the Bristol Channel proved my theory to be sound – we lost no aircraft on these difficult and dangerous missions.

'On 6 September 1940, I participated with 3/KG4 in three nocturnal raids against the East India Docks and London in retaliation for the bombing of Berlin. The weather was good. We suffered no losses, but I saw neither any hits nor fires in London proper.

'A few days later I received an order to personally fly a solo night raid against an industrial complex on the western edge of Newcastle-upon-Tyne. When I approached the He 111 that I was detailed to fly, and which was not my usual aircraft, I was astonished to see a giant bomb hanging beneath the plane, the like of which I had never seen before. I had trouble actually getting into the plane because the bomb was so big. I flew across the North Sea to Newcastle at about 2,000 metres. Again, the weather was good, but I could not find our specific target. In desperation I descended to about 100 metres or less, and criss-crossed Newcastle for at least thirty minutes without success. The response to the idea of indiscriminately dropping this huge bomb on Newcastle was "No". With the first rays of sunlight, I flew out across the North Sea toward our base in Holland. Once home I expected an unfriendly reception for returning home with the bomb, but fortunately I was wrong.

'On Friday 13 September 1940, all night missions were cancelled. An unusually bad weather front covered northern France, the Netherlands and Germany. There was thunder and lightning in every direction. At about 2100 hrs, I received an order for a crew of volunteers to fly a nuisance raid against Victoria Station in London. This came from a high level of authority, which was apparently unaware that there are limits to such bad weather! I was the *Staffelkapitän*, the Squadron Leader, of 3/KG4, so I did not ask anyone else to volunteer and flew the mission myself. However, I excluded a trainee pilot from our crew, although he felt somewhat aggrieved.

'I was concerned about where I could land upon return, due to the weather, but the Meteorologist was unable to provide the answer. At about 2300 hrs I switched on the plane's lights whilst I started up, and saw a car approaching from the left. It was the *Geschwaderkommodore* himself, *Oberstleutnant* Rath, who had come out in the heavy rain to salute our crew. I had never seen this before.

'I had hardly lifted the He 111 from the runway when I was in turbulent clouds. I had difficulty holding the plane on its course. Strong up and down winds played with our plane at their leisure. Frequently,

The wreckage of KG4 He 111 WN 2117, 5J+AC, the crash of which on a training flight in Germany, astonishingly, *Hauptmann* Kell survived – just.

I was unsure whether the plane was flying straight and level, the instrument needles going haywire. When a bolt of lightning illuminated the cockpit, I saw my good old navigator staring at me, the question of whether I could actually maintain control of the aircraft written all over his face. Sometimes I was unsure myself! When bolts of lightning hit the plane I often had no answer regarding what to do. Although I had previously flown many times at night and in bad weather, this flight taught me that in addition to ability and experience, sometimes you also need a little luck.

'We finally emerged from the clouds at 600 metres, to find a cloudless, moonlit night above the Thames Estuary, exactly where we were supposed to be. It was so peaceful and quiet that it was hard to believe that we were engaged on a war flight. The relaxation was rapidly terminated when we were coned by searchlights. I took evasive action, which shook them off momentarily, but after a while I had to accept that it was futile – I did not know then that London's searchlights were guided by radar and not acoustics.

'Orientation above blacked-out London was easy due to the recent heavy rain – the wet railway tracks reflected the bright moonlight. Where the glittering tracks joined many others but then suddenly disappeared was obviously Victoria Station. My navigator had actually guided me to this location with his homing device. Suddenly an endless stream of bullets

Hauptmann Kell and other KG4 *General Wever* personnel practice gunnery.

Hauptmann Kell (second right) and crew pose with their He 111.

smashed into our aircraft. It was a Blenheim which attacked from fifty closing to twenty metres, using all his ammunition in one continuous burst. I later learned that the pilot was a New Zealander, Pilot Officer Michael Herrick of 25 Squadron, who had already destroyed two *Heinkels* and after shooting us down received the DFC (sadly, he was later killed in action over Denmark, so I never got to meet this excellent and courageous young pilot after the war).

'After Herrick's attack the oil pressure of both engines rapidly dropped to zero. I knew that we had no chance. I immediately shut down both motors to avoid both fire or an explosion, but my actions were in vain. Flames spurted out of both engines and engulfed the plane. I called to the flight engineer and radio operator in the rear of the plane, telling them to bale out. There was no answer. I sent the navigator back to check them on them. He came back with news that both *Kameraden* were dead.

'By now I had changed to a northerly course and we glided down at as shallow an angle as possible, hoping to clear the outskirts of London before hitting the ground. The flames blocked all view of the outside, and prevented use of all escape hatches, except the small one above my seat. I was unsure whether the hatch was big enough to get through with my parachute on, but I had no option. My navigator stood silently beside me, calmly awaiting my decision. At 2,000 metres I guessed that we should be over open countryside. As the hatch was above my seat I had to jump first to allow my navigator to climb up on my empty seat and out of the hatch. I trimmed the plane for the last time into a steady glide. My navigator and I shook hands and wished each other good luck.

'I dived onto the left wing to avoid being hit by the tailplane, and fell into space. As I pulled the ripcord, I saw our burning plane continue its downward glide until exploding on impact with our dead comrades aboard. Beneath me I saw a parachute, but although I called out several times to my navigator I received no response. Suddenly a Blenheim emerged from the night and circled me, uncomfortably close, stood up on a wing tip. Obviously, there was a master at the controls. I pulled some strings of my parachute to drop faster. I hit the ground hard and found myself lying in a field. With the parachute beneath my arm, I hastened to get away from where I had landed. I climbed over several walls, but then the pain from my broken leg caused me to hide beneath some bushes on the banks of a stream.

Hauptmann Kell (third right) with fellow KG4 officers at their French base in summer 1940.

It gave me chance to rest and think. At first light I saw two AA guns about 300 yards away, so decided to surrender.'

Already in custody was Hermann's navigator, *Feldwebel* Werner Hobe; *Unteroffizier*s Müller-Wernscheid and Töpfer were both killed when their aircraft crashed at Downs Hall, Newman's End, near Sheering, at 0155 hrs GMT. Herman continued, explaining that after two nights in custody,

'My next "home" was in a bare room beneath the roof of a building in the Kensington Palace complex [the infamous interrogation centre known as the 'London Cage' commanded by Lieutenant Colonel A.P. Scotland]. During the afternoon I was led into a dark basement room. I sat in a small beam of light. In the other half, in darkness, a man in civilian clothes sat at a desk. After providing my name and rank, I was asked a question about my *Staffel*. My response was "Sir, I assume that you are or were an officer, and that you are therefore aware that I am unable to answer that question." To my great surprise, he replied that he already knew who I was, and closed my file in front of him. He switched on the light and invited me to his desk. We had a friendly chat and I was returned to my "room". It was 15 September 1940 – "Battle of Britain Day" – and I saw two Do 17s spin to earth. There were no parachutes. The next day I was escorted by an officer to the PoW camp at Grizedale Hall in the Lake District. There I joined 286 comrades, including some old friends.

'Shortly before Christmas 1940, we were all shipped to Canada. I spent the next six years there, behind barbed wire, as a "guest" of the strict but fair Canadian army. In January 1941, I was instrumental in helping *Oberleutnant* Franz von Werra, an Me 109 pilot also captured during the Battle of Britain, to escape. We were on a train travelling from Halifax to Camp W (100) at Neys, Ontario. I held up a blanket to conceal his exit via a window from which he had removed the screws. Franz, of course, made it to the USA, which was still neutral at that time, and was later sent home. He was later killed, sadly, when his engine failed over the North Sea. After the war he became infamous as *The One That Got Away*, in the book and film of that name, as the only German prisoner to escape from Allied custody during the Second World War.

After the war, Hermann was eventually reunited with his family in November 1946: 'My last mission, which had lasted over six years, had finally ended. Although the age of chivalry had largely passed, the example of some exceptional human beings whom I met during the war proves that decency and chivalry have still not entirely disappeared.' Later, together with his wife, Liane Friderike

Hauptmann Kell (centre) and crew during the Battle of Britain.

What now remains: Hermann Kell's pilot's qualification badges, rank collar patches, and compass. The 7.92mm cartridge case is from his He 111's crash site. (Derek Boyling).

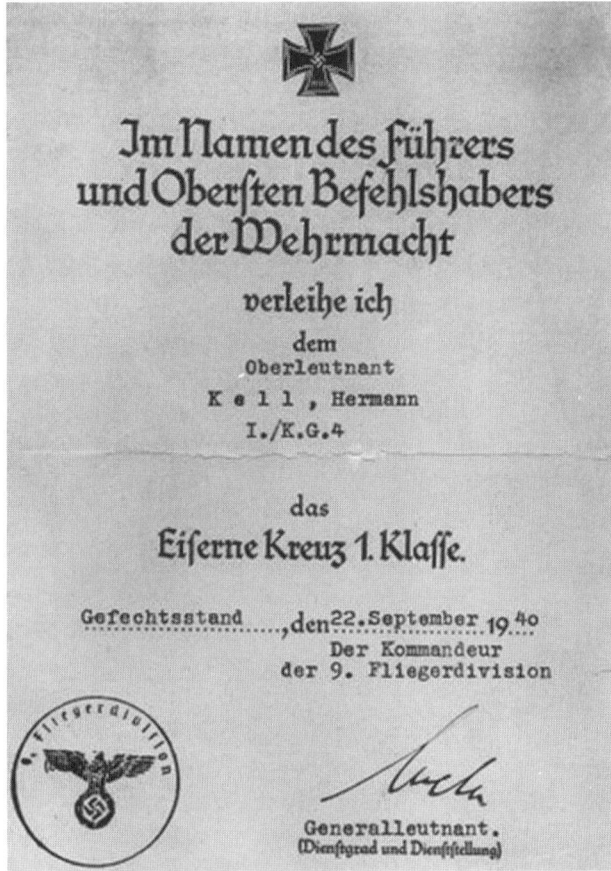

Im Namen des Führers
und Obersten Befehlshabers
der Wehrmacht

verleihe ich

dem
Oberleutnant
K e l l , Hermann
I./K.G.4

das

Eiserne Kreuz 1. Klasse.

Gefechtsstand ....,den 22.September 19 40
Der Kommandeur
der 9. Fliegerdivision

Generalleutnant.
(Dienstgrad und Dienststellung)

Hauptmann Kell was awarded the Iron Cross II Class on the Second World War's fifth day, followed by the I Class award on 22 September 1940 – by which time Hermann was a prisoner in England.

Kell, Hermann returned to Canada, once his prison, now a land of opportunity in which to make a fresh start. At first he worked in lumber, in the north, then moved to Sault Ste Marie, Ontario, to work for Algoma Steel as a laboratory technician. There, in Ontario, he lived out his days in peace, becoming a great-grandfather. Hermann died, after a long illness, on 26 September 2007, aged 87.

In closing, I refer to a letter Hermann wrote to me on 23 July 1995, in which he powerfully, yet succinctly, articulated why research into the Battle of Britain's human experience – and books like this – remain so important:-

'Getting older, or more accurately being old now, I live a lonely life, surrounded by scientific books and still hungry for knowledge.

'In my advanced age, I feel and recognize increasingly how time prunes our ego, expectations and desires, which we have created and nourished in our youth; how time, this puzzling and decisive cosmic power, which we have largely ignored in our youth, passes us always at increasing speed in an unknown direction; always away and never returning, and changing everything and ultimately ending everything in accordance alone with its superior unknown will or pleasure.

'What is the purpose of time? Of our life?

'Only historians, archaeologists and our memory can arrest the changing time and preserve a phase of our existence for a moment in our limited three-dimensional mind and intelligence, while the inconceivable power "Time" continues to reduce everything into negligible and changing matter.

'Again, who or what and why are we?

'Without historians, archaeologists and memories, we humans would soon be without a past, without parameters for our judgement and guidance; without hope and just a black hole as the future.'

Hermann Kell pictured at home in Canada during 1995.

Bibliography

Alcorn, J, 'Battle of Britain Top Guns', *Aeroplane Monthly*, September 1996

Alcorn, J, 'Battle of Britain Top Guns Update', *Aeroplane Monthly*, July 2000

Balss, M, *Deutsche Luftwaffe Losses & Claims Part: 1 September-15 October 1940*, self-published, Camarines Norte, Philippines, 2018

Bogle, J, Cluett, D, & Learmouth, B, *Croydon Airport and the Battle for Britain 1939-40*, London Borough of Sutton Libraries & Arts Services, Sutton, 1984

Brickhill, P, *Reach for the Sky: Douglas Bader, His Life Story*, Collins, London, 1954

Caldwell, D, *The JG26 War Diary: Volume One, 1939-42*, Grubb Street, London, 1996

Ellan, Sqn Ldr BJ, *Spitfire! The Experiences of a Fighter Pilot*, John Murray, London, 1942

Forrester, Larry, *Fly For Your Life*, Companion Book Club, London, 1956

Hillary, R, *The Last Enemy*, Macmillan, London, 1950

Lisiewicz, Squadron Leader M (Ed), *Destiny Can Wait: The Polish Air Force in the Second World War*, William Heinemann, London, 1949

Mason, F, *Battle Over Britain*, Aston Publications, Bourne End, 1990

Moseley, L, *Battle of Britain: The combined story of Harry Saltzman's production 'Battle of Britain' and the supremely dramatic events of 1940*, Pan, London, 1969

Ramsey, W (Ed) *The Battle of Britain Then & Now, Mk V*, Battle of Britain Prints International, London, 1989

Ramsey, W (Ed), *The Blitz Then & Now, Volumes 1 & 2*, Battle of Britain Prints International, 1987/8

Rawnsley, CF, and Wright, R, *Night Fighter*, Wm Collins Sons & Co, London, 1957

Robinson, A, *RAF Fighter Squadrons in the Battle of Britain*, Arms & Armour Press, London, 1987

Townsend, PW, *Duel of Eagles: The Struggle for the Skies from the First World War to the Battle of Britain*, Cassell, London, 1970

Townsend, PW, *Time & Chance: An Autobiography*, Methuen, London, 1978

Townsend, PW, *Duel in the Dark: The Sequel to Duel of Eagles*, Harrap, London, 1986

Wynn, K, *Men of the Battle of Britain*, Frontline Books, Barnsley, 2015

The Operations Record Books and individual pilots' combat reports were also consulted, all of which are preserved at The National Archives, Kew, London, in AIR 27 and AIR 50:-
www.nationalarchives.gov.uk

Anyone interested in commemorating the Battle of Britain should consider joining the 'Friends of the Few' and supporting the Battle of Britain Memorial Trust's efforts to preserve and maintain the National Battle of Britain Memorial: www.battleofbritainmemorial.org

Fighter Command's one-time HQ at Bentley Priory, in which Air Chief Marshal Dowding's office is preserved, now houses an excellent Museum: bentleypriorymuseum.org.uk

The Imperial War Museum at Duxford is the place to see Second World War aircraft fly, and with various museums on site not to be missed: iwm.org.uk/visits/iwm-duxford

The Kent Battle of Britain Museum provides a different experience and houses the remains of over 700 aircraft destroyed in the Battle of Britain: kbobm.org

Biographical information on the Few can be found online at the Battle of Britain London Monument website: bbm.org.uk/the-monument

Other Books by Dilip Sarkar
(in order of publication)

Spitfire Squadron: No 19 Squadron at War, 1939-41
The Invisible Thread: A Spitfire's Tale
Through Peril to the Stars: RAF Fighter Pilots Who Failed to Return, 1939-45
Angriff *Westland: Three Battle of Britain Air Raids Through the Looking Glass*
A Few of the Many: Air War 1939-45, A Kaleidoscope of Memories
Bader's Tangmere Spitfires: The Untold Story, 1941
Bader's Duxford Fighters: The Big Wing Controversy
Missing in Action: Resting in Peace?
Guards VC: Blitzkrieg 1940
Battle of Britain: The Photographic Kaleidoscope, Volumes I-IV
Fighter Pilot: The Photographic Kaleidoscope
Group Captain Sir Douglas Bader: An Inspiration in Photographs
Johnnie Johnson: Spitfire Top Gun, Parts I & II
Battle of Britain: Last Look Back
Spitfire! Courage & Sacrifice
Spitfire Voices: Heroes Remember
The Battle of Powick Bridge: Ambush a Fore-thought
Duxford 1940: A Battle of Britain Base at War
The Few: The Battle of Britain in the Words of the Pilots
Spitfire Manual 1940
The Sinking of HMS Royal Oak *in the Words of the Survivors (re-print of Hearts of Oak)*
The Last of the Few: Eighteen Battle of Britain Pilots tell their Extraordinary Stories
Hearts of Oak: The Human Tragedy of HMS Royal Oak
Spitfire Voices: Life as a Spitfire Pilot in the Words of the Veterans
How the Spitfire Won the Battle of Britain
Spitfire Ace of Aces: The True Wartime Story of Johnnie Johnson
Douglas Bader

Fighter Ace: The Extraordinary Life of Douglas Bader, Battle of Britain Hero (re-print of above)
Spitfire: The Photographic Biography
Hurricane Manual 1940
River Pike
The Final Few: The Last Surviving Pilots of the Battle of Britain tell their Stories
Arnhem 1944: The Human Tragedy of the Bridge Too Far
Spitfire! The Full Story of a Unique Battle of Britain Fighter Squadron
Battle of Britain 1940: The Finest Hour's Human Cost

Index

INDEX